NORMAN MacCAIG (1910–96) was born in Edinburgh. He lived there all his life, though lengthy annual visits to Assynt enriched his life and work. He attended the Royal High School, studied Classics at the University of Edinburgh and then trained as a teacher. Having spent years teaching in primary schools, he later taught Creative Writing at the University of Edinburgh, then at the University of Stirling.

As he became old, MacCaig's reputation grew and was recognised by the Queen's Gold Medal for Poetry and many other distinctions. However, his reputation as the 'grand old man' of Scottish poetry rested less on these than on his continuing creative work, his teaching and reading, and his fruitful influence on younger writers.

THE POEMS OF
Norman MacCaig

EDITED BY
EWEN McCAIG

INTRODUCTION BY
ALAN TAYLOR

First published in paperback in Great Britain in 2009 by
Polygon, an imprint of Birlinn Ltd
West Newington House
10 Newington Road
Edinburgh
EH9 1QS

www.birlinn.co.uk

ISBN 978 1 84697 136 5

First published in 2005

Reprinted in 2010

The publisher acknowledges subsidy from

 Scottish
Arts Council

towards the publication of this volume

British Library Cataloguing-in-Publication Data
A catalogue record for this book is available on request from the British Library.

Typeset by Koinonia, Bury, Lancashire
Printed and bound by Bell and Bain Ltd., Glasgow

Contents

Previously uncollected poems are denoted by an asterisk.

+ The following twelve poems were presented in sequence in their original
  publication.

Editorial Note

Ewen McCaig[1]

THIS is the third collected (paperback) edition of my father's poems. The first was published in 1985; the second, published in 1990, added later poems but was otherwise identical. Both bore the title, Collected Poems. This edition, The Poems of Norman MacCaig, contains more poems and other material. It is offered as the definitive (though not complete) MacCaig, because I believe the surviving poems not included here are below the standard set by the previous collection and therefore not suitable for publication.[2]

When my father died in 1996 he left a large number of unpublished poems. Ninety-nine were selected for inclusion here, giving 792 in all. Contextualisation of the poetry is provided in Alan Taylor's introduction and in a selection of my father's own words.

Two editorial issues had to be resolved. One was the order of presentation. Previous editions of the Collected Poems (compiled by my father) presented material from the original books in order of publication, though with exclusions and additions of individual poems. Here, the poems are presented in order of writing. The other issue was the inclusion of work unpublished at the time of his death. He usually disparaged the published gleanings from the estates of other poets and his admonition, 'Don't let them publish a lot of rubbish after I'm dead!' still sounds in my mind. I must now justify the inclusion of unpublished poems and describe the selection process undertaken to reject the 'rubbish'.

The specifics of producing another collection after his death would not have interested my father towards the end of his life and they were

---

1 Many people have questioned the spelling of my father's name. He used 'MacCaig' for writing and the original 'McCaig' for all other purposes.
2 This reflects my father's wishes although, as his literary executor, decisions on individual poems became my responsibility after his death. Unpublished poems and other writings can be found mainly in the Norman MacCaig Archive at Edinburgh University Library. Quotations from unpublished poems will be allowed when they are contextualised and their status acknowledged.

never discussed. However, I was helped in resolving these issues by knowledge of my father's way of working and a perception of his wishes based on many conversations.

Norman MacCaig was born in 1910. He wrote poetry from school age, but took many years to find his voice. The MacCaig his readers would recognise emerged in about 1947, when he adopted a more lucid and disciplined style. Poems written before then were disowned, including two early books: Far Cry and The Inward Eye. He later published fourteen 'slim volumes' as he termed them. These were: Riding Lights (1955); The Sinai Sort (1957); A Common Grace (1960); A Round of Applause (1962); Measures (1965); Surroundings (1966); Rings on a Tree (1968); A Man in my Position (1969); The White Bird (1973); The World's Room (1974); Tree of Strings (1977); The Equal Skies (1980); A World of Difference (1983); Voice-Over (1988). The Collected editions contain most poems from the slim volumes plus a selection of others that had not been published in books, or at all.

When altering his style in 1947 he also changed his approach to organising his work, writing on loose sheets rather than in notebooks. Each sheet contained a single poem, with its serial number and the month and year of writing. From time to time, usually in preparation for publication, he would unwillingly type a selection of poems, preserving their numbers and dates. Minor amendments were often made during, or following, this process. Many of the typescripts contain holograph amendments. The amendment process never entirely stopped, even following publication: his own copies of the books, including the final Collected Poems, contain a small number of amendments, which are reflected here.

He kept up this organisational approach for the rest of his life. The earliest poem included here is numbered 54 and was written in December 1947; the last, number 3,897, was written in January 1992. He therefore wrote about 3,900 poems during his forty-five years of mature production, of which 693 were published in the 1990 Collected and some 400 remain in manuscript. In total, about 1,100 still exist. The missing 2,800 were not good enough, so he destroyed them.

My father certainly never shaped his creative output with individual books in mind. The seed of each poem was a moment's inspiration or memory and, as he told me, the poems were often completely forgotten almost as soon as written (something entirely credible to those who knew him well). Despite the themes that run strongly through his work, the poems, with few exceptions, were discrete events and book selections were made from the stockpile available at the time. He always had a large supply of unpublished poems, even after completing the selection for a book. This is partly because he believed in selecting only from new material. Poems that had appeared in periodicals or been used in readings were not allowed in books, so many poems did not appear in the fourteen individual collections, despite having been disseminated by the author in other ways. While he held to this principle closely, a few may have been read and publication in the Collected editions was allowed.

On looking through my father's papers after his death I found about 600 unpublished poems.[3] About 200 predated his change of style so, as he had publicly rejected all this early work, they were not considered for publication here. The rest were from his mature period and could be considered. It would have been excessively precious and a negation of responsibility to interpret his injunction not to publish 'rubbish' as an all-embracing ban – principles apart, there were too many good poems. Considerations of principle vary, depending on when the poems were written. I have no concerns about publishing a selection of poems from the period approaching and following the 1990 edition of the Collected Poems, because they were not available for inclusion. However, even when considering work that could have been in the 1990 collection, it is far from evident that all the poems were decisively rejected. For one thing, he had kept them despite having destroyed most of his unpublished work. Also, although he was keen to reject poor work, he was often indecisive about individual poems. It appeared that the process of selection for books caused him far more difficulty than writing the poems in the first place. He told me on a number of occasions that there were poems he later wished he had included in the 1990 collection and our conversations in his old age sometimes touched on the topic of his recent work, without any suggestion that it should remain forever unpublished. What he objected to was indiscriminate publication of juvenilia and other unworthy relics.

Other considerations may explain why some individual poems were never published. One is that he felt some poems were more suitable

3 Though I refer to them as such, some will have appeared in periodicals and a very few appeared in the Selected edition by Douglas Dunn, now out of print.

for public readings than print and his productivity meant there were always plenty available for the books. It seems right that poems he read to the public should be available in print after his death. A small number of poems may have been withheld because of content that could be related to individuals then alive. A practical consideration is that his strategy for ordering his work methodically was not put into effective practice. I believe that numerous poems must have lain unnoticed for years in the chaos of his papers.

Much of the unpublished work included here is from his later years. Of the 99 poems selected, nineteen date from 1961–79 and 25 are from 1980–86. All of these could have been included in the 1990 collection, although his tendency to hoard recent work made those from 1980–86 more likely to be bypassed. Forty-four date from 1987–92. Many of these were from 1987–89 and may have been considered for the 1990 Collected. However, it seems unlikely that many were genuine candidates, although a few others from this period were included. Despite his age, he had hoped to cap the Collected with another slim volume so, feeling that his productivity was diminishing, he became reluctant to include many recent poems there. His words to me were, 'I'm not giving the buggers everything.' Not many of the poems from 1989–1992 were typed and very few of the later ones appear to have been amended at all. The ambition to produce another book was defeated by age and tiredness.

Thirteen of the unpublished poems are undated and a few of these have been taken from sources such as magazine cuttings found among his papers.

My father left quite a number of poems in the fourteen books out of the collected editions, especially from the earlier volumes. Although these were not considered for this edition, a few inadvertently made their way into the selection process and two made it through to the final list. Bearing in mind his expressed regrets about poems excluded from the Collected Poems, I have allowed these two to remain.

Having decided that including unpublished work would not disrespect the author's wishes, it remained to make a cautious selection. The 200 poems from his early period were disregarded. Some of the 400 mature poems were second-rate by MacCaig standards. Many others contained good things but were flawed, including some of the late poems that had not been revised. All such were rejected: editorial amendment has been limited to a very few corrections of obvious drafting errors. The chosen 99 are about a quarter of those remaining following the author's own ruthless cull from about 3,200 to 400 – a long way from the bottom of the barrel.

The first task of selecting from the 400 poems was to prepare a shortlist, which I did in consultation with my sister. The 130 short-listed poems were passed to Tom Pow and Alan Taylor, whose help in deciding the final set of 99 was invaluable. The objective was to select poems that, as a group, would not dilute the quality of the 1990 collection. I believe the objective has been met, although, as with any selection, others would have chosen differently. Inevitably, some poems are on the margin but that applies equally to some of those included in the Collected by my father. A few are among my personal favourites. The later poems may be of particular interest as they add significantly to the published work from his old age.

The other editorial issue was ordering the poems. An option was to complement the text of the 1990 collection. This followed the sequence of the fourteen books. Within each book, the order was retained, though some poems were excluded, mostly from the earlier books. Additional poems, from about the time of writing, followed each book. This format could have been retained, with the new poems added at the end or interspersed among the previous additional poems. However, I preferred to present the poems in the order of writing, while flagging the new poems as they appear in the text. His practice of numbering and dating his poems made this approach possible.

An objection to this is that the original order of the poems would have been selected by the author to provide a meaningful or, at least, readable sequence. This is a valid point: the order will not have been arbitrary. However, while my father discussed issues around the selection of poems with me on numerous occasions, he never referred to ordering. I don't think it was a concern that ranked highly with him. Even if it did, how far can the selection of order in individual books be sustained meaningfully in a larger collection? To some extent, it has been lost already, because poems were rejected. Also, he did not want the 1990 collection to be his last words. It is not possible to say whether, if he were alive to consider the presentation of his lifetime's work, my father would have retained an ordering system that, to me, now looks scrappy and piecemeal. Of the 792 poems here, 221 did not appear in the original fourteen books. Any attempt to retain elements of the original ordering would therefore have been partial and unsatisfactory.

Another reason to consider change is that this is no longer a book that readers might swallow whole. A book of 60 or 70 poems is not the same as a collection of over ten times that number: readers will browse, dip and refer. The principal effect of retaining the book order might be to give an impression that the collection consisted of two classes of poem, which I do not believe to be the case. The poems were not created in that way.

Therefore I adopted the principle of ordering by time. There is, of course, a correlation with the book ordering, especially in the 1960s and 1970s. The ordering task was possible because nearly all the poems were numbered and dated. Very occasionally, the number and date sequences did not match, although the differences were never significant. I have used the date in such cases. I believe my father would have got the month right, so his picking up the wrong 'last' sheet to get the next number is the most credible hypothesis.

There is one significant interruption in the presentation by date: I was unable to trace the manuscript and typescript of his fourth book, A Round of Applause. The poems from this book are inserted in a group at about the right time. A very small number of poems from other books have been similarly treated and 22 undated poems are placed at the end. Generally, though, the order is preserved very well.

There is only one sequence of poems in my father's work: the twelve Poems for Angus. They were written between March 1976 and January 1978. The sequence has been preserved and the poems are presented in the order in which they appeared in The Equal Skies.

The poems in the book are dated. The previously unpublished poems are identified by an asterisk following the date and are marked in the contents and index in the same way.

Clearly, the poems are the main substance of this book. However, three further elements are included. The introduction, by Alan Taylor, mainly discusses MacCaig's life and times. Quotations from MacCaig also gives context to the poetry. Most of the material comes from interviews with my father undertaken by Anette Degott in 1986 and 1988, as part of a PhD thesis on his work. Her interviews explored the topics of interest in more depth (and length) than in, for example, broadcast interviews. The material has been selected, edited and ordered by me. It mainly covers topics related to his own writing.

Acknowledgements

I am very grateful to Tom Pow and Alan Taylor for their help in selecting previously unpublished poems for inclusion here and to Anette Degott-Reinhardt, who provided transcripts of interviews with my father and was generous with her help in identifying and reviewing other material.

Norman MacCaig: an Introduction

Alan Taylor

THERE is every possibility that Norman MacCaig would not have approved of this introduction. When I first wrote about him in *The Scotsman* newspaper nearly a quarter of a century ago it took all the courage I could muster to ask him what he thought of it. 'All right as far as it goes, I suppose,' was the extent of his response. He insisted he was allergic to prose, which he wrote sparingly and reluctantly. Indeed he once claimed that he never read novels, which the many visitors to his flat in Edinburgh will testify was preposterous. When asked to write a note by way of a preface to *Scottish Eccentrics* by Hugh MacDiarmid, MacCaig vowed that it would be 'a limited note at that'.

MacDiarmid (with whom MacCaig is connected as Wordsworth was to Coleridge) was 'a tough subject' – a walking, talking, gesticulating mass of contradictions. 'Say something about him that is true and before the words are out of your mouth you remember that the opposite is also true.' MacDiarmid and MacCaig were chalk and cheese – physically, temperamentally, aesthetically, politically, you name it. They were bonded through poetry and friendship. MacDiarmid was built like a Border terrier, with a head of hair which seemed permanently to be on fire; MacCaig was as tall as a poppy, with the profile of a Roman emperor and the thin, sarcastic lips of a hanging judge. Some of MacDiarmid's best poems were written in Scots, which MacCaig chose not to use. MacDiarmid was a Communist and a Nationalist and, depending on the mood of the moment, a Fascist. 'He is a materialist and visionary,' wrote MacCaig. 'He is immoralist in principle and puritan in practice.'

MacCaig ought to be easier to sum up, but he is not. Genealogically, he said, he was 'a three-quarter Gael'. Three of his grandparents were Gaels and the fourth hailed from Dumfriesshire. 'He's the one who gets me to places on time,' he wrote in an autobiographical essay for *Chapman* magazine. Though he holidayed in the north-west of Scotland he was a city dweller all his life. He was apolitical and a pacifist and during the Second World War spent 93 days in Wormwood Scrubs as a conscientious objector. He was unshakeable in his abhorrence of all wars and suspicious of 'big words' such as glory, liberty, patriotism and democracy. He would surely have sympathised with MacDiarmid when he wrote that 'most of the important words were killed in the First World War'.

Throughout his poetry there is an unsentimental attachment to Scotland – its history, landscape, fauna, flora and people. In his longest poem, 'A man in Assynt', he rose to rhetorical anger at the injustices heaped on local communities by a distant government and imperious landlords:

> Who owns this landscape? –
> The millionaire who bought it or
> the poacher staggering downhill in the early morning
> with a deer on his back?
> Who possesses this landscape? –
> The man who bought it or
> I who am possessed by it?

Asked to sum up his religion, MacCaig invariably replied: 'Zen Calvinist'.

Norman Alexander MacCaig was born on 14 November 1910. His father, Robert, who came from Haugh-of-Ur in Dumfriesshire, was a pharmaceutical chemist in a shop in Dundas Street in Edinburgh's New Town. 'It was a white-collar job,' MacCaig recalled, 'and he wore fly-away stiff collars all his life ... very, very, very "boorjoysie".' His mother, Joan, née McLeod, was from Scalpay, a small island near Harris. Joan was sixteen when she arrived in Edinburgh and found work as a domestic servant. She and Robert married in December 1906. At first she spoke no English but she soon acquired enough to 'run circles round professors of Sanskrit'. According to her son, she thought predominantly in images and metaphors, a talent he inherited.

Around the age of twelve, MacCaig began to visit Scalpay, which was to have a profound influence on him:

> Those teenage visits to Scalpay, I didn't realise how important they were to me at the time but looking back it's the first time I began to realise that I had ancestors, not just my mother and father. They gave me a connection. It was meeting my aunts and my cousins there made me realise that I was a

miniscule and unimportant part of history. No, that's putting it too portentously. I felt I belonged to people in a way that I hadn't before, except to my parents.

Much as MacCaig liked Scalpay and could relate to its inhabitants, of whom there were fewer than one hundred, he was not at all attracted to their religion. They subscribed to Free Presbyterianism – the 'Wee Frees' are a byword for joylessness and deplore drinking, dancing and singing outside of church. In 'A man in Assynt' MacCaig describes how the:

> dark minds in black clothes gather
> like bees to the hive to share
> the bitter honey of the Word, to submit
> to the hard judgement of a God
> my childhood God would have difficulty
> in recognising.

Neither of MacCaig's parents was a Free Presbyterian, nor did they force religion on him or his three sisters. MacCaig himself joked he was a born atheist who uttered 'Down with Popery!' in Gaelic the minute he emerged from his mother's womb.

When he was five years old he was enrolled at the Royal High School on the south side of Calton Hill. It was not a private school but a small fee was exacted and pupils had to supply their own books. Among its illustrious alumni were William Drummond of Hawthornden, Sir Walter Scott, and Henry Mackenzie, who wrote the eighteenth-century bestseller, *The Man of Feeling*. In his autobiography, Paul Henderson Scott, ten years MacCaig's junior, remembered the 'dictatorial' rector, William King Gillies, who decreed that everyone should concentrate on the Classics and Mathematics, because he believed it was the best way to train the mind. MacCaig was not enamoured of King Gillies, the first of many authoritarian figures he was happy to lampoon. Ironically, in due course he too would become a schoolmaster, his model being a teacher called Young 'who understood bairns'.

How did MacCaig become a poet? In his usual diversionary, self-deprecating manner he claimed that what got him started was an English teacher who asked a class of fifth formers to produce an essay or a poem by the following week. Ever pragmatic, MacCaig opted for the poem because 'a poem is shorter'. He produced a poem to the tune of a Gaelic song, whose name he couldn't spell: 'Bruthaichean Ghlinn Bhraoin'. He never looked back.

'From then on,' he said, 'I wrote a tremendous number of "poems" of an elaborate and increasing awfulness.' Not all of them could have been terrible. In 1928, he won a prize for a poem called 'Autumn' and also the Walter Scott Prize, which was open to pupils in Edinburgh schools. Four years later, Muriel Spark won the same prize. MacCaig also wrote a prize-winning essay on Robert Louis Stevenson.

Destined to become a teacher, he won a bursary to Edinburgh University to study Classics in 1928, graduating in 1932 with Honours. At Edinburgh, at a dance, he met his future wife, Isabel Munro, who got a First in English. She, too, became a teacher; later, she was one of the co-editors of the *Oxford Dictionary of English Idioms*. They were married in 1939. Though Isabel was in the same class at university as Sorley MacLean, the Gaelic bard from the island of Raasay, MacCaig did not meet him until later. They became lifelong friends.

A formative influence on MacCaig's thinking at this period and thereafter was Socrates, none of whose own writing has survived but whose beliefs are communicated through the words of Plato, Socrates' student. MacCaig's poems are often exquisite examples of Socratic dialogues, in which the poet, in a quest for self-knowledge, interrogates himself. Like MacCaig, Socrates pretended to be ignorant of the subject under examination. The purpose of Socrates' method, which Plato described as 'midwifery', was to demonstrate to the student that if only he looked hard enough he would find the answer within himself. Socrates, said MacCaig, was one of his 'big men'. Plato, on the other hand, was 'just an up-market journalist'. In his final collection, *Voice-Over*, published in 1988, MacCaig invoked Socrates in 'Backward look':

> Or ugly Socrates, monolith-still
> in the middle of the battle, brooding
> on his beautiful, improbable abstractions:
> see his hand, without a tremor,
> raise the glass of hemlock to his truthful lips.

Edinburgh in the 1930s was a parochial, provincial backwater. The vertiginous Old Town, shaped like a herringbone, was mostly slums and there were signs that the New Town, built at the end of the eighteenth century, was going the same way. Behind the classical façades and doric columns, Edwin Muir, writing in 1935 in *Scottish Journey*, could not miss the poor and the unemployed. Only a few years earlier, Muriel Spark's Miss Brodie, traversing the sooty Scottish capital with the *crème de la crème* of the Marcia Blane School for Girls in her wake, was witness to a city of extremes. In the Grassmarket, the smell was 'amazingly' terrible. While children played barefoot, couples engaged in slanging matches and a man sat – 'just sat' – on an ice-cold pavement. Meanwhile, her charges held their noses, averted their gaze and listened to her lament John Knox.

This, then, was the nature of the city in which MacCaig embarked on his adult life. After a year at Moray House teacher training college, he emerged into an overcrowded job market and began looking for a job teaching Classics. After several months of unemployment and a number of temporary posts, he started teaching in primary schools, where he was to remain for thirty years. The job suited him and he liked children, though even he used the tawse from time to time. When war broke out in 1939, he was prepared to do anything but kill people. So he became a 'conchie', a conscientious objector. After his release from Wormwood Scrubs, he returned to Edinburgh and found a job in a nursery garden in Corstorphine. Though he didn't know 'a daffodil from an aluminous bullfoot' he spent two years there.

His first book, *Far Cry*, appeared in 1943; his second, *The Inward Eye*, in 1946. Neither collection was represented in MacCaig's *Selected Poems*, published in 1971, nor did they feature in his two volumes of *Collected Poems*, respectively published in 1985 and 1990. Nor do they figure in the present volume. Had MacCaig been able to, he would have bought and destroyed every copy or removed them from libraries and put them through a shredder. 'If you see any of them in people's bookcases,' he once said, 'offer to buy them for £10, or steal them, then take them home and burn them!' They represented a past he had no intention of revisiting, belonging to a period in his development when he was a member of The New Apocalypse, which one of its adherents, G.S. Fraser, described unappetisingly as a 'dialectical development of Surrealism'. Apart from Fraser and MacCaig, its members also included J.F. Hendry, Maurice Lindsay, Dylan Thomas and Vernon Watkins.

'Rubbish – incomprehensible rubbish!' was MacCaig's uncompromising verdict on these two rookie efforts. But while they may not have enhanced his reputation they taught him a valuable lesson, namely that to write obscurely is relatively easy. To write clearly and unambiguously is another matter. Inevitably, MacCaig turned adversity into an anecdote. He liked to tell the story of how he lent a friend one of the two offending books. When he returned it, he asked the poet when he was going to publish the answers. It marked the beginning of what MacCaig called 'the long haul to lucidity'. The first sign that he was on the right track came in 1955 with the publication of *Riding Lights*.

Every poem, said Dylan Thomas, should be a celebration, a sentiment Norman MacCaig keenly endorsed. In *Riding Lights* the things he celebrated, hymned, snapshot, captured, contemplated, memorialised, brought to life, were common to everyone. The titles are eloquently prosaic: 'I remember you', 'The last week of the year', 'Public bar', 'Cold wind in May', 'Back to Sutherland after a long absence'. The tone is conversational and the language requires no recourse to the dictionary. Like his mother, MacCaig communicates in images and metaphors and similes. One moment we're in Assynt climbing a mountain, the next in Edinburgh on a 'brown' – a favourite MacCaig colour – November night. He stares at the stars, listens to a bird's song and watches snow melt. It has been said of MacCaig that his poems give very little away about himself but it is hard to think of a poet who is more omnipresent. Whatever he is writing about, it seems, he relates it to himself and his being in the cosmos, as if he is trying to see where he fits in and learn what he has to contribute. 'Swimming lizard' is typical:

> He swam through the cool loch water
> As though not knowing whether he slanted down
> Or up to the brightness. Swimming was all he did.
>
> The tiny monster, the alligator
> A finger long, swam unhurried through the brown;
> Each eye glittered under its heavy lid.
>
> This was his witness and his protest,
> To swim unhurried; for an unknown Cause
> He twinkled his brief text through the brown and still.
>
> And I, like it, too big to be noticed,
> Hung over him in pity, and my help, too, was
> No reaching hand, but a loving and helpless will.

MacCaig once wrote:

> The thing is, art, whatever else it may be or do, is concerned with form, and that's to say, with order. I don't know whether artists see an order in the chaos of experience that other people don't or whether they impose an order on that chaos. But that order must be there. To defend formless and chaotic writing on the ground that it's an enactment of the chaotic times we live in is to commit that aesthetic sin, the fallacy of imitative form, and to renege from the primary duty of any artist, in whatever form he is operating.

MacCaig wrote prolifically and quickly. Asked how long he took to write a poem, he replied: 'Two fags. Unless it's a wee one, then it's one fag.' Over his career his method did not change very much. When he felt like writing a poem, he would sit down with a blank piece of paper and no idea in his head, into which, he explained, 'where there's plenty of room', would come the memory of a place, an emotional experience, a person, 'or, most commonly, a phrase, and the poem stalactites down the page from there'. Before he knew what the poem was about, it was finished. Often it turned out not to be about what he thought it was about but something entirely different. On the surface its subject might be a person or a plant or a place but its substance lay deeper in the poet's psyche. He did not revise much; he preferred to discard poems which he didn't like. The pleasure, he said, lay in their making, which he compared to the pleasure a craftsman takes in making a table, of producing something useful and beautiful that did not previously exist. But he was always the arbiter of what survived. MacDiarmid said his job was never to lay a tit's egg, 'but to erupt like a volcano, emitting not only flame but a lot of rubbish'. MacCaig's contract with himself was less violent and more discriminating. What he did not throw away is what he wanted us to read.

'Landscape,' MacCaig told Karl Miller, the writer and critic, who some decades later was also a pupil at the Royal High School, 'is my religion'. The landscape to which he and his family – Isabel, his daughter Joan and son Ewen – constantly returned was that of Assynt in the north-west of Scotland. The compensation for MacCaig's low salary as a primary school teacher was a long, uninterrupted annual summer holiday.

The further north one goes the more rugged and inhospitable becomes the terrain. Even today the road is fit only for rally drivers, rising theatrically then dropping precipitously. Outcrops of rocks and rippling, trout-filled lochans conspire to add to the area's otherness, its sense of remoteness. Stags stand sentinel while raptors hover in expectation. According to legend, the mountains of Assynt were deposited by the Norse gods, which seems all too believable when one first spies them bursting from the moorland like whales from the deep.

To MacCaig, their names and features were as familiar as those of his children: Suilven, Cul Beg, Canisp, Stac Polly, Cul Mor, 'my/ mountain of mountains,/ looming and pachydermatous in the thin light/ of a clear half moon.' No less hypnotic or evocative, however, were the names of the little towns and villages which cling like survivors of a shipwreck to the rugged coastline: Achiltibuie, Achmelvich, Inverkirkaig, and Lochinver. The MacCaigs stayed in rented accommodation, first in Achmelvich then in Inverkirkaig.

Assynt was MacCaig's idyll, his Eden. If he could have had his way, he would have spent half the year there, the other half in Edinburgh. In the early years, his children ran wild and barefoot, while he fished or smoked or imbibed his surroundings. Indeed, he called one collection just that. Published in 1966, *Surroundings* includes several poems set outside Scotland – 'The streets of Florence', 'Assisi', 'Hill streams of Abruzzi' – which were inspired by a Society of Authors' sponsored trip to Italy. But, significantly, they are surrounded by poems of home. Like Larkin, who would have liked to have gone to China if he could have returned the same day, MacCaig had no appetite for travel.

What differentiated Assynt from other parts of Scotland was its geology, a 'bamboozling' complex of low hills sitting on a bed of Lewisian gneiss. It was the geology of this landscape, said MacCaig, that was the bones of its beauty. It allowed him to imagine a time before man existed and a future in which he might no longer exist. In poem after poem he emphasises human temporality, the passing, injurious influence of people on the landscape and on themselves, the size of our egos in the face of eternity. He was no romantic or sentimentalist. In Assynt, he lived amongst real people making a real living against formidable odds: shearing sheep, poaching salmon, cutting peats. It had always been thus, since man – 'a man' – had first arrived, from prehistoric times through the Clearances to the present day when the crofters unite to buy back the land of their forebears. People make a place, people like A.K. MacLeod, one of the special few named by MacCaig throughout his oeuvre. But the place does not reciprocate; it just is.

> I can't pretend
> it gets sick for me in my absence,
> though I get
> sick for it. Yet I love it
> with special gratitude, since
> it sends me no letters, is never
> jealous and, expecting nothing
> from me, gets nothing but
> cigarette packets and footprints.

Who knows when MacCaig first met MacDiarmid? The chances are it was in one of Edinburgh's so-called Poets' Pubs, the Abbotsford at the east end of Rose Street or Milne's Bar in a basement on Hanover Street. In Alan Bold's biography of MacDiarmid, MacCaig first makes an appearance in MacDiarmid's orbit in May 1953, when Sean O'Casey and his wife Eileen were guests of honour at a party at the MacCaigs' flat in Leamington Terrace.

Whenever the pair met, they were soon inseparable if – on the face of it – incompatible. MacDiarmid, reported Bold, 'appreciated MacCaig's intellectual clarity, his acerbic wit, his capacity for keeping a clear head while drinking malt whisky, and the fact that he was one of the few Scottish poets of his generation who eschewed the MacDiarmid manner'.

By then, MacDiarmid had written most of the poetry that posterity may deem his best. MacCaig had yet to prove what he was capable of. Nearly three decades later, Alexander Moffat produced his famous painting of the Poets' Pub. MacDiarmid, not long dead, is the centre of attraction. Hanging on his every word are George Mackay Brown and Sidney Goodsir Smith. To the right sits Robert Garioch, his hands pensively clasped. Next to him is Edwin Morgan, jazzily dressed in a white checked jacket and red shirt. In the far background, as if looking down on the unfolding scene, stands the moustachioed Sorley MacLean, in front of him his younger fellow Gael, Iain Crichton Smith. MacCaig is the only poet presented full-length, a lean, languid, bored-looking figure, cigarette in his hand, like a Teddy boy who's gate-crashed the Mod. None of them looks as if he is having fun.

Much has been written about Milne's Bar and its denizens, much of it myth. Whether there ever was an occasion when all the poets in Moffat's painting were gathered there together is doubtful. They came and went as circumstance prescribed. Mackay Brown, a student at Newbattle in Midlothian, recalled dropping by in the late 1950s, peering through the smoke and the beer-fumes 'at the semi-legendary figures'. Goodsir Smith was a regular but the others were more transient visitors, not least because they had daytime jobs or lived outwith Edinburgh.

In his novel *Lanark*, published in 1981, Alasdair Gray described Mac-Diarmid, MacCaig and Goodsir Smith, 'the Rose Street Poets':

> The bar was crowded except where the three men stood in a small open space created by the attention of the other customers. One had a sombre pouchy face and upstanding hair which seemed too like thistledown to be natural, one looked like a tall sarcastic lizard, one like a small sly shy bear. 'Our three best since Burns,' a bystander informed me, 'barring Sorley of course.'

In the decades after the war the pubs in Edinburgh closed at ten o'clock, when things were just beginning to get going. On winter nights, when the leaves were glued to the pavement with frost and the sweet, yeasty smell from the breweries supplemented the intoxication, MacCaig would invite the throng back to his flat in Leamington Terrace, near Tollcross, 'burdened,' as Mackay Brown noted, 'with "kerry-oots"'. In the high-ceilinged sitting-room, one wall lined with books, another with photographs and drawings, MacCaig was the consummate host, glass in hand, frequently gurgling with laughter. Friends often knocked on the door well after midnight and were welcomed as if it were mid-day.

> 'One was aware always that for this particular man...,' wrote Mackay Brown, 'poetry was the thing that mattered most (however recklessly we squandered words in Milne's or the Abbotsford or Leamington). Subtle, invisible, passionate, the words that mattered were being gathered into the loom of his imagination, becoming at last, in the loneliness such as a poet must live in for much of the time, the magical web we call poetry.

To apprentice word-spinners like myself, he gave welcome and encouragement and benison always, without stint. We do well to salute him and be grateful.'

In total, MacCaig produced sixteen volumes of poetry, concluding with *Voice-Over* in 1988, all of which were published in London. In MacCaig's day, Scottish publishers, such as Callum Macdonald, who was based at Loanhead, William Maclellan and Duncan Glen, who ran Akros, were either under-capitalised, unbusinesslike or amateurish in their approach. In the circumstances, the books they produced were small miracles.

Throughout his life MacCaig received a pittance from his poetry. Not that he ever expected otherwise. Teaching remained his prime source of income. In later years he refrained from calling himself a poet, insisting he was a 'retired schoolteacher'. It was a profession which was slow to recognise his talent. Belatedly, he was appointed head teacher of Inch Primary School in Edinburgh. Many interpreted this overdue promotion as his punishment for being a conscientious objector, a reasonable supposition but unverifiable. Interestingly, MacCaig wrote very little about school life. He liked teaching and liked children. He addressed them as he would adults, without condescension. When he stopped teaching, he was regularly asked to give readings in schools. Rarely did he say no. His pocket diaries, deposited with the rest of his papers in the University of Edinburgh's library, read like train timetables.

In 1967, he was made the first fellow in Creative Writing at Edinburgh University and in 1970 he joined the Department of English Studies at the University of Stirling, in 1972 becoming a Reader in Poetry, a post he held until 1978. 'At the back of their heads,' he said, 'I think, they were offering me an Eventide Home.' He took the job on condition he did not have to attend committees. He preferred scholars to academics. Only occasionally did he give lectures, usually on MacDiarmid. Obviously at ease on a public platform, he nevertheless found lecturing a trial. Clocks in lecture halls seemed to tick slower than elsewhere.

Instead, he took tutorials and gave seminars on contemporary Scottish literature, American poetry and European poetry in translation. Sometimes he tackled writers who were deemed to have been influences on himself, the list of which is legion: William Carlos Williams, Robert Frost, Wallace Stevens, Bertolt Brecht, Miroslav Holub. MacCaig himself insisted he had never played the sedulous ape to anyone. 'My bump of mimicry was amputated at birth,' he said. No-one, however, ever seriously suggested that MacDiarmid had influenced him or vice versa. Their friendship came about because they liked one another. 'He liked me,' MacCaig said. 'He didn't admire me at all. I liked him, and didn't admire him at all.' One must take that with a pinch of the coarsest salt.

Age brought MacCaig awards and wider recognition – the OBE in 1979; the Queen's Gold Medal for Poetry in 1984 – but these were no consolation for the loss of those he loved. In September 1978 he gave the oration at MacDiarmid's funeral. 'He would walk into my mind as if it were a town and he a torchlight procession of one,' he said, having previously called on the nation to observe 'two minutes pandemonium' on the anniversary of his birth. A.K. MacLeod's death followed soon after. MacCaig took his pain out on an officer of religion:

> Over the dead man's house, over his landscape
> the frozen air was a scrawny psalm
> I believed in, because it was pagan
> as he was.
> Into it the minister's voice
> spread a pollution of bad beliefs.
> The sanctimonious voice dwindled away
> over the boring, beautiful sea.

In 1990, Isabel MacCaig died. At her funeral, the Shetland fiddler, Aly Bain, played a lament which melted into a jig.

The first edition of MacCaig's *Collected Poems* appeared in 1985, coinciding with his 75th birthday. Five years later, marking his 80th birthday, a revised edition was published, an occasion celebrated by a sell-out audience at the Queen's Hall in Edinburgh, with contributions from Sorley MacLean, Iain Crichton Smith, Liz Lochhead, Seamus Heaney and others. In 1995, his 85th birthday was celebrated in similar style at the Assembly Rooms in Edinburgh.

The following year, on 23 January 1996, Norman MacCaig died. The obituaries were generous and affectionate. *The Herald* remembered his multi-facetedness, his love of music, both traditional (in his youth he had played the fiddle, even attempting the pibroch) and classical, his devotion to smoking (advised to give up, he put a lit cigarette in each side of his mouth and said, 'One for each lung!') and drinking, his career in teaching, the hills he'd climbed and the rivers he'd fished, his determination to avoid pigeon-holing, his impatience with cant. *The Scotsman* wrote, 'He was an easy person to meet, an extraordinarily difficult person to know', adding:

> Critics have sometimes claimed that the poetry is lightweight, glib and lacking in political edge … But when one looks back across his *Collected Poems*, one is struck anew by the variety and profundity and lack of solemnity. He debunks our clichéd myths and stock responses, he forces a fresh awareness in such a way that we feel we have found something for ourselves.

It was left to Seamus Heaney to sum him up. A sentence was all that was necessary. 'He means poetry to me.'

Quotations from MacCaig[1]

The material here is mainly taken from interviews, hence the conversational style. The order is not taken from the sources and each quotation is separate. The selected topics are those of most relevance to the poetry – mainly MacCaig's thoughts on his own writing and writing generally. Although the material had to be ordered into a readable sequence, no attempt has been made to force a thematic structure and editorial intrusion has been kept to a minimum.

★

... there was a bit of surrealism in me when I was young, which I got from my mother, who was a Gael, a Celt. She expressed herself in metaphors and images to an extraordinary degree. So if there is any poetry in me, that's where it comes from. Often her images were really surrealistic, very funny very often. So there is a bit of that in me anyway, genetically. But I also got interested in surrealism round about university time. I bought magazines and things, you know, and I decided surrealism is all very well for painters, but it's no damn good for poets.

★

... poetry involves order. It has to submit to the control of the rational mind – it's not enough to lift the trap-door to the subconscious and lasso whatever crawls out. I say this, blushing with guilt, for there was a time in the Thirties and early Forties when that is pretty much what I did. Poem after poem was a splurge of hardly related images, sloppily bound together – and it wasn't enough – only by the blessed formalities of metre and rhyme. ... I was rescued by the only critical remark that was ever any use to me, when my second book came out and a friend, having read it, handed it back to me, saying, "When are you publishing the answers?" This took me several steps back towards my senses and I started on the long and difficult haul towards lucidity.

★

1 Mainly taken from: Anette Degott-Reinhardt: Norman MacCaigs lyrisches Werk (Frankfurt am Main: Lang, 1994).

xli]

I don't like vague words like that, impressionism, expressionism, I don't like them. I hate abstract words. I'm incapable of abstract thinking, that's why. I like to particularise. I hardly ever say a tree, I say what sort of tree it is, that sort of thing. A bird flew up from a cornfield. I would name the type of bird.

*

But you see, until these immediate experiences that occurred to me I have had an extraordinarily lucky life. A terrible thing about getting older is that your friends die on you. And suffering, therefore, comes into the poems much more often than it used to. They didn't use to come in very often because I didn't suffer. I went around in a continuous state of controlled hilarity. If I think of civilisation, I don't get off and dance in the streets. There's an awful lot of things wrong with civilisation and of course, I'm aware of them in a way. Take the big one, the war in Vietnam. The war in Vietnam didn't bother me at all, except when I was reading the news or discussing it; all the other hours in the twenty-four, I was concerned with my little, local, immediate existence and was a happy man. And I used to distrust people who went on and on about the atom bomb when I saw them drinking their pints with their friends and laughing and pretending they couldn't sleep at night because of the atom bomb. I think people lie about this. Most of the time they are not thinking of it at all. Only when it comes under their nose like the Assisi thing or the New York thing in my case, then you really feel it in the immediate way that is necessary for the creation of a poem. Otherwise you're just fictioneering. I'm only aware of the fact when you mention it. I don't have the mushroom cloud hanging over my head – except when I'm talking about it or reading about it. It's the nature of experience. What does a man know about death until somebody whom he loves dies? It's just an abstraction but if somebody you love dies then, boy, your nose is rubbed in absolutely nothing at all and it's a painful experience.

*

That is one theme that runs through everything I've written or damned near it. Well, now, put it this way. A tree that somebody hangs himself on isn't the same to that fellow who climbs up the tree with a rope as it is to the wee boy to pinch the apples. Every object, the tree, is different to everybody else. Pasternak in one of his poems says: "That tree outside the window is not a tree, it's a category of human passion," meaning that every object has a different meaning to every single person who looks at it. So have words.

★

Classical writing is generally very formal. I don't mean in the sense of formal manners, but very interested in shape more than colour, slightly more than colour. It keeps to the fact, which Romanticism doesn't. Romanticism glorifies and splatters the object with the writer's feelings, which I hate. Celtic art is very classical. In old Celtic art, all of their arts, songs, poems, sculpture … are very formal and I think I have always loved form, unconsciously. This is hindsight. But probably that's the reason I chose to take Classics at the university. And my native preference was, of course, reinforced by the study of Classics. So if I write a poem about an emotion, I don't inflate it. I write and I write as honestly as I can. I don't sit down and say: "Now we're going to have a tremendous love poem. Oh boy, everybody will admire it." No. Remember "We'll do it our way – / with a look, with a touch / and with the space between words / where the truths live / that we can find no words for." That is as far as I go. I won't go any further.

★

I disapprove terribly strongly of people who make references – say to classical or Greek literature or Chinese or anything else. When I write about classical figures, they are always very well-known ones like Hercules, Ulysses. And funnily enough, generally I take the Mickey out of them. … I don't know why I do that, but nearly every time I write about them – not always, but a lot of times – I use what's known as the reductive idiom, you know, I reduce them, I don't know why.

★

(*Is time connected with memory?*) … Oh, I suppose it must be, yes. Yes. I've got a – everybody has a strange memory. I'm a very – believe me, this is true – I'm a very ordinary person. I really am. I'm the O on the graph. The further away from me you are, the more eccentric you are. In many, many ways it's unbelievably weak and in other ways it's extraordinarily exact. For example, if I think of going once to certain lochs up yonder, miles and miles off the road, I can follow – and I was only there once – I can visualise every step of the way whether it was ten years ago or thirty years ago. On the other hand, the things I forget are unbelievable. People's names, straight off. Numbers. I'm innumerate.

★

… my writing habits haven't changed much. When I feel like writing a poem, I sit down with a blank sheet of paper and no idea whatever in my head. Into it, where there's plenty of room, enters the memory of a place, an emotional experience, a person or, most commonly, a phrase and the poem stalactites down the page from that. This means I'm into the poem, various distances, before I know what it's about. In fact, I don't know what the whole poem's about till I've finished it. This sounds daft, but I believe it's a common enough experience with poets.

★

Many poets polish and refine and eliminate and add, making version after version of the original attempt. I can't do that. The poem, whatever it's worth, generally comes easily and quickly and pretty often with no correction at all, and once it's on the page, that's that. This hit or miss way of writing means that I write a lot. It also means I write a lot of un-improvable duds. I reckon at least half, probably more, of what I write I put in the bucket – an act I relish almost as much as writing the things.

★

You know, often I write a poem in the morning and in the afternoon I can't remember anything about it. Not a single thing about it. I have to look it up.

★

I never get ideas. I don't mean there are no ideas in the poem. If there are, they are emerging in the writing of it. It sounds like a very stupid way, but that's the only way I can do it. I feel like writing a poem in the way I feel hungry, thirsty. Situation admitting it, I sit down with a blank sheet of paper with absolutely nothing in my head. No idea is coming. Into my head, pretty quickly – since there is nothing there to stop it – comes the memory of a place, person, event, or all three, but usually it's a wee phrase. A small phrase, quite unimportant. Any old phrase will do. This starts it off and the poem trickles down the page until it's finished. Now they come very easily. They are all short, of course. I don't write long poems partly because I can't be bothered reading long poems. Who can?

★

It is a fact that often enough in my poems, I self-deride myself, I deride myself and this leads into something I have to watch very carefully. I can so easily become flippant. Flippancy is my terrible enemy. I get on fine with him, mind you, but I have to watch it.

★

The pleasure in making poems lies in making them and seems to me not different from a true craftsman's pleasure in making a table or a meal to put on it, or a boat that marries the water as a boat should.

★

Well, the form of a poem depends on so many things. It depends on the language being used, whether it is conversational or more elevated. It depends on the actual visual shape and on the tone of the poem. Is it irony? Is it straightforward, direct, no ironical over- or undertones? And of course, the rhythm, not the metre because free-verse poems don't have metres, but the rhythm. I think rhythm is the absolutely fundamental thing. When young people show me poems – and my goodness, they do – I wish they were poems – if there is one of them which has a distinctive rhythm, not eccentric, then I think he or she has got the makings of a poet. I think it's the fundamental thing. All the rest is built upon that. The difference between free verse, roughly speaking, and strict form: the basic element in a metrical poem, of course, is the foot, the five-foot-line dá, dá, dá, dá, dá. The basic element in a free-verse poem is the phrase, which can vary very much in length. If your phrases are judiciously contrasted with each other, then you get a beautiful balance of lengths and phrases. So, in a free-verse poem, though it's not metrical, its basic unit is the phrase. These are adjusted because of sensibility and sensitivity keeping in your mind all the time which effect you are trying to produce. Then a free-verse poem will have a form just as much as a metrical one, and I think rather more difficult to achieve because in a strict metre one, there is a strict form, bang, bang, bang. Fill it and, there, with luck and skill, is a poem.

★

xlv]

(*Form and content*) ... Oh, yes, they are indistinguishable. If a poem is a complete poem, jampacked full of statements, words, ideas, images, rhythms, which are all relevant to the theme of the poem, then it has got form. No fat on it. No extra words. Kick them out of they're not earning their keep. Then you get a tight free-verse poem. It's easier to do that in strict form. That's why I think free verse is more difficult to write good poems in.

*

... I have always had a great and to some degree an exploratory interest in prosody and rhymes. Until about ten years ago, or less, I wrote only in stanzas that were metrical and used rhymes. But I was aware of the bullying authority of the compulsively iambic nature of English and particularly of the danger of adding to the thousand miles of banal iambic pentameters. But my way of "breaking the neck of the iambic" was not, for many years, the Poundian one of flopping into free verse and describing the basic element of the metrical foot in favour of the looser, more variable (and more difficult) basis of the cadence, or phrase. I tried to rescue my metrical lines from a rocking-horse Humpty Dumpty by using off beat stresses but not so off beat that the ghostly paradigm of the iambic pentameter (for instance) was not to be noticed behind the frailer metrics I was using. I also began to indulge more and more the ancient practice, publicised as "spring rhythm" and often overdone by G M Hopkins, of taking liberties with the number of syllables in the foot but, again, still preserving the fundamental iambic movement of the line.

There came an evening, however, eight or nine years ago, when I broodily sat down to hatch a poem and, to my surprise the little thing was fledged in free verse. I of course produced more of the same and got very interested in the techniques of this, to me, new form. Whoever it was – was it Graves or Auden? – who said, in contempt of free verse, that it was like playing tennis without a net, was talking through a hole in his own practice. The formal structure of a metrical, rhymed poem may be in some respects a restricting straitjacket, but it also keeps you from flailing your arms about in meaningless, shapeless gestures and it's my belief that to write a formally good poem in free verse is more difficult than to mosaic away with iambs and feminine rhymes. How many free-verse poems are ruined by the lack of a through-going rhythm to articulate the whole and by line endings which are purely arbitrary and serve no functional purpose whatever?

★

(Recognising a poet) ... Now, well, that's not because of the subject. That's because of the rhythm of the words. I think what distinguishes one poet from another poet above everything is the personal rhythm that he has. Much more than his vocabulary or his subject matters, or where he was born and brought up. You can tell two lines of any considerable poet if you have never seen the poem before because of the rhythm. And if that poem makes you think of me, it must be because in that poem, I managed to use a MacCaig rhythm.

★

('Energy') ... That's awfully hard to explain. I can't explain it, even to myself. I know that in the literary magazines, poem after poem after poem are most of them failures because of the lack of energy. You have books, magazines full of these poems. It's like a hospital ward, and on every bed, there is somebody dying of leukaemia and these are supposed to be poems. They just have no energy. They don't reach out and grab you. I don't mean by energy shouting and bawling.... So, an awful lot of poems, contemporary ones, just don't have – I can't explain it, but – no psychological energy. I don't mean the tough, stone-breaking stuff that Ted Hughes writes, which I'm not criticising. That is one way his energy is revealed. Poems can be written about trifles, you know, and – push that to an extreme – can even be written about rubbish. It has got this energy. "Full fathom five thy father lies;/Of his bones are coral made." Not true. "Those are pearls/that were his eyes." Rubbish. And then it goes on to a lot of balderdash about ding-dong belling. Absolute rubbish, but it has resisted the malice of time for three centuries because it has got this energy. It is not shouting and bawling. It's alive.

★

(Poems) are just other ways of speaking the truth. Nobody has been able to answer that. They have been talking about it since Plato's time. Most of the alleged definitions are incredibly short of the mark, you know, "the best words in the best order." That applies to prose as well. "Words, loaded with meaning" – that's one of Ezra Pound's. Well, good prose is

like that. There has not been an adequate definition of poetry. There
never will be. Hurray, hurray.

⋆

(Metaphors) … I don't find them. They present themselves. I know that's
dodging the question, but that's what they do. I don't think them up.
People used to praise a poem because of its beautiful metaphors or
images or something and think how hard I had worked to get them.
Not so.

⋆

(… balance between the emotional and the rational) … I don't like a poem to
be purely one or the other. It ought to be a balance of both, with the
elements of both. If it's purely rational, it should be in prose. If it's
purely emotional, have your hysterics in another room.

⋆

(Romanticism) … It's falsity and it's overblown rhetoric for feelings that
are trifling in the first place. It's sentimentality. It's too far removed
from reality.

⋆

I'm bombarded with things that are loveable.

⋆

An awful lot of my poems are celebrations. I think I probably told you.
There have been more sad ones in the last two, three books. I probably
told you why. Friends died. Close friends. And you never get over that.
Acquaintances, six weeks, six months afterwards, you know, come into
your mind occasionally. But really close friends, you never forget them.
So there are more sad things in the more recent books than there used
to be, which I'm rather glad about because it enabled me to write more
emotionally out of myself than I used to be able to. There is a big streak
of reticence in me. I think everybody has the perfect right to keep their
mouths shut about anything they want to keep their mouths shut about.
In other words, I'm not very fond of the idea of confessional poetry
although I like some confessional poems. Oh, I do, but I'm not a
confessional poet, not at all.

⋆

When I write about things, the poems really are celebrating. I've been such a lucky man all my days. When I write about Suilven or a grasshopper, anything, or a person, it's a celebration. In fact, I wrote a number of poems, as you know, about Angus after he died, and one of them says that even writing this sad, sad poem was, in fact, a celebration of Angus. So I was celebrating, really. I love them all. Earwigs, grass-hoppers, toads … people.

★

… it really is because I love things. I write a lot of poems about animals, all sorts of animals. I pat slaters on their heads and call earwigs by their first names. The difference between my animal poems, for example, and Ted Hughes's animal poems is that mine come out of affection. I love the little brutes and I love mountains, and people and waves and things. If you love something, surely it gives you an entry into their nature and also an elementary thing which I think hasn't been mentioned except I think by one reviewer. I find myself to be fascinated by movement, I love the movement of creatures and grasses, anything. And I think I'm sometimes not bad at describing things in movement. I'm not a static writer in spite of these snapshots.

★

(Identity of a 'thing' in poems – example of a toad) … For sure, for sure, I'm very conscious of that. I don't know what their identities are, of course, but I'm aware that they have them and I hate intruding on their identity. I loathe the pathetic fallacy. Makes it rain when you feel sad; makes it sunny when you feel gay. I loathe burdening outside objects with human feelings, making them some kind of sympathetic translator for my tiny small self. I hate it.

★

I'm not, of course, denying the special, unique and practical importance of poetry and the other arts. The nub and centre (pith if you like) of my thinking about that is this: An adult physique with the intelligence of a child is looked after as potentially dangerous. But an adult intelligence along with the emotional equipment of a child is even more so. Intellect and sensibility – the arts develop both. Poetry teaches a man to do more than observe merely factual errors and measurable truths. It trains him to have a shrewd nose for the bogus, the inflated, the imprecise and the dishonest. So, it compels him to resist stock responses, because it compels him to examine the emotional significance, as well as the rational significance, of whatever comes under his notice.

*

I think the biggest sin, the seven deadly sins you know, is cruelty which manifests itself in injustice and so of all the things I do hate it's cruelty and injustice. I do hate them. I have to flex my muscles to hate things; I am not a natural hater. I think a function of poetry is to recognise that words have an intellectual meaning, but they also have emotional meanings. Now, I think, an awful lot of the troubles in the world between two people or between two countries come from the fact that their emotions, their feelings and their beliefs are accepted as if they came out of a slot machine. They are unexamined. And of course, when a poem is doing its best, it compels the reader to examine the emotional and the intellectual meaning of the language so that the response to the poem isn't a stock response, a penny-in-the-slot response. And when you listen to politicians, trade unionists, teachers, in fact, all of us, we use words expecting a certain response. Mention liberty and people clap their hands. They haven't examined the idea of liberty. Mention a word like love. They have never examined the feeling of love at all. And poetry does examine the emotional and the intellectual meaning of any event and of any word. And therefore, the study of poetry is surely of the most ultimate significance. And in that poem you mentioned "A man in my position", I'm puzzled about myself. I'm examining myself and then I think, "Who am I?" What kind of stock responses am I expecting from the lady the poem is supposed to be addressed to? And how far am I lying?" That is linked with what we started with – what is the real me? – of course.

1]

Poems

The last week of the year

The last week of the year's no time
For contemplating days like orchards.
They hide below ground their tot of bushels
And would spill over a million baskets.

For you below ground are hidden too
And overspill my every measure.
I with my buried hands will be
Gathering you in all my future.

And in the last week of each year
I'll tell myself, 'Oh, why remember
This toss and shine of flowers that all
The winter winds now fail to scatter?'

December 1947

So many make one

There are so many deaths that go
To make up death, as a grown man
Is the walking grave of boy after boy.
– Sometimes we see in him the frown

Of a forsaken ghost, or a dead boy
Speaks suddenly in a petulant voice:
Six feet of blood have drowned so many.
And when death itself comes face to face

With us round that dreadful turning, will
All its ancestors be alive –
Will we, one moment, in its smile
See innocence and belief and love?

December 1947

Public bar

She went along these afternoons
So quiet and slow, so quiet and slow,
Making the year a miracle
Dreamt between June and July.

Now between the mirrors enters
Winter begging for a drink;
He coughs, and tugs my sleeve, and peers
To catch the frosty glasses' talk.

But I have empty pockets, all
My money squandered long ago.
We lean together and mutter of days
Dreamt after June, before July.

December 1947

Instrument and agent

In my eye I've no apple; every object
Enters in there with hands in pockets.
I welcome them all, just as they are,
Every one equal, none a stranger.

Yet in the short journey they make
To my skull's back, each takes a look
From another, or a gesture, or
A special way of saying *Sir*.

So tree is partly girl; moon
And wit slide through the sky together;
And which is star – what's come a million
Miles or gone those inches farther?

December 1947

Ophelia

Hours that were rockets laughing in the dark
With brilliant mild explosions now
Are flat water. Their leaf-gray palms
Hold up your eyes and drowning brow.

Shall I sing willow and scatter there
A wild vocabulary of flowers
To be your chambermaids and round you
Drift on the rambling and rocking waves?

They'll set like stars in your dispersal
And sail beyond the darkness's brim;
And beside the dulcet water I
Will raise your silent requiem.

I'll be your monumental shade
On the banks of darkness; and you will ride
In the long train of curtseying words
To meet my grief at the water's end.

                                        January 1948

Not yet afterwards

Can this be I that made your beauty greater?
Can I be suns swarming on the cold roofs
And with bright shots and snapping flares investing
The streets and shining on faces, hands and scarves?

Can I be March and drive away the winter
That lay so long white on your cold cheeks
And made shine there what's lovelier than crocus,
Oh, eloquent flowers I gather in your looks?

Can I be morning and end of separation?
Can it be I that hustles dreams away
Out of the room, that filled it with sad stories,
That made love possible, that heard you cry?

See, all the world trembles in you and lies
Safe in your hands, escaped from its own self.
Can I be what has made your beauty greater
And shown the world in it? Can I be grief?

March 1948

False summer

False summer's here and the canal's
Green water breathes with lovers' kisses,
And buildings deep as herons stand
In the whirlpool of their own wishes.

The buds that made our winter tender
Feel the leaf aching and begin
Its million-year-old two-inch journey
Into the parish of the sun.

But beyond the yellow light are lurking
Microbes of frost, and in the air
Are ghosts of claws that, one clear night,
Will pinch to ashes the cheated flower.

The water will be black and glassy
Against the brittle grass-stems, and
Bewildered lovers will remember
What once flew in the freezing wind.

April 1948

I remember you

The boat sits stuck in light, the water
Lies heavy as honey; and which
Is stiller, the supple air or the gray
Boulder lichened on the beach?

Here, one would think, is a whole legend,
Not to be added to, caught and held

In the still hallucination of summer
That honeys to blue the breathless wood.

But through the pine tops slants a mallard
Down to its gushing arrowhead;
It makes a whole mountain tremble;
It waves the arras of green shade.

April 1948

Early summer

The garden rolls its sleeves up, sweats
And labours in the fiery sun
To heave a flower into the air, and
Unclench a million fists of green.

Birds tip their sacks of sound – the morning's
Lettered like a calendar
With April growing like corn in the ground
And May hung yellow in the air.

The water in the gutters clucks
With light and flies into the sun.
Shadows crowd into doorways. Walls
Expand, forgetting to be stone.

And windows all are nests on fire;
And a million phoenixes now make
Arabia of these roofs and dart
From trees of incense-bearing smoke.

June 1948

Sun blink

On a steaming cloud the sun jumps, crowing light,
And the air opens like a book. Its blinding
Pages are stained with grass suddenly green
And water suddenly blue. Bracken is sending

Messages by mirrors, to anywhere,
Under the hawk that hangs like an apostle
Over his own bad news. The water rings
Clearer than coins. And with a whispering whistle

This heather clump that's forest to my head
Swarms in a mile of blue ... Time stirs his fire,
And here and everywhere begins to write
Another paragraph on the opened air.

June 1948

Private diary

This sick July that sits and shivers
Under a sackcloth sky is one
Fact that will creep into my book
And like a watch-dog shake its chain.

And other days will cry, 'Keep out',
Shaking a fist of snow or from
A cauldron of letters raising up
A spell of sorrow, a malicious dream.

There is a photograph of me;
Dreams behind my eyes are huge
And on my lap the future purrs.
I'll keep it for the opening page.

And a chapter will be given over
To say what you are and will be.
– You won't be there; for images
No more than clouds describe the sky.

Your name in days and months will be
A monument of your absence; through
The window of a word your hand
Will wave perpetual goodbye.

July 1948

No time, no time

The day's impatient, but you sit still
With weeks to spend, as though no roses
Ever yielded to a bitter air
And stepped out of their fallen graces.

The clouds busily go by; the light
Moves sideways, sniffing in every corner;
The wind seeks what it never finds,
Turning the glittering rubbish over.

And trees dance like children, roofs
Wink and blink like exclamations.
The precious minutes go by; and you
Sit in the ring of four seasons.

But you've no season; and on your hands
The loaded ships of days are stranded.
You prove no rose has ever died;
You prove that no song ever ended.

September 1948

Falls of Measach

The wind was basins slopping over.
The river plunged into its ravine
Like coins into a stocking. The day
Was like the buzzard on the pine.

It looked at us with eyes like resin
From some shelf of the scaly past
And could see nothing in between,
For it knew nothing it had lost.

But we were our continuation
And saw our graves behind us like
Waterfalls marking the stages
To some rich plunge into the dark.

Let the wind spill one other gust
And the day like the buzzard will
Sail, and sink invisible
As a fossil in the distant hill.

September 1948

Environment

The buildings and the frost in the air
Fill my ears with stern advice
And admonishments fall from the grimy hawthorn
And wag green fingers from between the cobbles.

What's there to do, you who surround me?
The air is pale with working in
A narrow room, and his shaking fingers
Twiddle the hawthorn like a ragged pen.

Shall I be automatic like
The cock I hear each muddy dawn
Spitting hot pennies from his throat and
Clapping an Orient down the grimy garden?

I'll pull the coverlet of frost
Up to my ears – like a saint in plaster
I'll snore the century out and wake
Only to call, 'Bring me my jug of winter'.

Or maybe with that drunken sun
I'll stagger over the rough horizon
Shouting a bawdy song of buildings
And making a chorus of the blowsy hawthorn.

But that's no answer. My own self
Is what surrounds me and it trembles
With my own winter. I hang in ragged
Branches and echo like these grassy cobbles.

October 1948

The year, only, goes by

And now November. And we should have
Forgotten all the charms of summer,
But there, framed in leafy branches,
It hangs on the wall, our favourite picture.

We should have learned the cold mornings,
Welcomed the fogs home from the sea,
Walked arm in arm with frost and greeted
The cold rains sighing in the sky.

We should have ceased to think, when burning
Leaves are acrid in the street,
'A gardener's burning up the summer –
Is this, of all that fire, what's left?'

And when the clanging tram comes grinding
Blue sparks from the frosty rails,
It should be carrying my wintry love
Home to its lair, its den of peace.

October 1948

In December

It was tonight the moon set glasses
Tinkling by the water side
And filled our throats with frost and stilled
The lights that shivered on the road.

Over the roofs the stars rushed sideways
Through skies as blue as milk. They fled
Making the buildings heel right over,
Perpetually plunging to the ground.

But in that cup of poison sipping
For truths to live for, we could find
Space that tingled on our tongues and
Silence that made our heads swim round.

It seemed that in the midnight's freezing
Utterance something had been said
As powerful as the childhood word
That turned the heaps of straw to gold.

December 1948

Charlatan summer

Now January. How often summer
Sold us his mats and tapestries
And birds entangled in nets of roses
And fish in cloudy pools, like glass.

His voice was thunder, sprawling over
The sky its vines and purple fruits;
Or crickets in wickerworks of grasses;
Or streams grown thin and hoarse with stones.

Now on green pools ice draws its shutters.
Still-lifes of trees are come to this
Naked whispering, and birds and roses
Put on the plumage of cold snows.

He sold us winter; and his fine speeches
Were all translations of the wild
And savage words that January
Mutters in the blustering wood.

And in the death of roses every
Season reads its epitaph
On air that snow, not roses, blanches
And frost, not flowers, makes still with grief.

January 1949

End of a cold night

The pond has closed its frozen eyelid,
The grass clump clenched its frozen claws.
The sky wheels like a millstone dropping grains
Of frost through air drawn thin and clear as glass.

The moon lies bleaching on the hedges.
A cock crows thinly and far away
– And a spell is broken; suddenly Time scratches
The hour on its box and up flares a new day.

January 1949

Morning

Here is the hand with flowers for chessmen.
Here's the light coming that will make
Another move towards the moment when
Over the fields he'll stoop and whisper, 'Check'.

Flocks of birds are his disguises,
And light rain rattling on the glass,
And feet going by to an unguessable somewhere,
And tea whirling brown specks in breakfast cups.

He has a long hand and it covers
With its one shadow seventy years.
He moves a flower, takes a bird from its branch
And brings his ambush to the deaths of kings.

We can't remember him. We welcome
The birds and the rain blurred on the glass.
And yet we'll recognise him when he's made
His final move and shows at last his face.

January 1949

Encounter

It disappeared, squeezed to nothing in a handshake,
The ghost that waves the traffic on in my mind.
And I've no thought to thank you for this silence.
And I've no word to tell how you are kind.

Spring's come to town. The gardens all are yawning.
Houses wear painters on their breasts like brooches.
And winds that roared along the streets of winter
Draw to the kerb and unload their secret parcels.

And my last muddy snow patch in the corner
Shrinks into trickling water. And I've no word
To say your look is Spring nor ask what's hidden
In the wintry gift you've put into my hand.

But in the silent streets you've wandered into
I'll cut the string, unfold the paper – and out
Will rush bright roofs and birds and gaudy dresses
And winds made vivid on glass and glittering paint.

February 1949

Wild and drunken night

The cold hour and the darkness sang
Drunk in the street and when the morning
Came dragging the distance with him
They crept into my room; and welcome.

I know them both. We hang our hands
Out to the fire. And never heeding
Miracles that move beyond the windows
They talk to me in sober earnest.

March 1949

Misty morning and no time

The sea puffs its breath along the streets.
The smell of seals and fishing-nets and a cold tide
Rolls between the buildings and cracks my footsteps
Like bladderwrack on the deserted road.

Who will explain my joy to these weeping stones?
Not only herring gulls between the chimneys
Circle with oceans like pebbles in their eyes
And long antarctics pale between their shoulders.

Not only winds like ice-floes lie deserted
In creeks of streets and jar against the headlands
Of so familiar buildings. Who will explain
What drifts to me along these silent eddies?

Who will describe the figure that walks beside me,
That the shop-fronts don't mirror, that says, 'My friend,
I will become you when the bristling sun
Sweeps the mist off this doorstep of the land;

'I will be you and walk in the shop-windows,
And you'll be lonely then, being without me
In the landlocked moment'. I smile and take his arm
And for once, for once am in no need of pity.

April 1949

Cold wind in May

There's nothing more to say to this North wind.
The buds peer from the entrances of their burrows
And come no further out, and the tortured thrush
Swings in delirium in its cage of branches.

It's all been said already. March and April
Held up their terms of truce deckled with all
Their youngest, tenderest flowers. But they're torn up
And whirled into space above the factory wall.

We still find fragments blown beneath the hedges.
Or, at some corner, at his café table
The sun lifts up his lazy glass of wine,
Says something charming, smiles for being fickle.

Be careful, passer-by. Where you are walking
Summer will scrawl its long nostalgia over
The panting stones and open gardens out
In drugged and dizzy manuscripts of flowers.

You'll read no stories there of the North wind.
Buds will have perished, thrush escaped from his song.
But you'll be singing still in your leafless branches
High in the dark, your year forever young.

April 1949

Lies for comfort

What our eyes say to us is fields
Are there for us to weave in baskets
To take a thought of murder home in;
Or they're a pool where silence beckons.

The long streets are our hearts' grammar,
And buildings where the sun comes up
Are coral islands where we face
Savages with bibles in our grip.

All that the eye names is disguises.
That's no tree but a way of feeling.
And in this May I've built I sit,
A rich man mumbling in his Folly.

The sun on his sierras rides
His ambling nag at windmill clouds
In the same Spain our castles are
Where poets paint their bowls of words.

And when my cheating tongue says, 'Look,
The hawthorn is a haze of green',
It means I've won this round and death
Sits in his corner looking down.

May 1949

After

Let's choose a pretty word, say, *evening*,
And climb through it into the past,
Or stand on a towering If, surveying
The rosy kingdoms we have lost.

From every corner creep a thousand
Boredoms saying, *Greet us. We're life*.
Let's round the sunset up and milk it
Into a jug and drink it off.

Or in the hawthorn let us tangle
Our dreary look like gossamer
To shudder with that sparrow's chirping
And when the dew falls be on fire.

Or drag the distance home and chain it
There in the corner of the room
To charm us with its savage howling
And beg for fragments of our dream.

There's a clue somewhere. Can you find it?
Can you say over and over again
'Love', till its incantation makes us
Forget how much we are alone?

May 1949

Separate

I can't help you. I can't reach out
And pin a miracle on your dress.
There's no sun in my fingers left
To be my thought's pure burning glass.

And all I write is darkness – see,
Night follows night all down the page
Where letters run like nightmares round
A certain black and crooked witch.

She had your name once and the sun
Grew it like gardens, full of weeks,
Where in a pond of summer all
The world leaned loving its own looks.

But now I'm darkness and can give
No blaze of days for you to wear –
Helpless as when I spoke your name
And gazed upon it full in flower.

May 1949

Same day

The window whitens; stars back into the sky;
A wind picks up the argument it had lost;
The horizon like a train of gunpowder
Smoulders from east to west.

A tree, comely as David, appears before
A stone-faced tenement, his Philistine.
Night sluices off the roofs, dives into drains;
And day dries on the stones.

Someone like me walks solitary in the street;
His footsteps put a roof over the morning
And a hollow under it. Someone like me
Drives by like a fire burning.

And someone like me, here, with a pen for crutch,
Limps out into the light, afraid to look back.
Will I be here to welcome him again
When other midnights strike?

August 1949

Always tonight

This night; and where are all the others
Whose shadows only stand behind me
Driving my pen to prove I never
Saw what they so clearly showed me?

All that was filmed against their darkness,
But seen no more than constellations
Over the windy roofs, fill
The obliterated town with visions.

But they are gone. What was done in them?
How did the light slant on the pavements?
Or did the rain puck on the cobbles
Dancing itself in watery mushrooms?

Now they've no east, but only shadows,
No heat or cold, but a thin finger
That mine is glove for and that makes me
Sign what is written by a stranger.

And every night's tonight. And Never
Stands at my back and whispers, 'Always'.
I send my coursing pen out, gazing
To catch a sight of what it follows.

September 1949

November night, Edinburgh

The night tinkles like ice in glasses.
Leaves are glued to the pavement with frost.
The brown air fumes at the shop windows,
Tries the doors, and sidles past.

I gulp down winter raw. The heady
Darkness swirls with tenements.
In a brown fuzz of cottonwool
Lamps fade up crags, die into pits.

Frost in my lungs is harsh as leaves
Scraped up on paths. – I look up, there,
A high roof sails, at the mast-head
Fluttering a grey and ragged star.

The world's a bear shrugged in his den.
It's snug and close in the snoring night.
And outside like chrysanthemums
The fog unfolds its bitter scent.

September 1949

Be easy

To shake an answer from one's sleeve is only
What the day does when it holds up a morning.
It never says, 'This lovely thing was chaos.
Fossils and earthquakes went to make it sunny.'

I walk into your answer – buildings bulge
Like lava down the streets, and in the meadows
Flat beasts pull into the stone cups of their mouths
Grass that by now should be all birds and ballads.

Last night has buried all its ancestors
And we're gravediggers too. Give me my answer
And see it clap and crow that new hour in
That sends my dead men bundling off together.

Buildings and fields will be the light's exhibits
Hung in a hall ten million miles high. Echoes
Will tell me of those spaces and those times
When all was morning and your look was daybreak.

December 1949

Something still

Was nothing begun? Nothing's a beggar
That soon transfers into his pocket
Your heart and soul and, without thanks,
Leaves you dumbstruck amidst the traffic.

He wakes your name up in the morning;
Your clothes walk out between the houses;
And when they meet a friend, it's nothing,
And not your face, that smiles and chatters.

But when I met you, curtains parted,
Suns were announced and weeks went by
All made of Saturdays. And we
Walked heart and soul into tomorrows.

Then too I met myself, the lost
And unfamiliar; and the traffic
Stormed round like planets, with hallelujahs.
Comets and stars were young and lovely.

Disregard your empty hands.
It is not nothing in your fingers
That aches, but the impossible greed
To hold at once all our tomorrows.

December 1949

Drifter

The long net, tasselled with corpses, came
Burning through the water, flowing up.
Dogfish following it to the surface
Turned away slowly to the deep.

The *Daffodil* squatted, slid ahead
Through the red kyle with thirty crans
Of throttled silver in her belly.
Her anchor snored amid its chains.

And memory gathered tarry splinters,
Put shadowy sparkles in her bag,
Slid up her sleeve the hills of Harris
And stole Orion and the Dog.

I sat with that kind thief inside me;
I sat with years I did not know
Heaped on my knees. With these two treasures
I sailed home through the Gaelic sea.

February 1950

Night no more real

What if the night walked from its frame
And shadows suddenly like accusers
Proved that the moon and I had met before?
Listen, the rain sobs in the frozen gutters.

Listen, the rain weeps on the roofs
And blinds with tenderness the windows.
The moon we walked in would have made them shine
And burned tall ghosts like candles in the gardens.

That moon is murdered and the night
Means nothing more to me. But what
If it should thrust a black knee in my back
And twist its cry of grief about my throat?

– I'd give it moons in millions, moons
To light up all the surly future,
Making a garden of the pearly rooftops,
Showing the ghost whose walking leaves my footsteps.

February 1950

Country house

Ruin creeps round the house, his wet hand fumbles
And smears the window with weeds; he shakes from the hollow
And coughing pines a rain of acid – invisible
As the wild cat skulking above on the craggy hill.

He roars, and one says, 'The burn's come down in spate'.
He sets the dogs barking, and goes by,
Swinging an axe and whistling, to the cottage below.
He taps on the door; there's a letter come for you.

Last night the birds perched under water; smoke
Hung flattened under fathoms of sodden air;
The roof, like a limpet, glistened; the lighted window
Was jelly-red, an anemone in flower.

But what does ruin care? We'll say tomorrow,
'Summer's come back'; he'll push hot grasses in
Between the stones, he'll file with a gay flame
The doorpost that your shoulder's leaning on.

Your thoughts come through the crippled gate, along
By the rheumatic fences to the door
With love to put in jugs in the smiling window;
But it's no good; something's been here before.

Something that leaves on the disordered slates
A thumbprint of green lichen, that sprawls the rose
Over the flaking wall, that on still nights
Rushes down headlong from the freezing stars.

February 1950

Back to Sutherland after a long absence

We'll pitch a tent in one past self
After another. Lochs will be lies,
The sky like an old nurse will babble
And mountains stand round in pretence.

Fictitious Nows will soak our shoulders,
Jump from our motor tyres, hold out
Over dark and scrabbled counters
Bacon and tea and cigarettes.

Now won't be there except for moments.
And you at the steering wheel will sit
Not knowing that on the seat beside you
Is a bundle of old and lively ghosts.

Long journey back, but never over.
One to make it, so many there.
So many faces to say, 'A stranger.
Why does he stop like that and stare?'

March 1950

Out from a lecture

The High Street sits drinking his swirling punch
Of buses, fruitshops, mackintoshes, windows
And a sour alley to bring out the flavour.
The High Street sprawls on his scruffy bed of shadows.

He lifts a ruddy eye to the clanging clock
And tosses down a smoky glass of sunlight
Bobbing with lorries, prickling with diesel gases.
A hundred scarves flame down his rusty gullet.

And my mouth chumbles words as dry as meal,
Is shaped like Correlations, choked with Quotients.
I munch on Visual Aids and what I gaze at
Dives in a book and scrubs off all its passion.

The High Street sticks his elbow in my ribs,
Lifts up a dram of shopfronts; shuts that book.
– And I raise my little glass where like a cherry
The sun's stuck on a chimney stack, and drink.

March 1950

Edinburgh spring

I walk my paint-box suburb. The clear air
Is flecked with green and ultramarine and rose.
The wind hangs nursery rhymes on branches;
The sun leans ladders against the apple trees.

And all my defence against the advancing summer
Is to trim hedges, gush the gutters sweet,
Tie the doomed rose against the wall
And watch myself being young and innocent.

Trams from my innocence thunder by like suns
Through my familiar city to where I know
Slatternly tenements wait till night
To make a Middle Ages in the sky.

A buzzing gas-lamp there must be my rose
Eating itself away in the ruined air
Where a damp bannister snakes up and
Time coughs his lungs out behind a battered door.

There craggy windows blink, mad buildings toss,
Dishevelled roofs, and dangerous shadows lean
Heavy with centuries, against the walls;
And Spring walks by ashamed, her eyes cast down.

She's not looked at. O merry midnight when
Squalid Persepolis shrugs its rotting stone
Round its old bones and hears the crowds
Weeping and cheering and crying, 'Tamburlaine'.

May 1950

Empty pool

The water moves no more than I.
Only the tottering reed-tips show
Where what I love, absurd with fear
And anguish, runs away from me.

I stand still as a post. Within me
There's anguish too, there's something trembling …
What's watching me? What tries to follow
Where I have gone, with love and pity?

May 1950

High Street, Edinburgh

Here's where to make a winter fire of stories
And burn dead heroes to keep your shinbones warm,
Bracing the door against the jackboot storm
With an old king or two, stuffing the glories
Of rancid martyrs with their flesh on fire
Into the broken pane that looks beyond Fife
Where Alexander died and a vain desire,
Hatched in Macbeth, sat whittling at his life.

Across this gulf where skeins of duck once clattered
Round the black Rock and now a tall ghost wails
Over a shuddering train, how many tales
Have come from the hungry North of armies shattered,
An ill cause won, a useless battle lost,
A head rolled like an apple on the ground;
And Spanish warships staggering west and tossed
On frothing skerries; and a king come to be crowned.

Look out into this brown November night
That smells of herrings from the Forth and frost;
The voices humming in the air have crossed
More than the Grampians; East and West unite,
In dragonish swirlings over the city park,
Their tales of deaths and treacheries, and where
A tall dissolving ghost shrieks in the dark
Old history greets you with a Bedlam stare.

He talks more tongues than English now. He fetches
The unimagined corners of the world
To ride this smoky sky, and in the curled
Autumnal fog his phantoms move. He stretches
His frozen arm across three continents
To blur this window. Look out from it. Look out
From your November. Tombs and monuments
Pile in the air and invisible armies shout.

May 1950

You went away

Suddenly, in my world of you,
You created time.
I walked about in its bitter lanes
Looking for whom I'd lost, afraid to go home.

You stole yourself and gave me this
Torturer for my friend
Who shows me gardens rotting in air
And tells me what I no longer understand.

The birds sing still in the apple trees,
But not in mine. I hear
Only the clock whose wintry strokes
Say, 'Now is now', that foul truth, over and over.

If I could kill this poem, sticking
My thin pen through its throat,
It would stand silent by your bed
And haunt your cruelty every empty night.

September 1950

21 October

Nothing to do, this little trickling wind,
Nothing to do with our loud-mouthed September
Whose each day was an oath, a canikin clinked
To death and treachery on an old map's island.

It's spilt from a sack of summer. It shines to show
By oddity that the tremendous star of June
Still burns invisibly in the freezing distance.
It buries time in the garden like a bone.

Can this, like all the others, be judgment day?
For what has its little voice to do with that
Black figure in our heart's red room
Whose lips are tombstones and speak monuments?

Green apples hang filled with December frost.
The petal cramps and chars the air with winter.
The moss is lightning. And falling from the air
The leaf sounds from the grass its clap of thunder.

September 1950

Double life

This wind from Fife has cruel fingers, scooping
The heat from streets with salty finger-tips
Crusted with frost; and all Midlothian,
Stubborn against what heeled the sides of ships
Off from the Isle of May, stiffens its drooping
Branches to the south. Each man
And woman put their winter masks on, set
In a stony flinch, and only children can
Light with a scream an autumn fire that says
With the quick crackle of its smoky blaze,
'Summer's to burn and it's October yet'.

My Water of Leith runs through a double city;
My city is threaded by a complex stream.
A matter for regret. If these cold stones

Could be stones only, and this watery gleam
Within the chasms of tenements and the pretty
Boskage of Dean could echo the groans
Of cart-wheeled bridges with only water's voice,
October would be just October. The bones
Of rattling winter would still lie underground,
Summer be less than ghost, I be unbound
From all the choking folderols of choice.

A loss of miracles – or an exchange
Of one sort for another. When the trams
Lower themselves like bugs on a branch down
The elbow of the Mound, they'd point the diagrams
Buckled between the New Town and the range
Of the craggy Old: that's all. A noun
Would so usurp all grammar no doing word
Could rob his money-bags or clap a crown
On his turned head, and all at last would be
Existence without category – free
From demonstration except as hill or bird.

And then no double-going stream would sing
Counties and books in the symbolic air,
Trundling my forty years to the Port of Leith.
But now, look around, my history's everywhere
And I'm my own environment. I cling
Like a cold limpet underneath
Each sinking stone and am the changing sea.
I die each dying minute and bequeath
Myself to all Octobers and to this
Damned flinty wind that with a scraping kiss
Howls that I'm winter, coming home to me.

October 1950

Wreck

The hulk stranded in Scalpay bay,
Hung like a hall with seaweed, stuck
Its long snout through my holiday.
It lay foundered on its own bad luck.

Twice every day it took aboard
A cargo of the tide; its crew
Flitted with fins. And sand explored
Whatever cranny it came to.

It should have carried deaths to give
To me stumbling across the stones;
It never spoke of what could live.
I saw no ghost between its bones.

It had not learned that it had failed;
Its voyages would not let it be.
More slow than glacier it sailed
Into the bottom of the sea.

December 1950

Old life for new

Why no, in a flowered field I see you walk,
Where the gentle tree says Hush. Under the grasses
A little earthquake travels where moles talk,
Shovelling your beauty aside, praising your graces.

Here by the tram-stops you can feel the dew
That lays a delicate fur of light all over
The branches that I can see you walking through,
That hang sad praises down on your buried lover?

Or the thick street of rosebushes and broom –
Can you count flocks there, animals all silvered
And baaing gravely, with a Latin gloom,
Of space and death, over the graves you favoured?

You died once but not here, wanting to die,
And to make a town of streets your hard disguises,
But a Spring of windows blossoms in the sky
And lorries stand like bulls among broom and roses.

And I, more than my height, watch you look out
From squares of epitaphs and psalms of buildings,
Preposterously undying, wearing about
Your minute's shoulders those immortal meadows.

March 1951

The rosyfingered

A dandling light and the world sings tremolo;
Even the grass, grown soulful, hangs its head
Over the prim winks of its daisies. Low
In a bush a blackbird trills then chirps instead.

And an old myth tries to heave itself to its feet:
The phoenix newly feathered in the east
Takes wing, blundering; and Phoebus not so fleet
Comes cantering after it, but comes at least.

And the dank grass is tangled with the song
Squirmed from a blackbird by the probe of light:
The hush is over … It will not be long,
Phoenix and blackbird. Bear it without spite.

Only a beauty with no rouge of myth
Walks plain in the plain field. Her decent hand
Will give you a meaning you can wrestle with;
Something to die of, not to understand.

June 1951

No escape

Bury my name in the ground and watch it grow.
The dead words fluttering from your mouth can waft
No nightmare stronger than this simple morning
Whose art is malice and whose kindness craft.

There's no escape. The colour of a dream
Falls into nowhere from your painting hand;
And there your fingers lie as pale and pleading
As refugees lost in my foreign land.

They gesture *Go*, and draw me closer in.
Your nightmare tongue says *Die*; and I swarm over
Your desert as green trees, and birds and lions
Come through the light to drink my singing water.

September 1951

Hero

Cuchulain
Or any other great legend's man
Salted white with the blue Aegean
Or ruddy on an Irish strand,
What was the simplicity that made
Time tender with you and your uncrooked shade?

No need to look
For plume, carved chessman, golden torque.
We, more than they, are your relic.
Passion remains; and south and north
Happen to us, as you. We seek
No other than gay Celt and subtle Greek.

Cuchulain
Fighting suffered a transformation
To still Cuchulain but more than man.
– Only once Time's repetition
Showed us in him, when, staring mad,
He died fighting the waves on a friendly strand.

September 1951

Frost and thin fog

The cold and melancholy sun
Hangs his red O above suburban gardens;
The smoking frost that's in his face
Glints on the stiff and sugared grasses.

The harsh air files the leafstalk through
And lowers the rattling leaf down through the branches;
A crust is lifted on the paths
And broken swords are heaped in borders.

Summer's bonfire has burned out
And left the air sour with the smell of ashes.
The tree the sun rolls through once was
A sky for moons and suns of apples.

Gas jets and fiery globes of flowers
Are all a darkness now in which there wander
Small, creaking voices that can say
Nothing at all but *Winter, winter*.

October 1951

Wet snow

White tree on black tree,
Ghostly appearance fastened on another,
Called up by harsh spells of this wintry weather
You stand in the night as though to speak to me.

I could almost
Say what you do not fail to say; that's why
I turn away, in terror, not to see
A tree stand there hugged by its own ghost.

January 1952

Swimming lizard

He swam through the cool loch water
As though not knowing whether he slanted down
Or up to the brightness. Swimming was all he did.

The tiny monster, the alligator
A finger long, swam unhurried through the brown;
Each eye glittered under its heavy lid.

This was his witness and his protest,
To swim unhurried; for an unknown Cause
He twinkled his brief text through the brown and still.

And I, like it, too big to be noticed,
Hung over him in pity, and my help, too, was
No reaching hand, but a loving and helpless will.

June 1952

Socrates

In the Greek air
So clear it seemed not there
He walked in his own clarity
That brought close to him what was lives away.

Nearer truths came
To shelter in his name
From hands that hunted them. And death
Gave them his life in exchange for his last breath.

In a rowdy street
He used to stop and greet
His friends with smiling news of these,
The Good and Beautiful, his executioners.

October 1952

Hugh MacDiarmid's lyrics

The tide goes over.
Not on my knees
These poems lie,
But the floor of existence.

Whelk and razorshell,
Delicate weight-lifters,
Supporting and made by
The crush of fathoms.

October 1952

Summer farm

Straws like tame lightnings lie about the grass
And hang zigzag on hedges. Green as glass
The water in the horse-trough shines.
Nine ducks go wobbling by in two straight lines.

A hen stares at nothing with one eye,
Then picks it up. Out of an empty sky
A swallow falls and, flickering through
The barn, dives up again into the dizzy blue.

I lie, not thinking, in the cool, soft grass,
Afraid of where a thought might take me – as
This grasshopper with plated face
Unfolds his legs and finds himself in space.

Self under self, a pile of selves I stand
Threaded on time, and with metaphysic hand
Lift the farm like a lid and see
Farm within farm, and in the centre, me.

January 1953

Sheep-dipping

Eyes, with one glimpse, can gather in
The simple details of the scene
Yet cannot gaze enough at all
The figures in it. For even those
That stand in idleness reveal
A ritual significance.

Two to dip and one to drive
And one, the tall saint up above,
Ticking in a glossy book
The tally of the just baptised
Who, skinny with new grace, look back
Nostalgically to the lost.

And dogs, hysterical with smells,
Sit high on haunches – sudden brawls
Explode, and scatter round a stick;
On the wall's top a labrador
Trots round and back and round and back,
Obsessed with doing nothing more.

Everything else is still. The lambs,
Cunning old ewes and surly rams
Jammed between drystone walls can move
Scarcely their Bourbon heads. Around,
Men lean on crooks and boys, more grave,
Spit wisely on the printed ground.

The unifying element is
The ceaseless consort of their cries,
Offended bass and lamentable
Contralto and passionate tenor, all
Quavering together, with one treble
Desperate and comical.

Supplication, hauteur and
Bewilderment rise in one sound,
A pillar of confession that

Stands high above the ritual saints
Who, stained to the elbows, sweatily thrust
Unwilling sinners into grace.

The lamentation dwindles. Night
Gathers, and the elect are quiet,
Except one; inconsolable
He rejects what the gods have given,
Bawling his affront from all
The steep slopes of his barren heaven.

May 1953

Birds all singing

Something to do with territory makes them sing,
Or so we are told – they woo no sweet and fair,
But tantalise and transfigure the morning air
With coarse descriptions of any other cock bird
That dare intrude a wing
In their half-acre – bumptious and absurd.

Come out and fight, they cry, and roulades of
Tumbling-down sweetness and ascending bliss
Elaborate unrepeatable ancestries;
And impossible deformities still to come
Rise like angels above
The tenement windows of their sylvan slum.

Not passion but possession. A miserly
Self-enlargement that muddles mine and me
Says the half-acre is the bird, and he,
Deluded to that grandeur, swells, and with
A jolly roundelay
Of boasts and curses establishes a myth.

The human figure underneath the boughs
Takes strictly down, as false as a machine,
The elements of the seen or the half-seen,

And with the miracle of his ear notes all
The singing bird allows,
And feels it innocent, calls it pastoral.

Creations clumsily collide and make
The bird and man more separate. The man,
Caught up in the lie the bird began,
Feigns a false acre that the world can't hold
Where all is for his sake;
It is the touchstone proving him true gold.

So he, his own enlargement also, thinks
A quiet thought in his corner that creates
Territories of existence, private states
Of being where trespassers are shot at sight;
And myth within myth blinks
Its blind eyes on the casual morning light.

Under or over, nothing truly lies
In its own lucidity. Creation moves
Restlessly through all its hates or loves
And leaves a wild scenario in its place
Where birds shake savage cries
Like clenched fists in the world's uncaring face.

And man, with straws of singing in his hair,
Strolls in his Bedlam transfiguring every fact,
In full possession of what he never lacked,
The power of being not himself – till with
A twitch of the morning air
Time topples bird and man out of their myth.

May 1953

Shadow in summer

Trees fall like weeping;
No summer ever told
A harder sorrow.

Time is not for keeping,
And a strange tomorrow
Already is taking hold.

The far boat, riding
Innocent blue waves
With clouds curled over,
In its hold is hiding
Its own deep-sea lover,
Its last of many graves.

And blackbird being
Phoenix in the tree
Is image only
That unsights with its seeing
What makes one of the lonely
And separate you and me.

In you a breaking
Shadow curves its head
Silently over –
Great tide, for ever making,
That will put loved and lover
At last in the one bed.

June 1953

Boats

The boat need carry no more than a live man
And there's a meaning, a cargo of centuries.
They make a hieroglyph on the sea that can
Cramp circumnavigations in one round gaze.

Hard sailors put out from books and ancient tales.
They have names that chink like gold or clash like ice.
They shred coarse fog or beat suns with their sails,
Pooled in iambics or tossed on hexameters.

Days jagged on skerries, nights signalling with foam
Were golden fleece, white whale, lost Ithaca.
No answering star could call these wanderers home;
Each cape they doubled jutted from history.

Watch this one, ancient Calum. He crabs his boat
Sideways across the tide, every stroke a groan –
Ancient Calum no more, but legends afloat.
No boat ever sailed with a crew of one alone.

October 1953

Still two

I'm not Arcturus who should go,
Colossal ploughboy, whistling through
The shocked sky; do not let those eyes
Hold me off in outer space.
    Distance has a hand can shrink
    Your heart in tighter than you think.

The blundering ant you fail to see
Deserves your foot no more than I
Who blunder towards a winter. Take
More than horizons in your look.
    For size is nothing at the most
    But variations upon dust.

Don't say Tomorrow. For too soon
Time will lift his lawyer's pen –
And when his mortgage is foreclosed,
Be sure you'll lose all interest.
    And Time and space and dust will be
    The indistinguished you and me.

November 1953

Brother

Frog and awkward angel can
Combine to be my brother man.
Louse and lion, he crawls in
The tunnels of my rotten skin.
I'll shake his hand, so long as he
Makes no boast of being me.

And with my fiercest lambkin glare
I'll sink my poison in him where
Immortality's kingdom come
Is contradicted by a drum,
That heart whose knocking will have rest
At last in my most private breast.

When that moment comes when I
Will sadly see the fellow die,
His contradictions falling in
Like my eyes and sunken chin,
I'll choke with his last breath and give
All my life that he should live.

November 1953

Botanic gardens

The keeper with a hating face
Skulks among the rosebushes
Whose useless flowers get on with their
Three weeks' explosion in the air.
His eyes, mad as a miser, glance
Through their unchilled extravagance.

Dangling from Pakistan, a blue
Flower reaches down into Peru;
A woman sits rocking a pram
Under the shadow of Assam;
From Norway two blue pigeons plane
To France; and China snows on Spain.

But in this Eden let two kiss –
The seraph in the trellises
Will drive them from the gates and stand,
A flaming by-law in his hand,
Directing their slow steps out of
This coloured no-man's-land of love.

For there's no season here to show
The way that any winds blow.
Frost and sun lie in one bed.
Winter-famished, summer-fed,
The naked and the clothed reveal
The contradictions of the real.

And time in more than one disguise
Jolts the cool logic of our eyes,
And man's intrusion proves that he
Is madder, only, than this tree
Which spends its virtue to contrive
That snow on fire should be alive.

December 1953

Accuser

I charge you with
Making a smaller of that greater death
Who on me, by your loss in some way dead,
Leans his cajoling head
And whispers his affection that once was
A look down cliffs and now's a looking-glass.

And the broad air
Is choked and stifled to the places where
We talked ourselves to ourselves (being mostly dumb);
All else is vacuum,
Emptied by you of mountains and strange men:
Geography's grown small, being born again.

And likeness dies
That was the enamourer of my learning eyes.
Since one thing's left, and that's your loss, no more
Can I by metaphor
Share the world's sharing, but must walk alone
My field of flesh and highway of hard bone.

Round circumstance
Shrunk to a point, to me, can in one glance
Be prisoned, where within myself I lie.
No ladder from the sky
Can slant for me where I lie in that cell
Under the cracked note of the warning bell.

All this I lay
Before your unjudging eyes that perch their May
Singing in storm clouds, and make drugged Julys
Dizzy the winter skies,
And see me go hilarious and mad
Through the dead pleasures that we sometime had.

So my words fall
Within the seed that is to grow them. All
Time's great treacheries keep you guiltless, and
Within your crooked hand
Your crime lies sleeping, and I your victim know
Less that you're lost than that I wish it so.

January 1954

Party

Watching your face
That makes an emptiness of this crowded place,
I stand, not speaking, terrified to see
You grown more lovely, and still lost to me.

January 1954

42]

By comparison

Staring at stars, stones, trees,
The rubbish and the backbone of what is
The helpless incarnation of death's will,
Is an exploration of innocence. See, the moon
Pours over the cold window-sill
A night, a midnight or a midnight's noon,
And its ambiguous beauty makes us feel
The guilt of knowing the real from the unreal.

Trees and stars and stones
Are falsely these and true comparisons
Whose likenesses are the observer. He
Stares, in the end, at his own face, and shame
Of his deep flaw, mortality,
Shines in the star, and from the tree the same
Pity is shed that weakens him when he knows
That he is going where even the stone goes.

February 1954

Information

Blunt shadows flutter to a warming flame
Since you came to my little greedy room
And with a word destroyed a long year's gloom
(Small candle that still burns and stays the same).
I who had nowhere else to go now do
Such journeys (here) as lie from me to you,
And think them nothing; which Time thinks them too.

For mile and moment are no larger than
Each other is; and that is less than what
Divides one thought of you from another thought;
And that is nothing – space to hold a man
It must be, though, since taking your thought from me
Leaves me and nothing; for I'm a fantasy
Your thoughts unghost into reality.

February 1954

43]

Dream world

In your loving arms there lie
Serious field and fickle sky;
Syllables of your breath compose
Arctic wind and desert rose;
And fidgeting Atlantics sigh
To sleep beneath your lullaby.

Let the presaging planets weep.
No nightmares from their mirrors creep
To touch you with their breath and show
The eyes of innocence how to know
The world you dandle into sleep
Rocks your cradle six feet deep.

February 1954

Quoting day

Today's the anniversary of when
What was lodged in the dark achieved the light,
And from a cloud descended the small rain
That deluged my whole world. For a year's night
I was my ark and animals, till that
Bow drizzled above today's green Ararat.

For you are gone out of my world and me,
The great storm over, the end of loneliness.
I croak as raven and coo as dove and see,
Swimming up from below, the remembered glens
Where is no echo, even, to prove once true
The story this day tells of me and you.

You are destroyed in you. The power you had
Consumed what contained it and now goes
Dispersed above the ruined good and bad.
Weak as today, your image comes and shows
A tiny raining cloud that will bring forth
Green fields and harvests, of whatever worth.

February 1954

Laggandoan, Harris

Bullock bellied in a green marsh,
Chinning his blockhead among white
And yellow tiny flowers, rolls
His brown eyes in a dark delight.

A dragonfly of mica whirs
Off and up; then makes a thin
Tottering grass its anchor-post,
Changed to a small blue zeppelin.

And Joseph-coated frogs tumble
Like drunken heralds in the grass
That tipples sweet marsh water and
Defies the sun's broad burning-glass.

Down from the moor, between two rocks
The furnace sun has calcined white,
Johann, humped with a creel of peats,
Comes leaning forward through the light.

Then everything returns again
To timelessness. A grasshopper scours
His little pail; and blissfully
The bullock floats awash in flowers.

March 1954

Maiden Loch

In the round bay a drifting boat
Rides on another's shadowy back
And unreflecting lilies float,
Whose whiteness makes brown water black.

Beyond the point, where islands are,
A black-throat diver wails and, there,
Making his own bill his Pole star,
Paddles himself into the air.

The glinting rod-tip bends and with
A customary brief struggle life
Gives in to a more lasting myth.
An oar-blade flashes like a knife.

The Minch breathes once across the land
And till that breathing dies away
Tall reeds stiffly whisper and
Gravely lean over all one way.

March 1954

Climbing Suilven

I nod and nod to my own shadow and thrust
A mountain down and down.
Between my feet a loch shines in the brown,
Its silver paper crinkled and edged with rust.
My lungs say No;
But down and down this treadmill hill must go.

Parishes dwindle. But my parish is
This stone, that tuft, this stone
And the cramped quarters of my flesh and bone.
I claw that tall horizon down to this;
And suddenly
My shadow jumps huge miles away from me.

March 1954

Contraries

Weather of disillusion. The green bays
Spit back the ferocious spray that batters up
From the broaching sides of waves. The wind has turned
Against the storm it made and from the cup
Formed of two mountains pours steep down and flays
The bitter skin of the sea, the water churned
By the one force to going two contrary ways.

The grass lies down and gallops. The sand once torn
Screaming from its sea bed flies out again
In its own thin storm. The land attacks the sea,
Boxing it back with sandstone fists. The rain
Spilt from a cloud bag rattles like hard corn
On the roof of the byre, where a crofter on one knee
Hauls on a calf unwilling to be born.

March 1954

Fiat

I cannot stammer thunder in your sky
Or flash white phrases there. I have no terse
Exploding passion, and cannot vilify
My dulcet world through flute-holes of a verse,
But gently speak and, gently speaking, prove
The everlastingness in which you move.

No superscription in a cloud need sign
Either my love or hate to show they are
Come from a source more terrible than mine.
And I need bow to no peremptory star:
A finger writes, and there is star – or me,
With love or hate to cloud identity.

And time's inflections cannot alter this
Most gentle truth, that fire and thunderhead
Are momentary metamorphosis
Of the most gentle word ever was said
Into what means not less of gentleness,
Being accepting being, and saying Yes.

April 1954

Harpsichord playing Bach

Translation, not transfiguration, of
The old conspiracy of space and time
Makes me conspirator too, huddling love

In my bosom like a bomb that will explode
A clock's precise and rigmaroling chime
And make a centre of the straightest road.

For space and time are those two clowns whose act
Seems all disruption. From sentimental rose
They squirt sad ink. They're the soprano's cracked
Most lamentable top note. Their stick brings down
The Hero from his nobility on his nose.
They are the itch beneath the royal crown.

Or they shake your hand and leave a death in it.
The world sits down – they pull the chair away.
From a bare hook they steal the Infinite
For the fisherman to grieve for. It's they who dowse
The lights at the quick crisis of the play.
They raise the rafters and bring down the house.

This loving music from their non-sense makes
An architecture of disruption and
Deploys a meaning in the air that shakes
The clock world off and lets the other in
Where atmospheres of meaning lead their grand
Galaxies through even a human skin.

The understanding and the loving are,
Of course, the same. Even the clock can chime
Sensibly with these notes. Six to the bar
The infinities accumulate; and I,
Drunk with the clarity of space and time,
Forget their fooling under the clownish sky.

May 1954

Dying landscape

Condolence makes no water speak, that still
Utters conversion of a crying rock
With slur and sibilance to a listening ear;

And pity hoists no hill
Other than such as these that dwindle here
By milligrams between cock and crowing cock.

The Summer Isles loiter towards the same
End as Stac Polly, laboriously bowing down
His sandstone head in tons of inches. These
Altering horizons frame
An ultimate constriction of cold seas;
The silver thorns, the blood that smooths the frown.

Only existence from its trivial cross
(Recalcitrance of tree and hill and bird)
Will descend in its lasting property,
The limiting differences
Making their huge withdrawal, selves away,
Behind the first simplicity of the Word.

May 1954

Too bright a day

I live invisible (in my whole sky
That is the light of where you are)
Calling the night to welcome my
Sad and procrastinating star,
Which will not leave, as it must do,
Its short conjunction here with you.

Light so engrossing cannot show
More than itself. I fade in it
And have no shadow even to throw.
But when I leave you, I'll commit
Such darkness on myself you'll stare
At the great conflagration there.

June 1954

Sad cunning

This light discloses you as if
It were death's hardest hieroglyph
And you its meaning. Yet in it I
Enfold you in a word whose noon
Will (brightening our mortality)
Diminish the devouring sun.

Or come in a stand of darkness whose
Leaf and bark might be my muse
Putting midnight on my lip.
I will speak such shadows then
As underwrite a sailing ship
Lest its grave fathoms shine too plain.

No parliament of beasts or flowers
Utters laws more fierce than ours
By which we burn the sun and kill
The dark with darkness; all to prove,
One useless moment, that death will
Go blindfold by our dying love.

July 1954

Poem for a goodbye

When you go through
My absence, which is all of you,
And clouds, or suns, no more can be my sky,
My one dissembling will be all –
The inclusive lie
Of being this voice, this look, these few feet tall.

The elements which
Made me from our encounter rich
Cannot be uncreated; there is no
Chaos whose informality
Can cancel so
The ritual of your presence, even gone away.

50]

You, then, and I
Will masquerade a lie,
Diminishing ourselves to be what can
Seem one without the other, while
A greater man,
In hiding, lies behind this look, this smile.

It's he who will
Across sad oceans meet you still,
Startling your carelessness with what once was.
His voice from this past hour will speak,
Cancelling Time's laws:
In the world's presence his hand will touch your cheek.

Foreign can be
Only that sound to you and me.
There is no thought that in its dying goes
Through such a region we do not
In it compose
Each other's selves, each in the other's thought.

You leave behind
More than I was, and with a kind
Of sad prevarication take with you
More than I'll be till that day when
Nothing's to do
But say, 'At last', and we are home again.

October 1954

Spate in winter midnight

The streams fall down and through the darkness bear
Such wild and shaking hair,
Such looks beyond a cool surmise,
Such lamentable uproar from night skies
As turn the owl from honey of blood and make
Great stags stand still to hear the darkness shake.

Through Troys of bracken and Babel towers of rocks
Shrinks now the looting fox,
Fearful to touch the thudding ground
And flattened to it by the mastering sound.
And roebuck stilt and leap sideways; their skin
Twitches like water on the fear within.

Black hills are slashed white with this falling grace
Whose violence buckles space
To a sheet-iron thunder. This
Is noise made universe, whose still centre is
Where the cold adder sleeps in his small bed,
Curled neatly round his neat and evil head.

October 1954

Golden calf

If all the answer's to be the Sinai sort,
The incorruptible lava of the word
Made alphabetic in a stormspout, what
Mere human vocables you've ever heard,
Poor golden calf, could overbear, I wonder,
   The magniloquence of thunder?

You're for another flame. The Moses in me
Looks with a stone face on our gaudy lives.
His fingers, scorched with godhead, point, and loose
An influence of categorical negatives
That make an image of love, a trope of lover.
   Our dancing days are over.

The buckles tarnish at the thought of it.
The winecup shatters. The bragging music chokes
To the funeral silence it was awkward in.
And before the faggot of salvation smokes,
Your knees are loosed, your wreathed neck bows lowly
   In presence of the holy.

What's a disgruntled cloud to you or me?
Listen to my multitudes, and beam for them,
Making a plinth of this dark wilderness.
Utter such rigmaroles an apothegm,
Doing its head-stroke, drowns in such wild water
    And proves itself no matter.

Or where's the desert cat, or hunching shade
That ambles hugely in the dark outside,
Or hospitable anguish beckoning
To its foul ceremony a sorry bride
Could bear the darts struck from your hide by torches
    That guard our pleasure's marches?

Forty years. Small wilderness to unravel
Such an unknotted thread of wandering.
The desert is in Moses' skull, the journey
To the white thalamus whose cradling
Enfolds the foetus of the law – gestation
    Of Moses as a nation.

A chosen people, since they have no choice.
The doors are locked, the fleshpots on the shelves,
And a long line of lamentation moves
Led by the nose through their own better selves
To buy with blood a land of milk and honey
    Where's no need for such money.

The smoke and thunder die. And here I stand
Smelling of gunpowder and holiness.
The great fire does its belly-dance and in it
You shine unharmed, not knowing what's to confess;
And the desert, seeing the issue grows no clearer,
    Takes one long slow step nearer.

December 1954

Fetish

Bangles and paper prayers and coins (the smallest)
Ward the gods off that narrow track where I
Skirt my own chasms, half-way between green jungles
And glaciers (of me) hung white on a black sky –
Useless precaution, to drive out hate and love
From the love and hate that I'm the contour of.

And the great sky, scattered with brilliances,
Trundles its lawfulness above the hope
(Fluttering or twinkling in the roadside bush)
Of pushing an evil out of its fated scope
Till it works elsewhere and infiltrates the good;
Stars fall to death because they do, not should.

I can resent this – and the resentment; neither
Being alteration of a destiny.
Hate of the pinprick leaves the pin as sharp.
But blood still speaks when it has leaked away –
It's the one law that thrusts the knife and cries
'Murder' (murder!) to unresponsive skies.

No word is big enough to enclose all this
Or small enough to wriggle into it. Words
Are a remembered climate where we viewed
A sort of landscape or spied on sorts of birds
Or were a (roughly speaking) kind of self.
Coffin the lot on some tall dusty shelf.

They'll not be silent. Their jaws will creak and out
Will buzz the revelations round the lamp
That we've no courage to put out. Great wits
Are branded with vocabularies and cramp
With the winter snowing in a syllable,
And nothing helps them, until nothing will.

So my ramshackle prayer-wheel clatters on,
Announcing me to my own self, who lies

Round any corner now. I'll know him for
The moment of obliteration. Cries
To the gods, or me, will be no service when
What had me once lays hold of me again.

December 1954

Ego

Stare at the stars, the stars say. *Look at me*,
Whispers the water and protests the tree;
The rose is its own exclamation and
Frost touches with an insinuating hand.
Yet they prefigure to my human mind
Categories only of a human kind.

I see a rose, that strange thing, and what's there
But a seeming something coloured on the air
With the transparencies that make up me,
Thickened to existence by my notice. Tree
And star are ways of finding out what I
Mean in a text composed of earth and sky.

What reason to believe this, any more
Than that I am myself a metaphor
That's noticed in the researches of a rose
And self-instructs a star? Time only knows
Creation's mad cross-purposes and will
Destroy the evidence to keep them secret still.

December 1954

Non pareil

If I could match you with an image found
Wedged amongst the measurable shapes
Embroiled in being by the four elements,
Or met like a possibility in dreamscapes,
Or figured in the motion of a mind –
Or anywhere – it's the last thing I would find.

Identity with you? – no chance of that:
No more than you can give me images for
Any experience other than yourself.
A ship sails clean out of its metaphor
And birds perch on no simile; and Time
Breaks all the rules of reason and of rhyme.

Find two identicals, and where's the world,
That's cross-grained out of fitting differences?
There's Time enough for eternity but not
For our abstraction from it. Going all ways,
That's where we end; but you're not eternal – yet –
And it's your differences I can't forget.

Sit in their solitude and speculate
On the identity of opposites.
The speculation joins them. You and all
The likenesses my greedy mind commits
To help its exploration of you are
As different as a slow-worm and a star.

Green grace of growing, fold of nowhere, shape
That visits between minutes, my whole thought
Is, measuring your separateness from all
That I can see or say of you, to plot
Where your invisible star must be whose force
Lurches my whole world from its easy course.

No wild impulsive planet flickering from
One private nowhere to another could
Engage my human notice. The one law
Governs my world and yours, whose solitude
Is guarded by those differences that are
Truth to the world and treason to a star.

December 1954

Pioneer

He went on further than he could not go.
Holding the waver of light in his green hand
He disappeared beyond the impossible. No
Word could befriend him in that friendless land.

Then the impossible grew its usual fruits.
The monsters withdrew beyond his ring of light.
We found him talking to us – the old disputes;
For we had been waiting for him, all the night.

And so we met ourselves again. And so
Once more we were one of him; until one day
Wanting to meet us, he prepared to go
Further impossibilities away.

December 1954

Growing down

*(There is a theory which finds language more and more metaphorical as it is
traced back in the past.)*

Call up those images and impoverish me
Till I become my ancient ancestor
Pendulous in his emblematic tree.
Will you destroy such generations for
A cage of pictures to imprison you
Somewhere in me, but in the public view?

I am, or should be, separated from
The ritual phenomena. Earth and sky,
Seasons, mad birds and flowers, journeys, home
Belong to all my training has put by
As childish things, and I, an adult man,
Am reason functioning – at least, that's the plan.

So when I leave the antiseptic room
Of my cold brainpan to discover where

A star may shine you on the elsewhere gloom
Or shadow figure you in the empty air,
My old ancestor, dropping from his tree,
Sidles through centuries and creeps into me.

And with a simian hand I pin some phrase
Upon your seeming. On one branch we sit
Above the world that stretches in the haze
With facts like mammoths wandering in it:
Our future selves creak by on leather wings;
The adult man crawls in the slime and stings.

– But back to the little room inside the skull:
A place you don't inhabit, though you visit there.
I search its pigeon-holes for something dull
That might mean you, but even its cold air
Is so transfigured by you that I gaze
At glittering row on row of images.

So I stand here, a guilty primitive,
My education down about my knees,
Caught in the act of living, if to live
Is to be all one's possibilities,
A sum of generations six foot high,
Learning to live and practising to die.

And what is adult, if it isn't that
(Besides being image among images,
Phenomenon among phenomena)? What
Can we communicate by except by these
Accumulations of ourselves which led
To our now separateness, from the common dead?

So, image, come and with your human hand
Call up the past, whose echo we partly are.
– Make even me an image to understand,
Till from my shadow or advancing star
You can discover where I am and prove
The everlastingness of common love.

December 1954

Celtic twilight

No waters here but make
Their sounding declination to the East,
Pouring between such islands we mistake
Where our selves lie and think ourselves at least
Engaged with some great overflow of what
Rubs us to death with everlasting thought.

Or their withdrawal is
Resilience only, proving its own law
And hinting of the monster in the abyss
Whose breathing shakes the Milky Way – that straw
That shows the way the wind blows, from what start
To some large ending in the human heart.

Ridiculously we gaze
With magic eyes towards an unfabled West
Whose largenesses are simply weather. Ways
Of knowing are many, but measuring is best;
The boat we rock in rises, that's to say,
A few feet nearer to the Milky Way.

Which stays a straw; and not
A beanstalk with a treasure at the top –
As all we see is a process, not a plot
That seeks its issue in a rich full-stop.
This incandescent hush of water is
Neither one sentence nor parenthesis.

So evening draws its piled
White adumbrations on a human sky
Where our ferocious dreams range through the mild
Incontrovertibles. The waves go by
Bringing no miracles, perhaps being one,
And facts on fire play-act a setting sun.

January 1955

59]

Sacred river

My knowing of you has reached the delta stage:
Mangroves and swamps and monkeys in the air
Are bred from silt that once, Himalayas high,
Was a moon-landscape. Now I disengage
Origins thus; but symbols everywhere
Obscure your countless depositions and I,
Prowling my steamy memory, must make
Crony and sage of tiger and water-snake.

Symbols of indirection – not of you
(Who stay diminished where you always were)
But of my knowing of you, creating my
Last environment, where the false and true
Are equally powerful and crueller
Than moonscape freezing under its black sky.
The chattering bright bird has no right to be
Bright in the darkness which is you in me.

No bird can sing that high Himalaya down.
The moon-striped tiger growling in my throat
Stares, with no blizzards in his eyes, at what
His only prey must be – himself; his frown
Narrows his eyes and mine. … These waters float
Something of you towards the sea, but not
Till this thick landscape blurs away will I
Be drowned with you where symbols are put by.

                                    January 1955

Ballade of good whisky

You whose ambition is to swim the Minch
Or write a drum concerto in B flat
Or run like Bannister or box like Lynch
Or find the Ark wrecked on Mt Ararat –
No special training's needed: thin or fat,
You'll do it if you never once supplant

As basis of your commissariat
Glenfiddich, Bruichladdich and Glengrant.

My own desires are small. In fact, I flinch
From heaving a heavenly Hindu from her ghat
Or hauling Loch Ness monsters, inch by inch,
Out of their wild and watery habitat.
I've no desire to be Jehoshaphat
Or toy with houris fetched from the Levant.
But give to me – *bis dat qui cito dat* –
Glenfiddich, Bruichladdich and Glengrant.

I would drink down, and think the feat a cinch,
The Congo, Volga, Amazon, La Platte,
And Tweed as chaser – a bargain, this, to clinch
In spite of *nota bene* and *caveat*
(Though what a feast must follow after that
Of Amplex, the divine deodorant!) –
If they ran – hear my heart go pit-a-pat! –
Glenfiddich, Bruichladdich and Glengrant.

   Envoi

Chris! (whether perpendicular or flat
Or moving rather horribly aslant)
Here is a toast that you won't scunner at –
Glenfiddich, Bruichladdich and Glengrant!

February 1955

Gifts

You read the old Irish poet and complain
I do not offer you impossible things –
Gloves of bee's fur, cap of the wren's wings,
Goblets so clear light falls on them like a stain.
I make you the harder offer of all I can,
The good and ill that make of me this man.

I need no fancy to mark you as beautiful,
If you are beautiful. All I know is what

Darkens and brightens the sad waste of my thought
Is what makes me your wild, truth-telling fool
Who will not spoil your power by adding one
Vainglorious image to all we've said and done.

Flowers need no fantasy, stones need no dream:
And you are flower and stone. And I compel
Myself to be no more than possible,
Offering nothing that might one day seem
A measure of your failure to be true
To the greedy vanity that disfigures you.

A cloak of the finest silk in Scotland – what
Has that to do with troubled nights and days
Of sorry happiness? I had no praise
Even of your kindness, that was not bought
At such a price this bankrupt self is all
I have to give. And is that possible?

April 1955

In no time at all

Yon calendar could not with a coloured air
Sidling come singing, proving to me with
Sugared insinuations you are there?
Then I shall go on being monolith
And he may take his nights and days away
Till they bring in that far, forbidden day.

I have a Spring where no flowers yawn desire
Nor birds make bright explosions in the green:
True vernal equinox – divided fire
Roasts my day's outward and my night's within
And, saintly with such torture, I propose
Myself as sun and holy, singing rose.

I am the pillar; on my self's top I squat
(A narrow squalor) and think it nothing hard

To be the centre of a genesis thought
Where I and time are each uncalendared,
Dragging ourselves from womb or tomb to see
The chaotic possibility of being me.

And you? Your hand shuts round me. I being twice
Most cruelly put to birth, see you must be
Continuous expulsion from a paradise
In whose false centre I stood like a tree.
Now like a tree I fruitless stand and house
Dreams of dead worlds in my dependent boughs.

Saints walk the world, blemished with holiness.
Hauling their eyelids down against the flesh,
They trespass on their future. So I, grown less,
Peer through the rotten honeycomb's torn mesh
My body is and blunder into bliss
Where shady notions exchange a phantom kiss.

See what your exile is, being gone from me.
Your vast idea swarms around me and
I am that concupiscence which might be
Your worlding forth in lip and brow and hand,
Where between rivers Edens could suppose
No prophecies more damaging than a rose.

I have no rose nor prophecy. I make
A knot of seasons where time's end is one
With his beginning, and for your graceless sake
Sit, a small chaos awaiting your word; for none
That I can speak has power unless you, too,
Utter what makes a world of me and you.

May 1955

Roses and thorns

Roses and thorns, the threadbare image is.
But it's the rose that hurts, the thorn that pleases.

63]

The treacherous rose – I've no belief in such
Loose wooing of the sun with an opening kiss.
Only the rankling thorn can show as much
Regard for truth as secrecy releases.

And you are secret – flowering wildly in
The space between us, blinding the air with colour,
And showing nothing of yourself. I touch
The little jagged word, and my torn skin
Carries your signature. The air, no duller,
Shouts your remonstrance and shows it nothing much.

So in your cruelty lies your truth. And I
Instruct my passion in its naked graces.
Fine food for love. Yet love grows fat on it
And, sourly staring at each pretty lie,
Rummages for the thorn in whose embraces
It finds at last a crime it can commit.

And that is murder, of your secrecy.
Then you become explicit and not lonely,
Forced to admit my share of you. And again,
Clinging and wounding, wildly you display
A daze of blossoms, a disguise that only
Some winter night will wither. And what then?

May 1955

Particular you

    What question will unmask
The hooded rose-tree, upright in its shadow?
Or show the steadiness that makes the stone steady?
    Or, knowing it, who would dare to ask
And change the pretty phenomena into one
Horde of disclosures blackening the sun?

    Reveal to me no more
Than what I know of you – your bright disguises.

The lie your body is only discloses
  The language of a rose-tree or
A stone; and universals gather where
Your hands lie still or light falls on your hair.

  But you are more and less
Than universals. I'd tremble to discover
That special, stubborn thing, that must forever
  Lie hooded between no and yes,
An affirmation which must always be
Incomprehensible and separate from me.

  I study to be wise.
Lift up the lesson of your hand. Then, gazing,
I lose the loss of what I must be losing
  And find the language of disguise
Says all I want and bear to know, that we
And all the world are three, but one in three.

July 1955

Stone pillow

The malediction that each moment is
Falls from your lips – or what I dream is there.
I fight with an angel, and a Jacob stair
Shuts me from heaven with heavenly distances.
Why should such dreams mock me? – that mock you, too,
  As any dream must do.

I need create no windy plain where gods
Might seem to insinuate themselves in what
Is matter for human lust and human thought
(My head to lie, a clod between two clods,
No doubt, while heroes briskly make a myth
  To immortalise you with).

For all the Helens made golden by a word
Are your projection on the marvellous screen,

A different wonder, the always might-have-been.
You're the dull fact, the mortally absurd
That gives sense to all Troys and makes them fall
    Into the possible.

Immortal ordinariness – is that
A meaning you can have? Cuchulain, changed
Extraordinarily, but still Cuchulain, ranged
Tall ranks of enemies and laid them flat.
The battle done, he became like other men.
    – Cuchulain once again?

Outward and inward equally in you
Display the other. Let no crisis be,
To loose you in depredation upon me;
How could I bear to be destroyed and through
My falling forces see you pass, no more
    Immortal than before?

My dreams are angel-like because their praise
Fills the distance between us, measuring
A space and time with what they are. You'll bring
Their heavenly ladder down when I can raise
My human head from this stone pillow and stare
    At you and the desert there.

                                                September 1955

Clachtoll

Ships full of birds, like sailing trees,
Add to the discourse of these seas
    Whose flouncing skerries wash and sigh
    A distance nearer with their cry.

Long islands at their cables ride
The double talk of the split tide
    And a low black rock pokes out
    From caves of green its dripping snout.

Coils of wind lie on that silk
That's flowered with shadows soft as milk
   Where rafts of duck crinkle and toss
   And plumping cormorants crisscross.

Persephone walks these plains and feels
Furrows of flowers break at her heels;
   And weeds that writhe on rocky shelves
   Are Proteus lost amid his selves.

And Icarus, see, is gannet, downed
And tombstoned by a fountain. Round
   Loops of dolphins carry their
   Singing Arions through the air.

An elegant confusion pours
A whole Atlantic on these shores
   Where seapods crack and pebbles cry
   And sandgrains whisper, trundling by.

Or guillemots urbanely edge
With rows of bottles that stone ledge
   That founders with each tide and then
   Gasps itself dripping up again.

One quality of colour ties
The seafoot to the upper skies
   And one decorum binds the sounds
   Of crofting lands and fishing grounds.

Till night lays sound and colour by,
Excepting where the skerries lie
   Cold as Sirens all the night,
   Opening and shutting fans of white.

December 1955

Spectroscope

Your threat to be a gormandising ghost
Is carried out too well. The world is you,
Digested into colour. And I, who learned
At least to pierce disguises, kowtow to
Perpetual images of what once was
    My lying looking-glass.

If there's a baby crying in its bed
That one day'll shuffle the elements of thought
And teach sensation somersaults, you might well be
The parodying star, the hanging nought
Over the roof-tree, and I your one Wise Man
    Arriving, as to plan.

Destiny's humour's far-fetched enough for that.
The spheres have rhymed in limericks often enough.
Bad jokes have died to keep the Scheme of Things
Safe from the risk of man calling its bluff
And perfection of imperfection is made one of
    Its claims for awe (and love).

Yet there is something flawless in us, too,
And it is I – your lucid spectroscope
That casts your separate elements on a screen –
And there's the world. If only I could hope
To reverse the process and reconstruct the bright
    Pure clarity of your light.

But all's digestion, translation, analysis;
The simplicity of infinites at ten removes;
A carcass of a god constructed from
A horn, a shred of hair and two split hooves;
And truth's extension's strictly governed by
    The limits of a lie.

All flesh is dreams, and nightmares, now. I see
Discolorations of you in the air;

You are my total of mutabilities
Whose images I make possible everywhere –
And will, till time in his old awkward way
    Demands to have his say.

January 1956

Another flood

Too many rainbows drizzle in
The broken promise that you gave;
Too many ghosts expose the grace
That cheated them into the grave.

Bend in the cloud your frenzied bow,
We'll take your false floods as they come;
Inevitable Ararats
Will lead our stiff survivors home.

Too many doves have died, for us
To be your image. Lightnings mark
Only a bestial darkness round
The pity of each floundering Ark.

Language of accidents and crimes
Exalts your mercy overhead:
The waters that you willed have drowned
The grain that grows your bitter bread.

February 1956

Insurrection of memory

The west wind and the small rain
Talk their subversions in my brain
And scents of July bogs bring down
With soft explosions this tall town.

A sea flower hoisted on his rock
Nods treason. – My prelatic clock

69]

That wags judgments and frowns graves
Is tumbrilled off by mobs of waves.

And by these rebels I am sent
Recorder to that parliament
Whose laws control the tides and tax
Seasons; and put men on their backs.

All in due time; for time will stir
(Being their grave prime minister)
At his true speed and have his say
When baubles all are taken away.

March 1956

Moor burns

Remembering the hilarity of these streams
(Half underground and twisted like an adder)
Puckers with sunlight any landscape; schemes

Of light fall down and formalise with their
Delusive intricacy such disorder
As any grayness makes, placing in air

Precisely this precisely here and that
In a place made due to it by planes of colour.
Distance goes off to distance; humped and flat,

That might be nowhere till you think of it,
Sociably emphasise, each one, the other.
Sound, so remembered, so can tangle wit

That senses in confusion speak more clear,
Sight being sound and light being born of water.
And with remembering I am scarcely here

As though space also were translated. I
Almost expect to see, and with no wonder,
A deer's horn formalise this branchless sky.

March 1956

Inverkirkaig Bay

Colour is comment of the cheating eye.
This bay, these islands walk themselves away
(When I have put my lust of looking by
And sink unnoticed into my natural gray)
To an odd world where senses never pry.

Even shape that advertises any man
Is lies to let us know him. That woman there,
Black on the steep road down to Badnaban,
Carts a whole fiction with her through the air
Whose shape's its title, reading 'Katie Ann'.

The seatrout nosing in along the shore
Taste the fresh water and the spawning beds.
They leap from their world into this, explore
A hidden sense of themselves and drive their heads
Into a knowledge they've not had before.

Sunrise and moonrise quietly get on
With their true miracles, which are never seen
For these explosions that we dote upon.
The roedeer hides in more than the bracken's green,
And round the stone gathers the sheltering stone.

But such a green, and such a shape in air
That with blunt fists boxes the sea away!
Such clarity of seeming can declare
More than my utter self to me, who say
In clouds of words less than that false cloud there.

September 1956

Feeding ducks

One duck stood on my toes.
The others made watery rushes after bread
Thrown by my momentary hand; instead,
She stood duck-still and got far more than those.

An invisible drone boomed by
With a beetle in it; the neighbour's yearning bull
Bugled across five fields. And an evening full
Of other evenings quietly began to die.

And my everlasting hand
Dropped on my hypocrite duck her grace of bread.
And I thought, 'The first to be fattened, the first to be dead',
Till my gestures enlarged, wide over the darkening land.

September 1956

Fishing the Balvaig

It is like being divided, stood on stumps
On a layer of water scarcely thicker than light
That parallels away to show it's water all right.

While underneath two sawn-off waders walk
Surprisingly to one's wishes – as though no man
Moved lumpishly, so, but a sort of Caliban.

The eel that tries to screw his ignorant head
Under an instep thinks the same; and goes
Like a tape of water going where the water flows.

Collecting images by redounding them
The stream is leafed, sunned, skied and full of shade;
Pot-holed with beer and shallowed with lemonade.

But in the glides is this thicker sort of light.
It blurs no freckled pebble or nervous weed,
Whose colours quicken as it slacks its speed.

As though water and light were mistranslations of
A vivifying influence they both use
To make a thing more thing and old news, news.

Which all the world is, wheeling round this odd
Divided figure, who forgets to pass
Through water that looks like the word isinglass.

October 1956

A man and a boat

It was his honey of environment
Where acquiescence was easy, the place where he
Became transparent and was heaven-sent.

He was easy in it as a fox is in his coat.
And it was his own idea, identity,
Large, better and battered self, and still afloat.

It was haunted by crabs and breathed of Stockholm tar.
It looked like melodeon music and took the waves
In a bucking jig-time, six to the blessed bar.

No meditative or senseless element
Loitering ashore lumber of planks and staves
But spoke their lingo and knew what they well meant.

And gibberish of horizons to him was clear
Comments to go by, explaining clause by clause
Their subtle story to his always listening ear.

His direction was all between the red and green,
Pacing athwart the Pole Star. His anchorage was
Indifference. He left no mark where he had been.

He used to drink in the waterfront pubs, aloof
Under the coiled smoke, speaking to nobody.
When he looked up, stars broke on the dirty roof.

– Not real enough. He'd go into the cold air
And the wider silence and smile in it to see
The friendly water and himself waiting there.

October 1956

Regatta, Plockton

Such expertise, such flimsies of blue air
Dizzy a drooped wing not a boat-sail there
And in blue parallels reveal a flash of red
On a trample of white curled as clouds overhead.

Clouds overhead swim winsomely their white
Cherubic hull-shapes on a race of light
Where boats might sail as truthfully as these
That swoop and dip in the half-dowsing seas.

Where wet the wet sails teeter down the kyle
Slanting the measured and unmeasured mile,
Through vogues of colour half-dissolving there
In flaws of water and flimsies of blue air.

October 1956

Goat

The goat, with amber dumb-bells in his eyes,
The blasé lecher, inquisitive as sin,
White sarcasm walking, proof against surprise,

The nothing like him goat, goat-in-itself,
Idea of goatishness made flesh, pure essence
In idle masquerade on a rocky shelf –

Hangs upside down from lushest grass to twitch
A shrivelled blade from the cliff's barren chest,
And holds the grass well lost; the narrowest niche

Is frame for the devil's face; the steepest thatch
Of barn or byre is pavement to his foot;
The last, loved rose a prisoner to his snatch;

And the man in his man-ness, passing, feels suddenly
Hypocrite found out, hearing behind him that
Vulgar vibrato, thin derisive me-eh.

November 1956

Nude in a fountain

Clip-clop go water-drops and bridles ring –
Or, visually, a gauze of water, blown
About and falling and blown about, discloses

74]

Pudicity herself in shameless stone,
In an unlikely world of shells and roses.

On shaven grass a summer's litter lies
Of paper bags and people. One o'clock
Booms on the leaves with which the trees are quilted
And wades away through air, making it rock
On flowerbeds that have blazed and dazed and wilted.

Light perches, preening, on the handle of a pram
And gasps on paths and runs along a rail
And whitely, brightly in a soft diffusion
Veils and unveils the naked figure, pale
As marble in her stone and stilled confusion.

And nothing moves except one dog that runs,
A red rag in a black rag, round and round
And that long helmet-plume of water waving,
In which the four elements, hoisted from the ground,
Become this grace, the form of their enslaving.

Meeting and marrying in the midmost air
Is mineral assurance of them all;
White doldrum on blue sky; a pose of meaning
Whose pose is what is explicit; a miracle
Made, and made bearable, by the water's screening.

The drops sigh, singing, and, still sighing, sing
Gently a leaning song. She makes no sound.
They veil her, not with shadows, but with brightness;
Till, gleam within a glitter, they expound
What a tall shadow is when it is whiteness.

A perpetual modification of itself
Going on around her is her; her hand is curled
Round more than a stone breast; and she discloses
The more than likely in an unlikely world
Of dogs and people and stone shells and roses.

November 1956

Country bedroom

It must have been the moon, because it was.
Because it was, it must have been a shadow
Uglily collapsing on the floor. Night spread,
For miles, around the snores of the villagers:
The separate mountains stood, anvils and jars.

It was a shadow that ought not to have been,
As though it had a knife in its back, as though
With a huge ho-hum about to heave itself to its feet.
Slow with damnation, it half-showed and half-hid
One arm that seemed to move, because it did.

Night spread around these darkest villagers,
Black in their deepest selves, illusive shades
That still achieved tall anvils and tall jars;
And the floor woke to its burden, the room became
Lived in and strangely, slightly not the same.

It was a night in August, 'fifty-six,
Temperature normal, no wind, ceiling high –
Oh, much too high that would hold such darkness in –
That this foul shadow was unnoticed by
Dark selves in bed and anvils in the sky.

December 1956

Haycock, Achiltibuie

Tanned in a solstice, fighting mackerel
In air half shore, half sea, it dwindles daily
To a hank of grass-hair, from a sopping hay-hill.

Hay-sweet, brine-salt, the air that bleaches it
Crisscrosses its fingers like a fan and salty
Flavours are tasted in the too honey-sweet.

It sinks into itself from blond to blond,
Wrecked on pure haycock, all its fat blades stranded.
Some saints, too, smelled of honey when they died.

A sort of holiness has been cut down
And heaped up in one hill, with many mansions
Where mice, its little sinners, can run in.

Till comes the wintry crofter, hoisting half
A Zion on his back, and pitiful
Small angels fall through nights and days of frost.

And even the crofter, shrugging by his fire,
Snug in his shaking house, will look up, hearing
Such execrations battering at his door.

December 1956

Turned head

The rose creeps in its thorn.
The bird flies into its egg and waits to be born.
The sun hauls in his rays, hand over hand.
You turn your head and stop the world from turning.
All meaning breaks off short, its last word 'and'.

Fine figures for what is
Not metaphor but metamorphosis.
No green girl changing to a greener tree
Left herself further than the world's existence
When you (no god pursuing) turn to me.

And everything begins
To be a beginning. Between widdershins
And deasil was this startle in the air
That now is settled in its solid shining
And mirrors you and April everywhere.

What will I make of it,
This huge enlargement of being you commit

To my greed and terror? Will a time come when,
Used to its reckless rolling to a future,
I shall forget when the world turned again?

Adam was grave, and I
Laugh with the substance of his gravity.
My beasts and flowers make Edens in my mind
And with you I will name them, not forgetting
The gate, the flaming sword and human kind.

March 1957

Creator

Fishermen haul fish from the strangling water.
Light birds thud on the ground, a thumping lie.
Out of the sylvan
Stink of various soils, never mind nettles
Cherries explode and handsome, bearded barley
Slants at attention.

The nosey-parker, thrumming at all his nerve-ends,
Saunters about amongst the husbandmen
And hard-fleshed hunters
Making translations he takes to be lovely
Of fish, bird, fruit: and the dead lives he mentions
Become immortal.

The poem he's in keeps on producing stanzas
That dangle and swim and grow remarkable beards
And tirelessly saunter
Translating into still-lifes their amazing
Mortalities. How hard to be so god-like
As one would fancy.

May 1957

Too cold for words

Sometimes old Gabriel lifts his aching chin,
Sick-tired of practising the tremendous note

That will bundle sinners into their earthy coat
Out of the nakedness they were peaceful in.

Or the Devil, even, bored with wickedness,
Chats with a dying saint without disdain
And, when all's over, leaves him to explain
The kiss burned black upon his holiness.

Girl, you're no resurrection, nor am I
Gabriel, nor the Devil. Yet, when I find
My rosy phrases bouncing off your mind,
I lay my horn, or sour seduction, by.

And little care, when we from nakedness
Put on our fleshly appetites again,
If you will have one black kiss to explain
The brimstone stink that haunts your holiness.

May 1957

Jug

With a toad belly and a horny lip,
It madly flourishes flowers
On an ill-lit shelf; as though trying to hop and skip
Into the beautiful world of allegories.

Plain reason sensibly deploys
Its furniture around
This odd neurosis that explodes its joys
Like a wild vice in the bosom of Mrs Grundy.

The revolution of the ugly, or
Only its pathos? Switch
The darkness on, that toads love; shut the door
On a midden-rose, on a Chaconne by Bach.

October 1957

Any Orpheus

His rich mind was a lusty boy
Swaggering towards the Styx,
Hailing all he passed – 'Are you
Basilisk or blubbing phoenix?

'Where's the dragon you begot
Or the tombstone crammed with angels?
Are you saint or drunken sot?
Do you ask, or answer riddles?'

Trees and heavenly hayricks, men,
Languages and space – them all –
Leapt up, livelier again,
From their ageing melancholy.

But the river got him and
The lusty boy went squeaking over –
'Is this end or ampersand?
Where's my lost and wailing lover?'

October 1957

Treeless landscape

Except in grooves of streams, armpits of hills,
Here's a bald, bare land, weathered half away.
It pokes its bony blades clean through its skin
And chucks the light up from grey knucklebones,
Tattering the eye, that's teased with flowers and stones.

Something to do with time has all to do
With shape and size. The million shapes of time,
Its millions of appearances are the true
Mountain and moor and tingling water drop
That runs and hangs and shakes time towards a stop.

Prowling like cats on levels of the air
These buzzards mew, or pounce: one vole the less,

One alteration more in time, or space.
But nothing's happened, all is in control
Unless you are the buzzard or the vole.

Yet, all the same, it's weathered half away.
Time's no procrastinator. The land thrusts
A rotting elbow up. It makes a place
By sinking into it, and buzzards fly
To be a buzzard and create a sky.

November 1957

Dude

    With goldmines in each corner,
Halcyons making ridiculous all my seas,
    Breakfasts with angels, cruises
    Through laughing Hesperides;

    One season, and it all summer,
And doom with a wreath of flowers to dance for me,
    With suns on my rubied fingers,
    Stars gartered below each knee;

    I giggle my tall love for you,
I stilt my praises, bow with a wooing grace
    And have no word of mourning
    To shade your turning face,

    But, glass of your smiling fashion,
Saunter in bliss and, quizzing the natives there,
    Discover them all your subjects
    With gold straws in their hair.

November 1957

Explicit snow

First snow is never all the snows there were
Come back again, but novel in the sun
As though a newness had but just begun.

It does not fall as rain does from nowhere
Or from that cloud spinnakered on the blue,
But from a place we feel we could go to.

As a great actor steps, not from the wings,
But from the play's extension – all he does
Is move to the seen from the mysterious –

And his performance is the first of all –
The snow falls from its implications and
Stages pure newness on the uncurtained land.

And the hill we've looked out of existence comes
Vivid in its own language; and this tree
Stands self-explained, its own soliloquy.

January 1958

By the canal, early March

The snow is trash now and the blackbirds sing
A gold and blue day trying to be Spring.
A gray sludge fringes the canal where swans,
Almost as gray, surge by, their wings like tents,
Hissing with love between the tenements.

Posters are peeled that once hung in the air
Their vulgar summers; but drab windows stare
Winking and blinking at the boisterous sun.
Low, the brown water breaks in glass and high
The tall mill cracks its smokelash in the sky.

And everything is headlong, rushing through
Spaces of sun and sky, their gold and blue,
Towards that still certain time when buds all break
And sparrows quarrel in the dust and men
Lounge their ways home and swans are white again.

March 1958

Edinburgh courtyard in July

Hot light is smeared as thick as paint
On these ramshackle tenements. Stones smell
Of dust. Their hoisting into quaint
Crowsteps, corbels, carved with fool and saint,
Holds fathoms of heat, like water in a well.

Cliff-dwellers have poked out from their
High cave-mouths brilliant rags on drying-lines;
They hang still, dazzling in the glare,
And lead the eye up, ledge by ledge, to where
A chimney's tilted helmet winks and shines.

And water from a broken drain
Splashes a glassy hand out in the air
That breaks in an unbraiding rain
And falls still fraying, to become a stain
That spreads by footsteps, ghosting everywhere.

March 1958

Half-built boat in a hayfield

A cradle, at a distance, of a kind:
Or, making midget its neat pastoral scene,
A carcass rotted and its bones picked clean.

Rye-grass was silk and sea, whose rippling was
Too suave to rock it. Solid in the sun,
Its stiff ribs ached for voyages not begun.

The gathering word was not completed yet.
The litter of its own genesis lay around,
Sunk in the bearded sea, or on the ground.

As though evolving brilliances could show
In their first utterances what would end as one
Continuous proclamation of a sun.

Only when these clawed timbers could enclose
Their own completing darkness would they be
Phoenixed from It and phoenixed into She.

And fit then, as such noticing reveals,
To split her first wave open and explore
The many ways that all lead to one shore.

May 1958

Ardmore

The track that stops there is a final one.
So absolute its ending that it seems
What other tracks are lesser copies of
– Paradigm of them all. The sea, the sun
Are the next stage, with nothing in between.
A quick place this to know your journey's done.

The journey, not the direction. It goes on
Beyond the wild rose and the barking dog
With a bird's rush to soar out into space:
It shows the lie the journey is, undergone,
It seems, for the direction's sake and not
The croft it set its endless love upon.

The sea rips in between two claws of stone
Or races out, as meaning does with words.
– So, here's a statement at its seeming end.
Only who makes it knows that it has flown
Into a space where dogs need never bark
Or roses in their thorns be overblown.

May 1958

Advices of time

Such exhortations, and how dull they get,
Appear as flowers or tides or a face ageing
Or a day done and nothing more than it.

No flimsy goddess comes to make a Spring
Immortal, these days, to her lucky lover.
    Such doubtless days are over.

And the admonishments surround us still
That time eats mountains, mice and emperors
And us, who listen till the senses tell
Such truths, about these strange particulars
That flower, or tide, becomes immortal as
    No god nor goddess was.

The bird flies in the mind, and more than bird:
Time dies somewhere between it and its flight.
The bird flies in the mind, and more than mind:
Sunsets and winds and roofs enrich the light
That makes it bird and more than bird, till they
    Can never fly away.

Queer sparrow this, the sparrow that it is.
And what a passion that can turn away
To a brown bird from gods and goddesses
And find it being what they fail to say
To me – whom, doubtless, time will one day pack
    In his deep haversack.

The recording mind goes down. The day goes down.
The mountain spills down its own side, the bird
Becomes a purse of maggots. Yet they mean
And are the ambiguities of the Word,
That vanishing-point beyond which Chaos sits
    Warming his timeless wits.

                                September 1958

Castles in Spain

Somehow above sierras they transpire,
Bone in the air, a clench of turrets. White
Invades the blue with soft and childish fire.
The littlest castle has a cloud on it.

Remarkable inventions of the air
Can never throw a shadow down on those
Off-humans toiling on the plain or shower
Fistfuls of raindrops on the dust they raise.

What sort of clarity is this that says,
'More legible – less meaning?' Dreams are thick
With their own understudies. Dreams have brows
Behind what stares, that cut short childish talk.

But this is visibility made pure,
Neat with horizons, meaning nothing else
Than snow and turrets in a milky fire
Above their brown and starving harvesters.

September 1958

Spring in a clear October

Light and a gay light cheats the world towards sleep,
Brocaded in thick gardens.
Spring that was dead returns in images.
Suns ride up handsome and all is heliotrope.

The difference is the distance of images:
The silver air booms bronze
And narrow flowers are wool-balls, discs, propellers
And buds are bulbed out bulging into fruits.

Yet the bell's voice rings clear, the fruit explodes,
Oddly, into fruition.
Chrysanthemums, that will smell of fog and lean
Sick from their stakes, whirl up their violent heads.

And the canal rocks sparkling in the sun
– As though no ashen frosts
Could swarm from their wide ambush, quenching this
Green glaze of water, incandescent swan.

October 1958

Standing in my ideas

Never did Nature, that vogue-mistress, give
An image from her slants and sighs and silks
Or make a figure out of froth and stone
That would not blush as your alternative,
– Though, trapped in a net of kins, a web of ilks,
The gorgeous rose is sibling to the bone.

You stand entrancing in my trance of woods,
Superlatively you; and bole and bough
Surrender Ariels rotting in their rind.
The dropped cone hiccups, the cherry branch intrudes.
And with such grace you breathe what, I allow,
Is foxglove vapours hazing in my mind.

Such elegant composure I suspect
Because I love it, and my loving charms
Environment from you. And, being wise
In my suspicions, can it be I detect
Something of innocent ivy in your arms?
Something of nightshade in those lucid eyes?

December 1958

Two ways of it

The duller legends are what you live in,
The girl who knew a man who once saw Helen
Or heard a hero howling in his pride.
I, knowing you, live in a larger one –
Where, all the same, no topless tower has fallen
Nor good man gone to Hell before he died.

You are no Helen, walking parapets
And dazing wisdom with another beauty
That made hard men talk of soft goddesses
And feel death blooming in their violent wits
With such seduction that they asked no pity –
Till death came whistling in and loosed their knees.

87]

For not death blooms but ordinariness;
And worlds and wits wake to a mundane glory
That, being its source, you can know nothing of.
This is the largest legend, that need not stress
A more than human distance or be fiery
With a god's grace that kills to keep its love.

Even a leaf, its own shape in the air,
Achieves its mystery not by being symbol
Or ominous of anything but what it is,
Such is the decent clarity you bear
For the world to be in. Everything is humble,
Not humbled, in its own lucidities.

No need to wander the dark lanes of Hell
Or be translated to a monumental
Sprinkle of stars, to mark our history:
But doucely, in your fashion, I will kill
Nothing but Time (until that final battle
When you and legends fade away from me).

To enrich the leaf and be enriched by it
And to be, both, your natural celebration,
Stating, by selves, what Time cannot outface …
A legend, this, with no curmudgeon plot
To make a martyr of a slave to passion –
Who am no slave, but freeman of your grace.

December 1958

Celtic cross

The implicated generations made
This symbol of their lives, a stone made light
By what is carved on it.
                              The plaiting masks,
But not with involutions of a shade,
What a stone says and what a stone cross asks.

Something that is not mirrored by nor trapped
In webs of water or bag-nets of cloud;
The tangled mesh of weed
                              lets it go by.
Only men's minds could ever have unmapped
Into abstraction such a territory.

No green bay going yellow over sand
Is written on by winds to tell a tale
Of death-dishevelled gull
                              or heron, stiff
As a cruel clerk with gaunt writs in his hand
– Or even of light, that makes its depths a cliff.

Singing responses order otherwise.
The tangled generations ravelled out
In links of song whose sweet
                              strong choruses
Are these stone involutions to the eyes
Given to the ear in abstract vocables.

The stone remains, and the cross, to let us know
Their unjust, hard demands, as symbols do.
But on them twine and grow
                              beneath the dove
Serpents of wisdom whose cool statements show
Such understanding that it seems like love.

                                        December 1958

World's centre

A common petal, tipped with its own self
And cockled in its crimson, velvet cup
For any finger wondering for it,
Shakes on the window-ledge, rocks in the draught
Squeezed through a crevice by the world's whole shape.

Sunlight lies broad and banded on warm wood
In a gold smell of dust. And, making planes,

It drifts a lake of light across the floor;
And, making angles, bores the blue with fire;
And is succession and one of origins.

Amid it all, with what exactness lies
The crimson curl, O of its natural graph
On whose huge web the hot sun flutters and
A lake of light drags sideways and the world
Thickens to place it: tight in its very self.

December 1958

Memory two ways

Along a road, all corners,
Into whose deepest secret
The huge Atlantic pokes
One of its crooked fingers,

Through tunnels damp with rowans,
Past Loch an Ordain, winking
With islands in its eye,
One of my selves is going

Ten years ago. Ten summers
Have quenched their flowery bonfire,
Ten winters have flamed white,
And there he is, dark figure,

A fact for time to curse at,
Sending on to my envy
A sky green as an egg
And two capsizing ravens

And moist ferns in a gully
And the sound of slapstick water
Perpetually falling downstairs.
If he could see his fellow,

His ten years older brother,
How many roads, all corners,
He'd have to look along
To find him here, dark figure

In enviable landscapes
Where space is of all meanings
And clownish times fall down
To beautiful Atlantics

Whose presence, breathing inland,
Enriches all it breathes on
With trembling atmospheres,
With sounds becoming soundless.

From *A Round Of Applause* (mostly 1959–61)

Sound of the sea on a still evening

It comes through quietness, softly crumbling in
Till it becomes the quietness; and we know
The wind to be will reach us from Loch Roe.
From the receding South it will begin
To stir, to whisper; and by morning all
The sea will lounge North, sloping by Clachtoll.

Gentlest of prophecies. The most tottering grass
Stands still as a stiff thorn, as though its root
Groped not in sand but in sand's absolute
And was itself disqualified to pass
Into a shaking world where it must be
Not grass but grasses rippling like the sea.

Three heifers slouch by, trailing down the road
A hundred yards of milky breath – they rip
The grasses sideways. Waterdrops still drip
From the turned tap and tinily explode
On their flat stone. An unseen bird goes by,
Its little feathers hushing the whole sky.

And yet a word is spoken. When the light
Gives back its redness to the Point of Stoer
And sets off cocks like squibs, pebbles will roar
At their harsh labour, grinding shells to white
And glittering beaches, and tall waves will run
Fawning on rocks and barking in the sun.

From *A Round Of Applause* (mostly 1959–61)

Rain on fence wire

What little violences shake
The raindrop till it turns from apple
To stretched-out pear, then drops and takes
Its whirling rainbows to the ground?

Once, I remember, you, too, fell,
Quenched, to the world, and in your vanished
Face I could see no call for help
Nor news of what had brought you down.

Was it the world itself that quaked
Enormously beyond my knowing?
Or tiny claws, that perch and shake
From yards away a rainbow down?

No difference … I look and see
The dry wings flirt, the small ounce soaring
And with its leap a shower of drops
Flames down, released into the grass.

From *A Round Of Applause* (mostly 1959–61)

Translations of innocence

Small girls on bibles sailed away
Through pinks and whites and curly clouds
And boys hung through a black Nor'easter,
Gallant upon the rattling shrouds.

They used to. But the heavenly shores
Are empty round the sea of glass
And oilwells gush on tropic islands
Gunboats scarcely dare to pass.

Yet restless in their present tense,
The little siblings, scarcely born,
Jostle around the same old places,
The gates of ivory and horn.

And paradisal images
Of pride and babies, blood and fear,
Obscure with trailing fumes of glory
The dreadful fact of being here.

And each one gulps his apple down
Under the dark forbidden tree.
Who would be angel now and notice
What's mirrored in the crystal sea?

From A Round Of Applause (mostly 1959–61)

Failed mystic

A stone remarked what he'd no answer to
And trees showered secrets he could only share
In remote reaches of himself – a country
He seldom travelled to. When winds were fair

He coasted with them, smelling of the Spring;
When they blew contrary he downed his head
And bullocked on, an ugly opposition,
Swearing to find himself – and found instead

What a wind is. He could not bear to be
The odd man out, the man out, or the man;
He grudged the grass the grass, he envied water
And coveted meaning's meaning. He would scan

Himself for monsters, or for dew. His mind
Leaked over being, trying to soak in
And by assumption to extend his empire
Beyond the confines of his rotting skin

To the remotest reaches of a stone
As though to look from there and see a place
That he could love, that he could, somehow, envy,
Although it had an only human face.

From A Round Of Applause (mostly 1959–61)

Crocus

Affiliations make no meaning to
The crocus single in the unheeded world
Nor, one would think, the force of being blue –

More than the world reflects upon itself
And hoists with expertise blue petals up.
Complacence is my way of feeling safe

Who make paternal, lover's, cousin's kin
Of all the world, something that a blue
Crocus can bear to find enlargement in,

As though a principle, pecked by sparrows, was
Sprung from a bulb and that bulb was the sun
And it a principle and I their cause

And fatherly, loverly, cousinly, by incest
Becoming all my creatures, survey them all
And, for the moment, think the crocus best.

From A Round Of Applause (mostly 1959–61)

Spraying sheep

Old tufts of wool lie on the grass.
The clipping's over. But once again
The small quicksilver flock come pouring
Down from the hill towards the pen.

Dogs coax them to the roofless steading.
They bunch, plunge forward, one by one.
When half's outside and half within, they
Make a white hourglass in the sun.

The dogs run on the ruined walls,
Swinging their tongues, their minds all sheep.
The zinc bath winks, the stirrup pump
Guzzles the primrose one foot deep.

Then out they come, bounding high over
Nothing at all, and ramble on
The shining grass – not quicksilver
But golden fleeces, every one.

From A Round Of Applause (mostly 1959–61)

Lighthouse

Gorgon in greed, but not effect, it glares
A thing to life and back again.
A hill jumps forward, then it isn't there.
A tree explodes in tree shape. Flashes devour
This house's natural death – it has more than twenty
Punctual resurrections every hour.
Bad Christians think that one is more than plenty.

Bad disbelievers, too, are troubled by
Their disbelief – how weak it is;
And in the dark look for that whirling eye
Whose maniacal rigidity might swing
Them into high relief … The sea, too busy
Inventing its own forms, bucks by, leaving
The mind to spin, the dark brain to grow dizzy.

From A Round Of Applause (mostly 1959–61)

Culag Pier

A moderate jargon – winches, cries in Gaelic,
Cordage against the sky: most moderate when

A gull slews in with icefloes in his eyes
And a seal of crimson dapper on his beak;
A frosty distance follows where he flies.

Yet see him, pick-and-run, as he hauls a herring
Through slats of a fishbox, ululating oaths
In a sort of Eskimo at whatever stands
Between his greed and his belly – see him swerving
Out of infinity, steered by guts and glands.

The moderate jargon takes the two things in –
The winged etcetera in his etcetera wastes
Or small town gangster pillaging a slum –
And, puffing incense of brine and oily iron,
Jubilates briskly of its kingdom come.

The moderation is, of course, no mask.
Grace is hilarity; and this scene has
Good nature, in two meanings, as its meaning,
Where a transcendence feeds on guts and makes
No bones of it, nor thinks it worth the screening.

And the observing mind, in its own sun,
Takes it as so. Fishboxes swing between
The darkness and the light and herrings go
Where they could not have guessed in their broad ocean,
And ropes seem tangled, but they are not so.

From *A Round Of Applause* (mostly 1959–61)

Always first morning

And spaces, with no sound at all
Assembling like a threatening crowd,
Contracted into selves – a wall
Between each cloud that touched a cloud.

On mountain tops, round ptarmigan
Grunted from burrows in the air

96]

And with a flash of red began
Plumply to whirr to here from there.

Salmon deduced themselves from what
Became a brown froth over stones.
They winked and sidled into thought,
Wavering their long monotones.

And hayfields gently lurched. And slopes
Were buckled with red cattle. Tracks
Tangled green parishes with ropes
And laid tall fields upon their backs.

Larks climbed the air, more cliff than tree,
Each improvising shelf on shelf.
A roof, discovering how to be
Ran helter-skelter through itself.

Horizons prowled. How could they pounce
Out of the cage that distance is
To tear rose bush and water flounce
Or fawn on homely presences? –

Like that small curdling of the air
That played with two white stones and smiled
To see a sparkling Everywhere
Perched on the knuckles of a child.

And everything unfolded till
A naked Eden gathered round
The tree that on a distant hill
Laid its crossed shadow on the ground.

From *A Round Of Applause* (mostly 1959–61)

Other self

My inmost creature, Caliban perhaps,
Perhaps St Francis (at least, a sort of dunce)
Sits, like a Chinese sage listening to

A colloquy of summer afternoons,
Inscrutable understanding on his brow.

The panegyric that his silence is
Comes clear to me (that other sort of dunce),
Written with smallest wrinkles, the stillness of
A sleeve, the half-beginnings of a glance,
An air of sensuous contemplative.

What pool rocks what white petal in his gaze?
What fluffed out bird is blobbed upon its bough?
I can see mountains, but they are not his
Tressed with cascades and single in the sky,
Removed by poems from glittering paddy fields.

If I could make the epigram he is,
The seventeen syllables saying exactly what
They exactly do not say, this other man
Would see such blossoms frosting with their light
The barbarous province he is banished in.

From A Round Of Applause (mostly 1959–61)

All being equal

A black wave bangs on timber
And slavers past. We go
Bouncing by lucky shores.
The sky sways overhead
Where blue stars spurt and crumble.
The sea turns in its bed.

All that is in this narrow
Abridgment of what is
Bulks big and equal. Thin
Spatters of water are
No less themselves nor nearer
Than cliffhead or than star.

As though skies could remember
And winds be filled with all
That winds are, no line falls
As treacherous boundary
Beyond which myth and monster
Are told, are as they say.

You make it so. You, sitting
Dark in the sternsheets, break
Webs of perspective. Space
Hauls all its treasures in
And time, with plots for plotting,
Has no time to begin.

The moon climbs up, converging
With miracles. It shows
How running waves can go
Against but cannot halt
Our rakish island, forging
Past bays as white as salt.

And the black wave bangs on timber
And hoists you up against
The sky and not its mask,
The rock and not its stone
In time and not its minutes,
Where nothing is alone.

From A Round Of Applause (mostly 1959–61)

Ordinary homecoming

All that had been before had led to this
Hand in the air, about to knock. It was
The funnel tip from which events fanned back,
Through which they'd pour, and with no filtering gauze.

The night had measured out miles that were long
Under the Plough – but not to be shortened by

99]

The looking all ways mind, balanced between
Its once upon a time, its by-and-by.

Not one shade could be grudged, one oily glint
From the black sea. All that had been before
Must be in the narrow moment, that held it all,
When the clenched fist knocked lightly on the door.

Chair scraped, steps sounded. Light shot violently
Across the grass and quenched the shaking Plough.
The purse upon the doorstep gave a jump,
Turning to toad. A bouncing dog said *How*.

And resolutions filled the lighted room.
Click went the wireless, off. And words were said
That in an hour would lay a future down
Beside a past, safe in one narrow bed.

From *A Round Of Applause* (mostly 1959–61)

In a level light

Sheep wander haloed, birds at their plainsong shed
Pure benedictions on water's painted glass.
The gentle worm rears up her hooded head
And weaves hot sermons under her steeple of grass.
Saints objurgate from thickets, angels bank
Over the sea: and its crisp texts unfold,
Silvering the sand's ecclesiastic gold.

Accepted in it all, one of its moods,
The human mind sits in its sense of sin,
Hacking a cross from gross beatitudes,
The price to pay warm in its purse of skin,
And sees out in that bliss, and out of its,
An angel tilt, dive into texts and float,
Working his god down his rebelling throat.

From *A Round Of Applause* (mostly 1959–61)

Midnight, Lochinver

Wine-coloured, Homer said, wine-dark …
The seaweed on the stony beach,
Flushed darker with that wine, was kilts
And beasts and carpets … A startled heron
Tucked in its cloud two yellow stilts.

And eiderducks were five, no, two –
No, six. A lounging fishbox raised
Its broad nose to the moon. With groans
And shouts the steep burn drowned itself;
And sighs were soft among the stones.

All quiet, all dark: excepting where
A cone of light stood on the pier
And in the circle of its scope
A hot winch huffed and puffed and gnashed
Its iron fangs and swallowed rope.

The nursing tide moved gently in.
Familiar archipelagos
Heard her advancing, heard her speak
Things clear, though hard to understand
Whether in Gaelic or in Greek.

> From *A Round Of Applause* (mostly 1959–61)

Things in each other

To fake green strokes in water, light fidgets,
A niggling fidget, and the green is there,
Born of a blue and marrying into blue
With clouds blushed pink on it from the upper air.

And water breathing upwards from itself
Sketches an island with blurred pencillings,
A phase of space, a melting out of space:
Mind does this, too, with the pure shapes of things.

Or the mind fidgets and a thought, grown green,
Born of nowhere and marrying nowhere,
Fakes a creation, that is one and goes
Into the world and makes its difference there.

A thing to be regarded: whose pure shape
Blurs in the quality of the noticing mind
And is blushed pink and makes the hard jump from
Created to creator, like human kind.

A Round Of Applause (mostly 1959–61)

The shore road

The sea pursued
Its beastlike amours, rolling in its sweat
And beautiful under the moon; and a leaf was
A lively architecture in the light.

The space between
Was full, to splitting point, of presences
So oilily adjustable a walking man
Pushed through and trailed behind no turbulence.

The walking man
With octaves in his guts was a quartertone
In octaves of octaves that climbed up and down
Beyond his hearing, to back parts of the moon.

As though things were
Perpetual chronologies of themselves,
He sounded his small history, to make complete
The interval of leaf and rutting waves.

Or so he thought,
And heard his hard shoes scrunching in the grit,
Smelt salt and iodine in the wind and knew
The door was near, the supper, the small lamplight.

From A Round Of Applause (mostly 1959–61)

High up on Suilven

Gulfs of blue air, two lochs like spectacles,
A frog (this height) and Harris in the sky –
There are more reasons for hills
Than being steep and reaching only high.

Meeting the cliff face, the American wind
Stands up on end: chute going the wrong way.
Nine ravens play with it and
Go up and down its lift half the long day.

Reasons for them? the hill's one … A web like this
Has a thread that goes beyond the possible;
The old spider outside space
Runs down it – and where's raven? Or where's hill?

From *A Round Of Applause* (mostly 1959–61)

Preacher

The cloud he speaks from has another voice
That, needing no words, minces none and splits
No doubtful hairs with stropped and shining wits.

Its thirdly fourthly and its brethren are
All one to it, and it makes nothing of
Division and distraction, hate and love.

He pounds his metaphysics, and its dust
Joins all the rest, waltzing above the pews
Where chosen people wonder what they choose.

The infiltration of an angel would
Gloze the proceedings; but his fiery face
Would burn like brimstone this defenceless place.

And what pedantic lunacy could bear
The logic of a presence? – Or could raise
Blind eyes to that mild and catastrophic gaze?

The crow voice caws. The mind saws up and down
And thinks to follow the first Word and Will
By trying to divide the Indivisible.

The other voice speaks things into the air,
Its own disguises, utterances that fall
As kirk and congregation, angel and all.

One word pronounced all ways – hard text to read,
That spells out heaven and pronounces hell
And rings a steeple when it builds a bell.

And the congregation (that disguise), led out
From sorts of Egypts, singing as they go,
Cross more and wider Jordans than they know.

From A Round Of Applause (mostly 1959–61)

Moorings

In a salt ring of moonlight
The dinghy nods at nothing.
It paws the bright water
And scatters its own shadow
In a false net of light.

A ruined chain lies reptile,
Tied to the ground by grasses.
Two oars, wet with sweet water
Filched from the air, are slanted
From a wrecked lobster creel.

The cork that can't be travels –
Nose of a dog otter.
It's piped at, screamed at, sworn at
By an elegant oystercatcher
On furious orange legs.

With a sort of idle swaying
The tide breathes in. Harsh seaweed

Uncrackles to its kissing;
The skin of the water glistens;
Rich fat swims on the brine.

And all night in his stable
The dinghy paws bright water,
Restless steeplechaser
Longing to clear the hurdles
That ring the Point of Stoer.

From A Round Of Applause (mostly 1959–61)

Christmas snow in Princes Street

Slush on the ground. Taxis
Go slurring by. The railing
Holds up its snowy wicks –
Beyond, the castle sails.

Pale on the dirty clouds,
High in the air, not climbing,
A second moon announces
A second sort of time.

The night shrugs distance off,
But it won't go. It whispers
Of wastes, migrations, gulfs
And swarming memories.

Here windows glow for Aladdins –
No Sesame to open
But coins that children jingle,
That taste just like the snow.

Fine to be them. But lonely
To be the tall man staring
At tinsel sprawling down
On snowfield and shambling bear

And on that globe of crimson –
Cottage where crooked women

Keep strange children for ransom;
As he in his red room

Keeps what was once his childhood.
Who will redeem it? A moment,
Only, may go by riding
And toss him his purse of gold.

What more than a moment matters –
Small wizard, whose small whisper
Lays the tall champion flat
And makes songs sing in earnest?

The high clock there, glum angel
Whose self is his own halo,
Measures off Edens; clangs
On each its sullen gate.

– Yet still a tree of gardens
And snowy windows, rooted
Deep in a dark field,
Holds up its dangerous fruit.

And a strange will in its branches
Twinkles its scales. It hisses
Like wheels in the watery slush.
It coils in these dark minds.

And inklings grope in spaces
And breathe up from dark cellars
And lie like newspapers
Scuffed round the drinking well;

Where a drunk man, blunt lips pouting,
Sucking a thumb of water,
Is joined by a silver string
To nightblack watersheds.

From A Round Of Applause (mostly 1959–61)

Poachers, early morning

The net was spread upon the ground.
As though a sort of cloud it lay
Where fish had failed to fly. They cleaned
Their choking cloud, their Milky Way
Whose constellations bulged in sacks
Soon to be heaved upon their backs.

Enlarged in the enlarging light,
Two bustling primitives, they shook
A sixty yards long diagram out;
Four huge deft hands reached out and took
Precisely knots of weed and wrack,
The smooth, the varicose, the black.

Centuries, generations made
A natural ritual of a crime
And with their less than human hand
Lifted two rascals out of time
Till, each his own ancestor, they
Carried their holy spoils away.

From A Round Of Applause (mostly 1959–61)

Byre

The thatched roof rings like heaven where mice
Squeak small hosannahs all night long,
Scratching its golden pavements, skirting
The gutter's crystal river-song.

Wild kittens in the world below
Glare with one flaming eye through cracks,
Spurt in the straw, are tawny brooches
Splayed on the chests of drunken sacks.

The dimness becomes darkness as
Vast presences come mincing in,

Swagbellied Aphrodites, swinging
A silver slaver from each chin.

And all is milky, secret, female.
Angels are hushed and plain straws shine.
And kittens miaow in circles, stalking
With tail and hindleg one straight line.

From A Round Of Applause (mostly 1959–61)

Still life

Three apples, if they are apples, and a jug,
A lemon (certain), grapes, a fish's tail,
A melting fruitdish and a randy table:
Squared off from other existences they struggle
Into a peace, a balancing of such power
As past and future use in being Now.

Still life, they call it – like a bursting bomb
That keeps on bursting, one burst, on and on:
A new existence, continually being born,
Emerging out of white into the sombre
Garishness of the spectrum, refusing the easy,
Clenching its strength on nothing but how to be.

Nice lesson for a narrative or for
A thing made emblem – that martyrs in their fire,
Christs on their crosses, fêtes and massacres,
When purified of their small history,
Cannot surpass, no matter how they struggle,
Three apples (more than likely) and a jug.

From A Round Of Applause (mostly 1959–61)

Water tap

There was this hayfield,
You remember, pale gold
If it weren't hazed
With a million clover heads.

A rope of water
Frayed down – the bucket
Hoisted up a plate
Of flashing light.

The thin road screwed
Into hills; all ended
Journeys were somewhere,
But far, far.

You laughed, by the fence;
And everything that was
Hoisting water
Suddenly spilled over.

From A Round Of Applause (mostly 1959–61)

Mutual life

A wildcat, furfire in a bracken bush,
Twitches his club-tail, rounds his amber eyes
At rockabye rabbits humped on the world. The air
Crackles about him. His world is a rabbit's size.

And in milky pearls, in a liquefaction of green,
One of ten thousand, spattering squabs of light,
A mackerel shuttles the hanging waterwebs,
Muscling through tons, slipping them left and right.

What do you know, mind, of that speck in air,
The high insanitary raven that pecks his claws
A thousand feet up and volplanes on his back
And greets his ancient sweetheart with coarse caws?

You tell a hand to rise and you think it yours.
It makes a shape (you have none) in a space
It gives perspective to. You sink in it
And disappear there, foundered without trace.

And dreadful alienations bring you down
Into a proper loneliness. You cry
For limits that make a wildcat possible
And laws that tumble ravens in the sky.

– Till clenched hand opens, drowning into you,
Where mackerel, wildcat, raven never fall
Out of their proper spaces; and you are
Perpetual resurrection of them all.

From *A Round Of Applause* (mostly 1959–61)

Loch Sionascaig

Hard to remember how the water went
Shaking the light,
Until it shook like peas in a riddling plate.

Or how the islands snored into the wind,
Or seemed to, round
Stiff, plunging headlands that they never cleared.

Or how a trout hung high its drizzling bow
For a count of three –
Heraldic figure on a shield of spray.

Yet clear the footprint in the puddled sand
That slowly filled
And rounded out and smoothed and disappeared.

From *A Round Of Applause* (mostly 1959–61)

Outsider

I watch the lush moon fatly smirking down –
Where she might go, to skirt that smouldering cloud,
Is space enough to lose your image in.

Or, turn my head, between those islands run
Sandpapering currents that would scrub the dull
Picture away in suds and slaverings.

Even this grass, glowered at with force enough,
And listened to with lusting, would usurp,
In its beanstalk way, this walking, talking thing.

I choose it should not go. I turn from these
Paltering beautiful things, in case I see
Your image fade and myself fade with it –

A dissipation into actual light:
A dissolution in pure wave: a demise
In growth of a good greenness, sappy and thick –

And think myself a foreigner in this scene,
The odd shape cramped on stone, the unbeastlike, clear
Of law and logos, with choices to commit …

Thump goes the wave then crisscross gabbles back –
As I do now till, wave to wonder at,
I come again, to tower and lurch and spill.

From A Round Of Applause (mostly 1959–61)

Dunvegan

High in the air, the air
Lies like an open secret;
It loosens its fist and lets
Islands float in to where

Round heads bob on the green –
Their dogs' eyes follow the dinghy
Crabbing across the tide.
Two cliffs and a sea between

Have stolen a space of time
And squander it all in being;
The sea thrills like a silence
Between a chime and a chime:

And the rowan digs its claws
Into the heart of the matter

And a rose is Lazarus and
Shuffling ripples are flaws

Through which the mind can see
What way the wind is blowing –
As this one, that drifts in
Over the boulder scree,

Where ducks squatter in mud
And, cubed on a kilted stone,
Stands the grey honeycomb
Filled with claret and blood

Where a great music arose
And Mary, Red Alasdair's daughter,
Made poems and ladled her snuff
Into her randy nose.

From A Round Of Applause (mostly 1959–61)

Loch na Bearraig

It makes no claim – as though a claim could be
Colour of islands, absence of a tree
Or cliff on one side sailing to the sea.

And no solution can be made to fit
The clues it gives, however composite
Of ravens above Glen Canisp, deer in it.

If two mergansers, beak to beak, swim round
Their kissing centre, that is what they've found
And flouncing water is their loving sound.

And drifting flies, whose jury sails can do
No more than keep them head to wind, pursue
Their own solution and a different clue.

Even light stays universal – though it has needs
That it expresses, trailing in long screeds
Or sparking epigrams in a bed of weeds.

And trout swim separate in their private cold,
Even if it seems, so closely are they shoaled,
It is their wavering turns the water gold.

It has no claim: is one. Its water makes
For beaches other than those on which it breaks
And its waves die for more than their own sakes.

A true decorum, where an abstraction finds
Easy admittance and haunts these rocky wynds,
Filthy and roaring for its sidling hinds.

From A Round Of Applause (mostly 1959–61)

John Quixote

Where he jogs dusty, trailing a horn of dust,
Ironic windmills signal through gray air
Their huge tall jokes and a lousy innkeeper
Spreads evil blankets, swansdown to his pelt;
Princes in pigsties scratch their scurfy crust
And heads of heathens stutter at his belt.

No lark so ravishing as to be a lark
Nor dirt so true as nourish one poor seed.
His mad eye twitches, hands grope for a deed
That would free heavenly hosts to sing and soar
Over gold acres, dancing round the Ark.
(He halts at byre-ends, snuffing the devil's spoor).

No fat self follows him to keep him wrong.
High in his proper sun his high casque jogs
By scarps and enfilading gorges, dogs
Snarling in worlds below where wit and grace
And bestial scholars and thin priests belong.
– By tumbling in the dust he proves his case.

His chattering armour squeaks there as he sprawls
Under the laughing bellies, and his lance,

Clenched in his claw still, wavers through mischance
To point, true North, at his old target, till,
His beard cocked high, he clatters off and bawls
Tremendous lovesongs to the tiny hills.

From A Round Of Applause (mostly 1959–61)

Work in progress

Curl creamy angels on the blue,
With every cloud a puffing boy
And dolphins blowing to the true
North in every corner.

Ships, elegantly wrecked, toss out
Toy mariners, caught as they sprawl,
As though all threaded down the snout
Of an old gin bottle.

A few crimped waves will frill the foot
Of paradisal reefs whereon
Brown seabeasts scurf their scales and flute
A minuet of Mozart.

And now a mermaid, fancy-free,
Blank-eyed and draggle-tailed in surf –
Erotic image that the sea
Has not a thing to do with.

The whole thing's framed. The artist, faint
With visionary exertions, knows
A storm howls underneath the paint
And wrecks rot under canvas.

And now, a pastoral, perhaps? –
With haywains, carting judgments home
And lowing cows (God's thunderclaps)
And pert milkmaids (the Furies).

From A Round Of Applause (mostly 1959–61)

Romantic sunset

The purple flare made images, of course,
In the image-mad; and was a purple flare
Of one huge pulse upon the darkening air.

Proximity, too, rolled up its sleeves and took
From nothing there engaging miracles
To make sand more sand and hills sudden hills.

Even a mind, made numinous of itself,
Achieved the image of being an actual fact;
Aesthetics painting what its substance lacked.

And gods, of kinds, and meanings, of a sort,
Emerged from a worn seascape and became
Its substitute, and seemed the very same.

A revelation, murmured the mad mind,
Expanding through affinities till it was
So near divine it was almost its own Cause.

And contemplations of pure being breathed
Serenity and grace where, overhead,
Blue seduced green and purple savaged red.

From A Round Of Applause (mostly 1959–61)

Explorer

Trampling new seas with filthy timbers, he
Jotted down headlands, speculated on
Vestigial civilisations, ate strange fruits
And called his officers Mister. When sails were gone

Bundling and tumbling down the shrieking dark,
He trailed the Bible as sea-anchor; when
Reefs shaved the barnacles from the keel, he took
His gentlemanly snuff. Each night at ten,

Under the lamp from which his cabin swung,
He logged the latest, drank his grog and spread,
With only one uncomprehending sigh,
His wild uncharted world upon his bed.

From *A Round Of Applause* (mostly 1959–61)

July evening

A bird's voice chinks and tinkles
Alone in the gaunt reedbed –
    Tiny silversmith
Working late in the evening.

I sit and listen. The rooftop
With a quill of smoke stuck in it
    Wavers against the sky
In the dreamy heat of summer.

Flowers' closing time: bee lurches
Across the hayfield, singing
    And feeling its drunken way
Round the air's invisible corners.

And grass is grace. And charlock
Is gold of its own bounty.
    The broken chair by the wall
Is one with immortal landscapes.

Something has been completed
That everything is part of,
    Something that will go on
Being completed forever.

From *A Round Of Applause* (mostly 1959–61)

A good day

Sun-stunned the water; trees hold their breath.
The bracken smell is six foot deep

And never stirs. I feel green crumbs of heather
Crawling on cheekbones … Stillness but not sleep.

A heron, folded round himself,
Stands in the ebb, as I in mine.
I feel my world beneath me, like his, shelving
To darker depths of dark and bitter brine.

Suddenly round the cliff face bolt
Pigeon and falcon – they tear the air
And are gone in it. And the day stands, without motion,
As though nothing had drawn that savage blue stroke there.

What has been wounded? Only false
Images. Nothing can betray
Wise heron, shattering light or breathless alder
Or water slipping soundlessly away.

From *A Round Of Applause* (mostly 1959–61)

Old man by himself

The moonstreak shone green-gilded through the room,
Apprentice ghost, no proper revenant,
But matchlessly aloof; and softly, boom!

And softly, boom! The waves crushed on the sand
And night spread its immaculate distances.
He sat in darkness and his heavy hand

Lay clenched in other times. His face was stone
Or timber, rather, rejected by long tides:
Experience, not feeling. Men long gone

And small pragmatic ships and curving shores
Loosened the mind they were composed of through
Weddings and storms and nettle-foundered doors

And into blazing immaculate distances.
How a carved eyelid shuts no sunlight out
Or knotted tongue finds nothing to dispraise

Or hand fails to unclench and reject it all –
Till the green moonstreak lipped his foot and he
Scraped the chair sideways, closer to the wall.

From A Round Of Applause (mostly 1959–61))

Purification

Winds whirl in their hooded caves
And tawny rocks are all asleep.
Easy to see the moon walk on this desert,
Easy to see her, smiling to her herself.

Yesterday winds howled overhead,
Lions loped in the cruel light,
Cities crawled in the glare, and the horizon
Flickered with journeys, dreams, abandonments.

Wearing your self as though it were
the lightest of all garments, moving
As though all answers were a mode of movement,
You came and were as though to be were easy.

And now there is an end of storm,
Of rage and lust and wild horizons.
Desert is purely desert, in itself...
To be a desert, even, is difficult.

From A Round Of Applause (mostly 1959–61)

Thaw on a building site

The strong sun changed the air; drops
Trembled down, expired upwards.
Saucer crusts of earth collapsed.
Extraordinary pools appeared.

And reddish planks turned yellow;
A concrete mixer cleared its throat
For a boring speech, all consonants. Slow
Troglodytes came from the hut.

They swarmed in air, on earth, beneath it,
Crept in and out of space, informed
It with a ghost of shape – breathing
Not yet a language, but its grammar.

Wheelbarrows shot up thirty feet.
A ripped plank screamed. And slowly, buildings
Backed their way into the light;
They crumbled upwards into being.

From A Round Of Applause (mostly 1959–61)

Dinghy skirting a reef

Ploughshare that leaves no furrow
Slides through the crumbling water
Where tigerish mackerel go
Slashing through shoals of fry –
That seething brine is bitter
But not because they die.

A cormorant, unfrocked priest
Gross on the groaning skerry,
Parodies holy Easter.
He hangs on the cosy Cross
Of his own skeleton there
Gorged on his natural Logos.

Up feathers a naked figure,
Pauses, collapses, shot
In the hollow breast by a rainbow
And, pattering sideways rests,
In his Abraham's bosom of water,
His lecherous old ancestor.

The brown sail wags, leans over
And the whole world spins around
The solid brain at the centre –
Blobbed in the middlemost middle

Of a web of grace abounding,
At once shrill fly, cold spider.

From *A Round Of Applause* (mostly 1959–61)

Ambiguous snow

Snowfalls make no insinuations.
Silence in a white disguise
Happens, without rhetoric
Of slamming clouds and slipshod raindrops.

Posts are mushroomed, roofs are frilled;
Light bangs on the sparkling snow-crust;
Thin wires balance mountain ranges;
Branches break off at the wrist.

Pretty ambiguity, where
Great stags smother, armies founder
In a mad pastrycook's mad vision.
Pretty in the Christmas candles.

And the word creeps through the snow,
Black as pavements, green as crocus;
And the snuggling bud is warm;
And the thrush dies in his feathers.

From *A Round Of Applause* (mostly 1959–61)

Canal in winter

The wind makes flags of posters;
Small grins of bubbles break
Uneasily on the thick
Scum matted on green water.

Slowly a rotting warehouse
Steps down another inch
Into the mud, from which
Weeds float on dying journeys.

The towpath creaks with wintry
Cat-ice; pincushion grass
Is frosted on walls where slime
Draws maps of every country.

Doom and decay, inflicting
Their beauty here, disclose
Themselves as vocables:
A human mind's reflection.

The other facts care nothing;
They ease a landscape towards
New forms, through filth and mud
Where a new life is seething.

And the corrupt reed, leaning
Over its own downfall,
Sets out on a never final
Stage of its endless journey.

                          From *A Round Of Applause* (mostly 1959–61)

Crofter's kitchen, evening

A man's boots with a woman in them
Clatter across the floor. A hand
Long careless of the lives it kills
Comes down and thwacks on newspapers
A long black fish with bloody gills.

The kettle's at her singsong – minor
Prophetess in her sooty cave.
A kitten climbs the bundled net
On the bench and, curled up like a cowpat,
Purrs on the *Stornoway Gazette*.

The six hooks of a Mackerel Dandy
Climb their thin rope – an exclamation
By the curled question of a gaff.

Three rubber eels cling like a crayfish
On top of an old photograph.

Peats fur themselves in gray. The door
Bursts open, chairs creak, a hand reaches out
For spectacles, a lamp flares high ...
The collie underneath the table
Slumps with a world-rejecting sigh.

April 1959

Moon

Moon and fence lie together
On the pavement; moon builds
A lean-to of blackness
On one side of walls.

She stirs light into the sea
With a long gold finger
And lies, naked and tawny,
On innumerable shores.

She paces the smouldering
Magnesium of clouds
And like a beggar slips
Into dark cellars.

And skulls of sleeping
Women grow radiant.
They turn on the pillow.
They murmur in the night.

May 1959

Green water

Green pool – green pool, the first I ever saw.
An Asiatic swarming of green life
Curdled the clear, the crystal with no flaw,

Soggily see-sawing, a soup of woods,
A brew of sappy stems, emulsion of
Peagreenest mosses – slipslopping under hoods

And howdahs of great clouds whose herds stood still
Over the sliding wind – a wind too small
To heave a cloud on like a glittering hill

But large enough to glaze with glints not green
The broth of greenness till the crystal showed
As liquid diamond, lost when scarcely seen

But traitor to it all, till one could stare
At this very self of greenness and see there
The source of all clouds humped high in the air.

October 1959

Perfect morning

No idle corner in the air,
No formless seeking in a cloud
Marred the completeness everywhere –
As though defects were disallowed

By some huge order that would not
Permit a disobedience.
The real thing was the same in thought
As trembling on a naked sense

And with a permeation full
Of present moments could compose
Beside a thorntip, white and cool,
The encyclopedia of a rose

Out of a kingdom newly come
Where sunken treasures in the world
Thrilled into sight like radium.
The ladders of the air were curled

With goings up and down that made
The air a shore of sandpipers
Beneath a wave of blue and jade;
– Till, having nowhere to disperse

Its secret selves, even the unreal
Emerged and took its real place,
With civil looks admitting all
The actual world into its grace.

October 1959

Early Sunday morning, Edinburgh

Crosshatch of streets: some waterfall
Down pits, some rear to lay their forepaws
On hilly ledges; others bore
Tunnels through lilac, gean and holly.

A stretch of sky makes what it can
Of ships sailing and sailing islands.
Trees open their rustling hands
And toss birds up, a fountain, a fanfare.

A yellow milkcart clipclops by
Like money shaken in a box,
Less yellow than the golden coxcomb
Gallanting on St Giles's spire.

And people idle into space
And disappear again in it –
Apparitions from nowhere: unseen
Distances shine from their faces.

And, fore and hindpaws out of line,
An old dog mooches by, his gold
Eyes hung down below hunched shoulders,
His tail switching, feathery, finely.

January 1960

Black cat in a morning

Black cat, slink longer: flatten through the grass.
The chaffinch scolds you, pebbling you with chinks
Of quartzy sound, where the green lilac banks
White falls of stillness and green shades of peace.

A shape where topaz eyes may climb and find
The fluttering gone, the dust smelling of green,
The green a royal deshabille of the sun
Tossed on a tree and stitched with its own gold.

And chaffinch rattling from another bush
Shakes with his furious ounce a yard of leaves,
Strikes flints together in his soft throat and moves
In out, out in, two white stripes and a blush.

Black cat pours to the ground, is pool, is cat
That walks finicking away, twitching behind
A stretched foot: sits, is carved, upon the ground,
Drubbing soft tomtoms in his silky throat.

He changes all around him to his scale.
Suburban suns are jungle stripes of fire
And all the mornings that there ever were
Make this one mount and mount and overspill.

And in their drenching where time cannot be,
Amiably blinking in ancestral suns
He swallows chaffinches in stretching yawns
And holds the world down under one soft paw.

March 1960

Granton

A shunting engine butts them
And the long line of waggons
        Abruptly pours out
Iron drops from a bottle.

125]

A flare fizzes, discovers
Tarry sheds, a slipway
    Tasselled with weeds
And a boat with oars akimbo.

On the oily skin of the water
Are coils and whorls, all oily,
     Of green and blue;
They sparkle with filthy coal dust.

Night crouches beyond the harbour,
Powerful, black as a panther
    That suddenly
Opens a yellow eye.

December 1960

Man at sea

He drives his long oars, colouring the green,
Through waves like feathers and through light like waves.
A glistening snail's track shows where he has been.

And where he goes, uplifting waters mount
Behind each other, rounding onwards, more
Than makers of mythologies could count.

Riffled with mackerel, bombed by gannets, curled
With snakish cormorants, the water smooths
Between its hands the huge ball of the world.

He leans and lifts, and leaves on green, going blue,
Long lines of whorls and trinkling drops that are
Each one a point where the light breaks in two.

He stares astern to where the sea is pinned
Down by the sky. Above his rocking head,
Graying the clouds, gulls warp across the wind.

January 1961

Hare

The hill rears up to where
Trees tuft the bare horizon;
Beyond it, metal skies
Make nothing of the air.

No variations mount,
Except the close ones only
Of grassblade and small stone,
For a starved eye to count.

Monstrous, then, the hare.
He rocks ahead, sits sideways
With ears like antlers; wide
Miles pour into his stare.

He jerks on over the rig
In knight's moves, easy and lightly,
Wild as a tugging kite –
Two zigs, one zag, one zig.

He's gone – but still, so high,
So gently the hill curves over,
Two ears like antlers move,
Pricked on a pewter sky.

April 1961*

Harris, East side

Stones crowd and shine
As though a Christ preached, they his multitude.
(Weather's their gospel, and they need no sign).

The narrow bay
Has a knuckle of houses and a nail of sand
By which the sea hangs grimly to the land.

A boat, deflowered
Of its brown sail, pokes its bald pistil up,
Fattening the seed of miles it has devoured.

It rocks upon
The rocking world and sends its small waves back
Against the waves that turned its blue to black.

On a green sward
A woman stands kneedeep in hens and from
A flashing pail scatters their peaceful Word.

Around altars hung
With holy weeds, ducks, as they skid and lurch,
Quack soft, like laymen working in a church.

And light bends down
In seeming benediction, though it comes
From where hail buds and vicious thunder drums.

Its storms lie round,
Already here where a roof shows its bones
Or where a child sits in a field of stones.

February 1962

A voice of summer

In this one of all fields I know the best
All day and night, hoarse and melodious, sounded
A creeping corncrake, coloured like the ground,
Till the cats got him and gave the rough air rest.

Mechanical August, dowdy in the reeds,
He ground his quern and the round minutes sifted
Away in the powdery light. He would never lift
His beady periscope over the dusty hayseeds.

Cunning low-runner, tobogganing on his breast
He slid from sight once, from my feet. He only

Became the grass; then stone scraped harsh on stone,
Boxing the compass round his trivial nest.

– Summer now is diminished, is less by him.
Something that it could say cannot be spoken –
As though the language of a subtle folk
Had lost a word that had no synonym.

February 1962

No accident

Walking downhill from Suilven (a fine day, for once)
I twisted a knee. Two crippling miles to walk.
Leap became lower. Bag swung from a bowed neck.
Pedant of walking learned it like a dunce.

I didn't mind so much. Suilven's a place
That gives more than a basket of trout. It opens
The space it lives in and a heaven's revealed, in glimpses.
Grace is a crippling thing. You've to pay for grace.

The heaven's an odd one, shaped like cliff and scree
No less than they are: no picnicking place, but hiding
Forevers and everywhere in every thing – including
A two-mile walk, even, and a crippled knee.

You reach it by revelation. Good works can't place
Heaven in a dead hind and a falcon going
Or in the hard truth that, if only by being
First in a lower state, you've to pay for grace.

February 1962

Bull

Black bull denies
The world is bright. He tramples
It to his own blackness
And burns it with his eyes.

129]

Space yields, rebuffed
By him in this order:
Head's box, body's barrel,
Pinched haunches – tail's tuft.

Caged in his cage,
He dwarfs the dyke he smoulders
By; is a cloud of thunder.
He moans, with lust and rage –

Black Jove, on fire,
Locked in his ruinous heaven
From the sauntering filmstar heifer
Mincing towards the byre.

February 1962

Appearances

Strung green in fire-glows, this cloud was,
A net for catching nothing; light leaked through it.
It aimed south – had a darting look; a posture
That told a lie – it died there without warning.

On the damp rock a limpet sloped
Towards the cloud, snuffed by its hat and bearing
Wrong sorts of fathoms on it. (How look like groping
Sideways, when one is round?) It left no trace.

And over it the sea flipped up
A soapy loop of water. How it shone – then dully
Went faintly nowhere, the same lie in its cupful
As limpet was, all hat, and cloud, all colour.

May 1962

Signs and signals

The Loch of the Wolf's Pass
And the Loch of the Green Corrie

Are both hung high in the air.
Rock, sphagnum and grass

Set them there. They shine
With the drenched light of the sky.
Round them the deer: and, over,
An eagle rules its line

Straight for its nest, midge-speck
On a ledge of Ben More Assynt –
Ptarmigan crouch in the stones …
Now the hinds move off, on trek

To Glen Coul; they unhurriedly wind
Round the Loch of the Green Corrie
And the Loch of the Wolf's Pass
That are hung there in my mind

And drenched with meaning – where the high
Eagle tears apart
The wind, and the ptarmigan, each
A stone with a crimson eye,

Crouch on my self's ground.
The water rocks, and the meaning
Tilts to its brighter self
And flashes all worlds around –

I see them jump in the air,
They wheel in the tall cathedral
Where space tumbles before
The altar of everywhere.

September 1962

Construction site

In its own swamp
A clanking beast, painted like a toy,
Guzzles a ton of muck, then, stretching up thin,

Turns its head in disgust to spew
Its horrible mouthful out, raining it down
On a battered truck that lurches towards the dump.

High overhead
A little insect, constructed like a man,
Crawls on a foot-wide thread on a web that catches
Only a space with a cloud in it. A crane
Staggers, peeps over, drops its long neck and clutches
In tiny mandibles a steel straw from the ground.

The cloud goes by.
The space is patient, lending itself to be
New forms, new spaces. Growing like crystals in
A depth of space, they order it and say
Ascending fiats in the chaos between
The grovelling beast and the pecking crane in the sky.

October 1962

Fire water

The water was still, dead black.
In it comets shot off
From the drifting boat, their track
Ten yards of greenish fire.

Corks bobbed. Arms plunged in
And were arms of fire. They plunged
Through the black water-skin
To a boiling cloud of fire.

From the fiery cloud they plucked
A salmon, cold as a saint.
Clout him. Stuff him in the rucked
Neck of the slimy sack.

Two fires quenched … The boat
Crept off, with a string of fire
Trailed thinly round its throat
And comets under its keel.

October 1962

Sandstone mountain

The bare rock hill turned out to be
A rocky sponge – it leaked all round
A maze of trickles. There's a broad shelf that is
A lace of them. Deer love it. No-one can see
Them couched there on the plumped and quilted ground
Except by being half raven. Let a bullet miss,
It crosses gulfs: cliffs clip back the short sound.

Of any place, a place to see
Light being water, quirking down.
Half raven, in my feathers, I was there.
Hinds raised their heads in V's. They stood to me
In bonny broadside, then moved off, a brown
Cloud going. The hill streamed ribbons everywhere,
Perpetual conjuror, from his sandstone gown.

October 1962

True ways of knowing

Not an ounce excessive, not an inch too little,
Our easy reciprocations. You let me know
The way a boat would feel, if it could feel,
The intimate support of water.

The news you bring me has been news forever,
So that I understand what a stone would say
If only a stone could speak. Is it sad a grassblade
Can't know how it is lovely?

Is it sad that you can't know, except by hearsay
(My gossiping failing words) that you are the way
A water is that can clench its palm and crumple
A boat's confiding timbers?

But that's excessive, and too little. Knowing
The way a circle would describe its roundness,

133]

We touch two selves and feel, complete and gentle,
The intimate support of being.

The way that flight would feel a bird flying
(If it could feel) is the way a space that's in
A stone that's in a water would know itself
If it had our way of knowing.

                                                                    October 1962

Same new start

Stone sparrows perch in air all stone;
The petrifying morning looks
A tree to stillness; a fossil flower
Clutches the light with stony hooks.

As though a moment had come to stay:
As though a river, hard as flints,
Stood solid still, its whirls and whorls
As motionless as fingerprints.

Till memory jolts the dozing world
And in an eyeblink sparrows flit,
All feathers, into time. The river
Comes to itself and flows in it.

The petrifying mind that is
A moment's morning lurches and,
Back into business, throws up worlds
And sparrows from its juggling hand.

                                                                    November 1962

Street preacher

Every Sunday evening at seven o'clock
He howls outside my window. He howls about God.
No tattered prophet: a rosy bourgeois, he lifts
His head and howls. He addresses me as *Friend*.

One day I'll open the window and howl at him
And so betray his Enemy. I'll call him *Brother*.
Who'd laugh the louder, the Devil or God, to see
Two rosy bourgeois howling at each other?

When he goes coughing home, does he speak to his wife
Of the good fight well fought, the shaft well sped,
Before he puts God's teeth in a glass and, taking
His sensible underclothes off, rolls into bed?

November 1962

Hugh MacDiarmid

When he speaks a small sentence
he is a man
who presses a plunger that will
blow the face off a cliff.

Or: one last small penstroke –
and the huge poem rides
down the slipway, ready
for enormous voyages.

He does more than he does.
When he goes hunting
he aims at a bird and
brings a landscape down.

Or he dynamites a ramshackle
idea – when
the dust settles,
what structures shine in the sun.

November 1962

Solitary crow

Why solitary crow? He in his feathers
Is a whole world of crow – of a dry-stick nest,
Of windy distances where to be crow is best,

Of tough-guy clowning and of black things done
To a sprawled lamb whose blood beads in the sun.

Sardonic anarchist. Where he goes he carries,
Since there's no centre, what a centre is,
And that is crow, the ragged self that's his.
Smudged on a cloud, he jeers at the world then halts
To jeer at himself and turns two somersaults.

He ambles through the air, flops down and seesaws
On a blunt fencepost, hiccups and says *Caw*.
The sun glints greasy on his working craw
And adds a silver spot to that round eye
Whose black light bends and cocks the world awry.

November 1962

Sleet

The first snow was sleet. It swirled heavily
Out of a cloud black enough to hold snow.
It was fine in the wind, but couldn't bear to touch
Anything solid. It died a pauper's death.

Now snow – it grins like a maniac in the moon.
It puts a glove on your face. It stops gaps.
It catches your eye and your breath. It settles down
Ponderously crushing trees with its airy ounces.

But today it was sleet, dissolving spiders on cheekbones,
Being melting spit on the glass, smudging the mind
That humped itself by the fire, turning away
From the ill wind, the sky filthily weeping.

November 1962

Sheep dipping, Achmelvich

The sea goes flick-flack or the light does. When
John chucks the ewe in, she splays up two wings
That beat once and are water once again.

Pushing her nose, she trots slow-motion through
The glassy green. The others bleat and plunge –
If she must do it, what else is there to do?

They leap from ledges, all legs in the air
All furbelows and bulged eyes in the green
Turned suds, turned soda with the plumping there.

They haul themselves ashore. With outraged cries
They waterfall uphill, spread out and stand
Dribbling salt water into flowers' eyes.

November 1962

Old crofter

The gate he built last year
hangs by its elbow from the wall.
The oar he shaped this summer
goes through the water with a swirl, a swivel.

The hammer in his great hand
pecks like fowl in the grain.
His haycocks are lopsided.
His lamp stands on the dresser, unlit.

One day the rope he has tied
will slither down the rock
and the boat drift off idly
dwindling away into the Atlantic.

November 1962

Likenesses

It comes to mind,
Where there is room enough, that water goes
Between tall mountains and between small toes.

Or, if I like,
When the sun rises, his first light explores
Under high clouds and underneath low doors.

Or (doing it still)
Darkness can hide beside all that it hid
Behind a nightfall and a dropped eyelid.

Why do I add
Such notions up, unless they say what's true
In ways I don't quite see, of me and you?

November 1962

By Achmelvich bridge

Night stirs the trees
With breathings of such music that they sway,
Skirts, sleeves, tiaras, in the humming dark,
Their highborn heads tossing in disarray.

A floating owl
Unreels his silence, winding in and out
Of different darknesses. The wind takes up
And scatters a sound of water all about.

No moon need slide
Into the sky to make that water bright;
It ties its swelling self with glassy ropes;
It jumps from stones in smithereens of light.

The mosses on the wall
Plump their fat cushions up. They smell of wells,
Of under bridges and of spoons. They move
More quiveringly than the dazed rims of bells.

A broad cloud drops
A darker darkness. Turning up his stare,
Letting the world pour under him, owl goes off,
His small soft foghorn quavering through the air.

November 1962

A corner of the road, early morning

The thorny light
Scratched out a lanky rose bush in the air.
Goats had been at it, leaving five flowers there.

Scrabbles of bright
Water ran linking down the pink road. Pink
Rocks shouldered it to the left. The ditch ran ink.

I felt the night
Inside my head, like the one outside it, fade
Till its last shadow swallowed its last shade.

And into sight
Of inner as of outer eye there grew
Shapes into shape, colours becoming true.

By holding tight
To loosing every hold, I began to see
What I was not helping myself to be.

I looked up: white
Against a blue – five suns. And this I wrote
Beneath the constellation of the Goat.

November 1962

Skittles

Fine alley this. A ball
That ought to trundle smooth on its small thunder
Has two legs, seemingly, one shorter than the other:
It hops, steps, hobbles towards the scattering fall.

Flat on my face, I stare
At my brown round toad crippling away. It hasn't
Much of my intention left. Far off, the wizened
Bottle shapes stand: brown penguins. The ball's now square.

From snake to mantis to man
I stand upright and turn away. Behind me
A demolition says my fate has found me.
My lost intention has done what I once began.

December 1962

Neglected graveyard, Luskentyre

I wade in the long grass,
Barking my shins on gravestones.
The grass overtops the dyke.
In and out of the bay hesitates the Atlantic.

A seagull stares at me hard
With a quarterdeck eye, leans forward
And shrugs into the air.
The dead rest from their journey from one wilderness to another.

Considering what they were,
This seems a proper disorder.
Why lay graves by rule
Like bars of a cage on the ground? To discipline the unruly?

I know a man who is
Peeped at by death. No place is
Atlantics coming in;
No time but reaches out to touch him with a cold finger.

He hears death at the door.
He knows him round every corner.
No matter where he goes
He wades in long grass, barking his shins on gravestones.

The edge of the green sea
Crumples. Bees are in clover.
I part the grasses and there –
Angus MacLeod, drowned. Mary his wife. Together.

December 1962

Remembering old Murdo scything

A place where sand
Drifts white on the road
And the knees of the Split Rock
Are frilled with white water.

Curved back, claw hands
Bring more to the ground
Than walls of grass.
They scythe a whole city.

Edinburgh falls flat.
Its swathes of streets
Jump with grasshoppers
And clover petals.

And a spurred hawk rides
Bareback on the wind
Whose cantering makes
Bright water brighter.

December 1962

Not only there

By Leader Water
In the dead mirk of night, I grasped a fencepost
And squashed a slug. All that I think I am
Struggled to break from that wet gray web in my palm.

By Leader Water
In the deadest dark of the night, under my foot
The world became rabbit. All my ancestors were
Tossed me a couple of clear feet in the air.

By Leader Water
Behind my back, in the quietest hush of the night,
An old ewe coughed. All that I think of men
Raised my hair up then stroked it down again.

December 1962

Icy road

The world skates by on whatever is its icerink,
Paying out a chain in lamplight of long waltzes.
We crouch in our tiny van,
Four intellectual cavemen and a woman.

A fire of dung, one feels, should be our centre,
With fishbones here and there, and on the cave wall
Bourgeois fluently hunting
Startled ideas through a wood of cant.

Chins jolt on knees. We brush the floor with knuckles
Or clutch at the ribbed roof with a simian gesture
And bandy to and fro
Our beetlebrowed ideas, all for show.

A show to hide the show outside, the newsreel
Flickering past, projected on the darkness,
That any moment will
Come to a stop with us its stars: a still.

December 1962

Traffic stop

The policeman stands on a plate of dirty light –
Statue of liberty, angel with flaming sword
As the whim takes him. His coat is white, not bright.

Screenwipers click and wheeze. Your sideways face
Wears its Etruscan look. How still we sit,
Staring from nowhere through two fans of space.

We, too, are in neutral. My one hand on the wheel
Has an underwater look, a growth look. I
Pick it from there to make it seem more real.

Completely other people come and go
In the completely other world. They'd speak
Black cubes and cones – some tongue we do not know.

The space between your shoulder and mine is full
Of space – you are ten million miles away …
The angel shuffles in his sleazy pool.

– We're off. You're back. Through fans of space I see
Comets and constellations and, glancing down,
A glove-black scorpion perched on one bright knee.

December 1962

Tired sympathy

Come sigh no closer than a sigh can do.
The wind that tramples on the house can bear
On it with no more weight than bulging air.
I can support no more in you than you.

The Christmas holly shrivels on its stem
And ghastly January is ill in the long street.
Greetings are done with. For what's left to greet?
All days are yesterdays, and we know them.

And all your sighing is last year's, until
You invent a Spring to freshen grief again
With cruel contrasts. I will listen when
My wells, like yours, rise, blink and overspill.

January 1963

Heron

It stands in water, wrapped in heron. It makes
An absolute exclusion of everything else
By disappearing in itself, yet is the presence
Of hidden pools and secret, reedy lakes.
It twirls small fish from the bright water flakes.

(Glog goes the small fish down). With lifted head
And no shoulders at all, it periscopes round –
Steps, like an aunty, forward – gives itself shoulders
And vanishes, a shilling in a pound,
Making no sight as other things make no sound.

Until, releasing its own spring, it fills
The air with heron, finds its height and goes,
A spear between two clouds. A cliff receives it
And it is gargoyle. All around it hills
Stand in the sea; wind from a brown sail spills.

January 1963

Summer waterfall, Glendale

I watch a rock shine black
Behind thin water that falls with a frail sound
To the ferny pool. Elvers are roping upwards,
Tumultuous as hair. The rippling ground
Is elvers only, wriggling from crack to crack.

Above, a blackfaced ram,
Its viking head malevolent on the sky,
Peers down, stamps and is gone. A rowanberry
Skims and swims, a scarlet coracle, by.
Between two stones a grassblade breathes *I am*.

Small insect glitters run
On the water's skin … I turn away and see
Distances looking over each other's shoulders
At a black cliff, a ferny pool and me
And a tress of elvers rippling in the sun.

January 1963

Aspects

Clean in the light, with nothing to remember,
The fox fur shrivels, the bone beak drops apart;
Sludge on the ground, the dead deer drips his heart.

Clean in the weather, trees crack and lean over;
Mountain bows down and combs its scurfy head
To make a meadow and its own deathbed.

Clean in the moon, tides scrub away their islands,
Unpicking gulls. Whales that have learned to drown,
Ballooning up, meet navies circling down.

Clean in the mind, a new mind creeps to being,
Eating the old ... Ancestors have no place
In such clean qualities as time and space.

January 1963

Sleepy passenger on a wild road

When the dark lurches, or the car does, I
Am jolted from sleep to see our lights leap wildly
Up, down, across a hidden landscape: or
They soar and drain to nothing in the sky.

I grunt from symbols, wedge my chin and feel
Towards a more hidden landscape. Stones ping loudly
From pinching tyres. A pale hand draws small arcs
Whose circle is an invisible steering wheel.

Now, so flowed through by motion I am it,
I am all forward, I am all swerving blindly,
An abstract passage, bodiless going, till
A stillness soaks me inwards, bit by bit.

And I am hulk: luggage in space ... But head
Hangs from a thin stalk, head is hard and heavy.
The road bucks and I see through rainbow lids
A startled house jump, staring, from its bed.

January 1963

Struck by lightning

The tall transformer stood
Biblically glorified, and then turned blue.
Space split. The earth tossed twelve hens in the air.
The landscape's hair stood up. The collie flew,
Or near it, back to the house and vanished there.

Roofed by a gravel pit,
I, in a safe place, as I always am,
Was, as I always am, observer only
– Nor cared. Why should I? The belief's a sham
That shared danger or escape cures being lonely.

Yet when I reached the croft
They excluded me by telling me. As they talked
Across my failure, I turned away to see
Hills spouting white and a huge cloud that walked
With a million million legs on to the sea.

February 1963

By an overflowing stream

From a cloud this stretch of the stream
Would look like a straight insect
With two lacy wings of water.
Their sparkling is a sort of movement.

Live branches are gallows
For dead branches. Some rot
On their feet, elegant
In coats made of green velvet.

The battered fence sends out
Suckers of wire – thorny
And tufted with wool. The fenceposts
Lean on what they supported.

Too much life has choked
Itself to death; so abundant
The death, the air hangs rotten
Like webs of filthy sacking.

If the cloud stood still, it would watch
The silvery insect daily
And infinitely slowly
Folding its wings of water.

April 1963

Firewood

Sad handfuls of green air
Hang in the gloom. The sun
Nails tatters of foxfur
On the bark of larch and fir.

I find a tree poleaxed
By a hammerhead of wind –
Its roots a miser's fist;
Its slender branches crushed.

Death's scavenger, I lop
Them off. To the sawing-horse
I drag the dismembered corpse.
I saw the sunlight up.

– As though I have released
What was still imprisoned there,
The air is filled with scent,
The tree gives up its ghost.

April 1963

Saturday morning

The fire, new lit,
Gulps down the air and hiccups out a flame;
Young as a lamb, it dances just the same.

Pictures, a bit
Earthquaked off line by buses, remind me by
Still life of stirring life: and so do I.

Grave books commit
Their legal indiscretions round the room.
I ranked them there and am their ghost and tomb.

Outside, birds flit
In the hawthorn tree. It's old. Its 'leafy bowers'
Are dabbed with a pinkish lotion of small flowers.

And huge clouds spit
Small raindrops on the window. Each one has
A bright antipodes: buttoned on glass.

This page I fit
Cockled upon my knees gathers the light,
Doing what pools do in the darkest night.

And here I sit,
Flameswallower who gulps down flame and then
Puffs out stale air that turns to flame again.

April 1963

Winter

Shepherds, tramping the frozen bogland
Beside the sheeted ghost of Quinag,
Hear guns go off in the shrivelling air –
Not guns, ice on the frozen lochans
Whose own weight is too gross to bear.

Crofter, coughing in the morning,
Sees the pale window crossed with branches
Of a new tree. He wipes a rag
Across the glass and, there, a beggar
In his own tatters, a royal stag.

Six black stumps on the naked skerry
Draw the boat close in. The oarsman,
Feeling a new cold in his bones,
Sees cormorants, glazed to the sea-rock,
Carved out of life, their own tombstones.

                                        May 1963

Drenched field and bright sun

I saw a crow swallow a silver worm
On a ploughed field so dazzled that it was
A puzzle to make a ploughed field out of – and
Then find the crow. The one thing that was clear
Was the stretched worm, the twirl, the thing not there.

As though a little chaos of colours tossed
A flake in the air, the crow flopped up and turned,
Suddenly black, into what made him black.
He cawed *Brother!* and, shrugging his graceless shoulders,
Ambled away behind some happening trees.

                                        May 1963

Wind in the city

The day is flapping coats and hair
Going ahead of faces. Flags
Crack on the National Bank of Scotland.
A paper bag's a kite in the air.

Cars bare their radiators, snarling by,
And boys on bikes jump up and down,

Climbing the level street. A policeman
Stands eighty degrees against the sky.

Everything's combed slick in a gale
Of horizontals and streaming slants –
Except where, in that stony corner,
A cobra straw stands on its tail.

June 1963

Among scholars

On our way to a loch, two miles from Inveruplan,
Three of us (keepers) read the landscape as
I read a book. They missed no word of it:
Fox-hole, strange weed, blue berry, ice-scrape, deer's hoof-print.
It was their back yard, and fresh as the garden in Eden
(Striped rock 'like a Belted Galloway'). They saw what I
Saw, and more, and its meaning. They spoke like a native
The language they walked in. I envied them, naturally.

Coming back, we dragged the boat down to Inveruplan,
Lurching and slithering, both it and us. A stag
Paused in the thickening light to see that strange thing,
A twelve-legged boat in a bog. Angie roared at it
Like a stag in rut. Denying its other senses
It came and paused and came – and took itself off,
A text, a chapter and verse, into its gospel.
We took up the rope and hauled on, sweating and gasping.

We left the boat in the hayfield at Inveruplan:
The tractor would get it. A moon was coming up
Over the roof and under it a Tilley lamp
Hissed in its yellow self. We took our noise
Into the room and shut it in with us
Where, till light broke on a boat foundered in dew,
I drank down drams in a company of scholars
With exploding songs and a three-days ache in my shoulder.

September 1963

Miracles in working clothes

Not over clouds or under stones
My homely apparitions. They gather,
Quiet and noisy, fat and bony,
No age at all, on any path.

Why should I drench them with false light?
Why should I soar to make them tiny
Or grovel to make them huge? A brighter
Space contains them: I keep to mine.

In it I'll shout or sing or cry,
Play all the parts in one small drama,
Send the disordered hours all flying
And fight with me to prove I am.

And when I'm sick of it, I'll go
Amongst worn aprons, clumsy trousers
And listen to their gossip, knowing
What wisdom lies behind their brows.

Shapes, colours, movements filled
With leaves and taxis, girls and treetops
Are a history that only killing
Time can take away from me.

Can I understand them? Can
I lie to them and call it glory,
The light they move in, that is only
A light that creeps beneath a door?

September 1963

Coral island

Jumped from a tree, I grew up and began
To take a shape a man might take as man.
I grew a cubit, added on a span.

The filthy bellings of a tropic night
Sank from my ears, loose jaws sank from my sight.
I learned to croak, say, cry, *Let there be light*.

Pacific time reached long tides and withdrew
A coral island and its coloured zoo.
Clothes and right minds, it seemed, were all I knew.

Till I looked in, and I grew in, and found
A jungle and a figure slouching round
Whose brow was low, whose knuckles brushed the ground.

October 1963

Fetching cows

The black one, last as usual, swings her head
And coils a black tongue round a grass-tuft. I
Watch her soft weight come down, her split feet spread.

In front, the others swing and slouch; they roll
Their great Greek eyes and breathe out milky gusts
From muzzles black and shiny as wet coal.

The collie trots, bored, at my heels, then plops
Into the ditch. The sea makes a tired sound
That's always stopping though it never stops.

A haycart squats prickeared against the sky.
Hay breath and milk breath. Far out in the West
The wrecked sun founders though its colours fly.

The collie's bored. There's nothing to control …
The black cow is two native carriers
Bringing its belly home, slung from a pole.

October 1963

Falls pool, evening

The level blaze poured up the Kirkaig gorge
Straight from the sun, projecting technicolour
Rowan berries and birch bark and bell heather
On the dripping crags. Keeping its restless place,
A pillar of flies juggled itself in space.

Eight feet by two. Downstream another one
And then another stood in the powerful brightness –
Nebulas, distaffs, fiery figures, weightless
As the thick light that they were fiery in.
They kept their shape however they might spin.

Up from the drumming water (salmon curved
In a torque of silver from one hand) we clambered
To the stalker's path and, pausing there, remembered
And looked in the fiery furnace down below
At Shadrach, Meshach and Abednego.

October 1963

Movements

Lark drives invisible pitons in the air
And hauls itself up the face of space.
Mouse stops being comma and clockworks on the floor.
Cats spill from walls. Swans undulate through clouds.
Eel drills through darkness its malignant face.

Fox, smouldering through the heather bushes, bursts
A bomb of grouse. A speck of air grows thick
And is a hornet. When a gannet dives
It's a white anchor falling. And when it lands
Umbrella heron becomes walking-stick.

I think these movements and become them, here,
In this room's stillness, none of them about,
And relish them all – until I think of where,
Thrashed by a crook, the cursive adder writes
Quick V's and Q's in the dust and rubs them out.

October 1963

Vestey's well

We raised the lid. The cold spring water was
So clear it wasn't there.
At the foot of its non-depth a grave toad squatted
As still as Buddha in his non-place. Flaws
Breathed on the water – he trembled to no-where
Then steadied into being again. A fretted
Fern was his Bo-tree. Time in that delicate place
Sat still for ever staring in its own face.

We filled the jam-jar with bright nothing and
Drank down its freezing light
That the sun burned us with (that raging planet
That will not stand and will not understand)
And tried to feel we were each one a bright
And delicate place with a philosopher in it –
And failed; and let the hinged lid slowly fall.
The little Buddha hadn't moved at all.

November 1963

Straggling geranium

Lusting for light, one takes it. Which seems to mean
Getting as far as possible from its roots.
The pot sits under balconies of green.

Stems all grow spindly, blanching upwards. Flowers
Are knobs, not mops. Leaves dwindle to green florins.
It topples over as its high head towers.

Different from me, whose light is in the mind –
I crouch over my roots. And what's the light?
And what's the soil I grow from – human kind?

And what's the pot – worst question of them all?
Geranium doesn't tell, but keeps on showing
That love, like pride, can go before a fall.

December 1963

Threshing

The corn stack dwindles in
The wintry air. Jess,
The terrier, has killed twenty
Rats and looks for more …
He heaps chaff in a hill;
His eyes are red and sore.

They see him as he was
Twenty years ago,
Ruddy and tall and glowing,
Filled with his natural Spring –
Full of grace as a cornstalk,
His fat seed ripening.

Time clanks and smokes in the thin
And wintry air. He sees
The stack fall in and easy
Straws lying all about
While chaff heaps up in a hill
And hidden rats run out.

February 1964

Another pause

The crab's mouth bubbled and its eyes were squint.
I – well then, more than I – and a purple cloud
Were above the sea. To prove it I tossed a flint.
The sound it made was short and sharp, not loud.

Extraordinary ambiguities were
Nowhere to be seen. I wished my knees
Did not pretend (they failed so) to appear
Humped in the air above the Hebrides.

How could a boat be more boat, or be less,
Than that one dragged south by a paltering breeze?
Caves in my mind accepted me. My guess
At what was in them cleared, and failed to please.

The crab lay on its back, its legs and claws
All pointing to itself. I wished it would
Stop all that silly bubbling ... Just because
It was going to die ... The world swayed as I stood.

Then settled down around me. My whole mind jumped
From a mica glitter to the crawling cloud
And to prove nothing I threw a flint that plumped
Into the sea with a short sound, not loud.

February 1964

Inarticulate

A flower as possibility, burning with more
Ambiguity than a flower's, melts and grows
In the foregarden of my mind; and never
Its lapsing selves are narrowed to a rose.

How give to you, with only this to give,
One flower that would be one and include
(Even though it should die) in its strict sculpture
All the wild roses in the wilder wood?

April 1964

A noise of stumbles

Stones in the throat make the hill burn sing.
Without you to choke me, my life would be
A sliding silence. This is the noise I make,
Bickering over your image: for your own sake.

A blundering noise, a noise made out of stumbles
And bawled out broadcast, decorating space
With interruptions. How can it be so gay
That's caused by you and me and gravity?

Sometimes I pull my moorland over me
As hill burns do and gallop in its shade;
Yet still you'll hear me, if you bend your brow,
Go chuckling underground: as I do now.

April 1964

A writer

Events got him in a corner
and gave him a bad time of it –
poverty, people, ill-health
battered at him from all sides.
So far from being silenced,
he wrote more poems than ever
and all of them different –
just as a stoned crow
invents ways of flying
it had never thought of before.

No wonder now he sometimes
suddenly lurches, stalls, twirls sideways,
before continuing his effortless level flight
so high over the heads of people
their stones can't reach him.

May 1964

Stages

The wave's grip loosened and it fell
off the rock, leaving in cracks and crevices
snuffling sponges of yellow froth.

I sat on stones that had been taken
from a derelict house to patch
a house now derelict.

Through its staved walls I could see
the wrecks of objects that had been made
from the wrecks of ships.

It made me boast of me,
not quite derelict, not quite a wreck, not yet
lodged in a cosy crevice.

I walked off, striking my foot
against a rotten sheep crook, tied down
and left to die in Lilliput.

May 1964

Hill streams of Abruzzi

Through Florentine palaces
and the basilicas of Verona
flow the green streams of Abruzzi.
The canals of Venice slipslop under their water.
And frescoes by great dead men
waver in an aqueous light that has trickled
wooingly down
from a desperate landscape
of wolves and bears.

They have dug channels
in their yellow rocks.
They have dug channels
in the substance of my mind.

They flow by bell-towers
of ferocious crags.
Between murals of mountains,
through the harsh mosaics of dead avalanches,
they speak the world language of hill streams.

I listen and understand
that watery Esperanto –
I am
a new valley for them to flow through.

May 1964

Summer drowse

Nets to catch nothing (which a cloud is) hang
Still in the sun
And seaweed crackles, drying into powder:
And time hangs fire behind his aiming gun.

The creeping bracken halts up on the hill.
No shivering grass
Bows a breeze over. Everything looks inward,
Making itself its drowsy looking-glass.

There have been tides; there have been voyages.
There have been stems
Shrapnelling seeds – but they are all forgotten,
Outwitted by a summer's stratagems.

Parched timbers will suck salt, shingle will feel
New tides begin
When time's long finger squeezes on the trigger:
Ropes will reach out and draw cold salmon in.

And bracken's slow invasion will creep down,
Frail seeds will roam.
Through yards of air, a blistered door will open
When time stands up to cart his quarry home.

Not yet. No movement crisps this idle air
And stone stock still,
As though his world were not yet to be discovered,
Lies time, the marksman, sleeping on the hill.

May 1964

Three invisibles

The sea is invisible
under a sun-scatter of light.

What are you invisible under?
From what hard foreland of being
do I fail to see you?

I could put a boat
into that baffling glitter
that would tame it, that would slide
on the veriest water …

Inland, the mountains
withdraw
behind a beautiful blue haze.

I could walk through that haze
and reach those mountains,
I could measure them
with legs and lungs.

Is it your beauty
that comes between me and you?
Is what strips me
to my unwilling self
your closest shelter?

What wrong place am I in
who, of three invisible things,
love most the one
no voyage will take me to,
no journey will ever take me to?

June 1964

Nothing so memorable

Like an orange pip squeezed from between fingertips
the roebuck shot from the bracken bush
and into the wood. Sudden things
are apparitions, if they're over
quickly enough – like a trout
a foot above the water it extravagantly
emerged from – you remember it
a foot above the water, not coming out
or returning to it: a still.
Can you tell me
how you manage to be an apparition
all the time?

Or, when I hear that music
which is my miracle of music, it shows
how much my memory falls short
of its always new and never changing utterance.
But this requires,
between my experiences of that music, time

for memory to work in,
and time is that unavoidable process
you disqualify, when
you startle me
to an apprehension of your still self
by an unbroken presence
of suddennesses:
stills
of your stillness.

June 1964

Two shepherds

Donald roared and ran and brandished
his stick and swore
in all the languages
he knew, which were
some.

Pollóchan sauntered, stood
six feet three silent: with a small
turn of the hand
he'd send the collie flowing
round the half-mile-long arc
of a towsy circle.

Two poets –
Dionysian,
Apollonian
and the sheep in the pen.

June 1964

Loch Roe

Not even the tide
sighed, being brimful. The moonburnt water
lay inert and silent as
a deserted city square. Hills rose from it

as steep as tenements. The citizens of the place
had gone to roost, in cellars
and flats and attics. No trafficking here
except with silence and stillness.

Enter two policemen, two
puffing porpoises, that
patrolled the place, found everything
in order and went off side by side,
good boys in blue, down the narrow street
they came in by.

It wasn't for some moments after they had gone
that the whole place was again
under arrest.

June 1964

Assisi

The dwarf with his hands on backwards
sat, slumped like a half-filled sack
on tiny twisted legs from which
sawdust might run,
outside the three tiers of churches built
in honour of St Francis, brother
of the poor, talker with birds, over whom
he had the advantage
of not being dead yet.

A priest explained
how clever it was of Giotto
to make his frescoes tell stories
that would reveal to the illiterate the goodness
of God and the suffering
of His Son. I understood
the explanation and
the cleverness.

A rush of tourists, clucking contentedly,
fluttered after him as he scattered
the grain of the Word. It was they who had passed
the ruined temple outside, whose eyes
wept pus, whose back was higher
than his head, whose lopsided mouth
said *Grazie* in a voice as sweet
as a child's when she speaks to her mother
or a bird's when it spoke
to St Francis.

June 1964

Responsibility

They left the horse standing for two days
with a shattered leg
till the vet signed a paper.
Then they dug a hole beside it
and put a bullet in its skull.
They didn't consider its wishes
when they did either of those things.

This could have been worse only
if they had had to wait
till the horse signed a paper.

Some day they'll dig a hole
near enough to the vet's bed
for him to know it's there.
Let him write that off,
let him sign himself out of that
when he's lying there with a face on him
as white as bone.

June 1964

An ordinary day

I took my mind a walk
or my mind took me a walk –
whichever was the truth of it.

The light glittered on the water
or the water glittered in the light.
Cormorants stood on a tidal rock

with their wings spread out,
stopping no traffic. Various ducks
shilly-shallied here and there

on the shilly-shallying water.
An occasional gull yelped. Small flowers
were doing their level best

to bring to their kerb bees like
aerial charabancs. Long weeds in the clear
water did Eastern dances, unregarded

by shoals of darning needles. A cow
started a moo but thought
better of it … And my feet took me home

and my mind observed to me,
or I to it, how ordinary
extraordinary things are or

how extraordinary ordinary
things are, like the nature of the mind
and the process of observing.

June 1964

Porpoises

In twos and threes and fives
they made a circus-ring of the Minch,
wheeling over, and leaving behind them in the air

164]

two puffs, three puffs, five puffs –
audible plumes.
One looked to see on their backs
or in the carved car they might well be pulling
some plump mythical boy
or sea-green sea-nymph
or Arion himself, twangling from his lyre
audible spray.

But not
these days.

All the same, I myself
(in a mythical sort of way)
have been drawn over metaphorical waters
by these curving backs, till,
filled with an elation
I don't want to have explained to me,
I lifted a pagan face and shouted
audible nonsense.

June 1964

Smuggler

Watch him when he opens
his bulging words – justice,
fraternity, freedom, internationalism, peace,
peace, peace. Make it your custom
to pay no heed
to his frank look, his visas, his stamps
and signatures. Make it
your duty to spread out their contents
in a clear light.

Nobody with such luggage
has nothing to declare.

June 1964

Flooded mind

When the water fell
the trees rose up again
and fish stopped being birds
among the branches.

The trees were never the same again, though,
and the birds
often regarded him
with a very fishy eye
as he walked the policies of himself,
his own keeper.

Also, he was afraid to go fishing
in case he landed a fish
with feathers that would sing
in his net.

No wonder his eyes were
noticeboards saying
Private. Keep out.

July 1964

Cold song

The doctor gazed
at the sack of guts passing
and saw
my pretty girl.
The lawyer looked at
a ringless finger
and saw my
pretty girl.

The professor noticed
eyes quick with intelligence
and
saw my pretty girl.

166]

I met my pretty girl
and saw an intelligent
sack of guts with
a ringless finger.

July 1964

Leader of men

When he addressed ten thousand
faces worked by automation
he was filled, exalted, afflated
with love and ambition for
his fellowcountrymen – in so far,
of course,
as they were not incompatible
with the love and ambition he felt
for himself. No sacrifice
would be too great. No
holocaust. No bloodbath. He
was so affected by the nobility
of his vision, his eyes were,
naturally, blurred.

How was he to know
the mindless face of the crowd
broke up, when he finished, into ten thousand pieces – except that,
when he went home,
he found the tea cold, his wife
plain, his dog smelly?

July 1964

No nominalist

I'll say a sunshiny thing
and breed grasshoppers in any
grass there is, to rollick there,
playing their green fiddles. Or
I'll say a moonshiny thing and

fish will curl in the glass wall
of any wave going by: you'll smile
at their bright commas. Or I'll say
a rainy thing and snails
will shine on walls under
their cocklehats, peaceful pilgrims
without staffs.

All this so that I won't say
a saying thing, that would uncurtain
a world too real, of
grasshoppers, fishes, snails and
me, grinning all round
at such inventions and frightened
to name you in their midst – I'll not
be Adam and name them, or you,
in case I anger
the friendly archangel and
learn the meaning
of the snake's hiss.

July 1964

Absorbed

Each footstep parted
from the sodden earth it clung to
with a vulgar kiss. I breathed webs
and gossamers of water – if you clenched your fist,
I thought, you'd squeeze waterdrops
from mid-air. A hawk flew by,
almost leaving a wake, and buzzards
aquaplaned over the ridges.

My mind, snug
in its wren's nest, was its own element,
as it has to be. Yet it could creep into
a tormented thorn bush, a flat palm
of water, a reed in the wind

playing an invisible fish. It could wear
the curved nose of an affronted ewe
and tug so, like this, with
a rocking lilypad.

Now at home it spreads out that landscape
like a chart and follows the course
pricked on it by a line
of vulgar kisses. And it knows
that for it this journey will never end.
A transference has been made. A squelching
countryside has become
a dry thought, and square miles
fluff their feathers in the wren's nest.

To be one's own element
seems more inhospitable
than it is.

July 1964

Progress

When the armies marched off,
cursing the criminal stupidity of their leaders,
to fight for the glory and prosperity
of the motherland,
the leaders
did their bit
by putting the prices up;
and when the remnants came back,
cursing the criminal stupidity of their leaders,
their leaders did what they could for them
by putting the prices up again.
This so reduced
the prosperity of the country
that new leaders were appointed
whose criminal stupidity was no less
than the first.

169]

The only consoling thought is
that somewhere along the line
the idea of glory
was lost sight of.

July 1964

Waiting to notice

I sprawl among seapinks – a statue
fallen from the ruins
of the air into
the twentieth century – and think:
a crowd of fancies is not so easily come by
as you suppose. They have to happen
like weather, or a migration, or a haystack
going up in flames all on its own
half way through some time or other.
When they happen, the mind alerts itself –
it's as if this landscape were suddenly
to become aware
of the existence of its own elements –
possessive rock, possessing
only itself: huge lumbering sea –
that fat-fingered lacemaker who,
by sitting on shells, gives them
their shapes: mountains
reaching half way to somewhere or other:
and heather and grass and me
and a gull, as usual
tuning his bagpipe
and not going on to the tune.

Things there to be noticed.

It takes a sunshaft
to reveal the motes in the air. I wait
for that weather, that sunshaft
to show in the dark room of my mind
that invisible dancing, that

wayward and ceaseless activity, and I bend
my stone arm up till the hawk
hovering over the hayfield
perches fluttering
on my wrist.

July 1964

Go-between

Out of a night
that felt like a grape's skin
an owl's voice shuddered.
Out of the running
blackness of a river pool
a white salmon unplugged
itself and fell back
in a smash of light.
Out of the throat of
a duck flying over,
delicate, Japanese
on the blue plate of the sky,
came a croaking grunt,
catarrhal and fat-living.
Out of your never
averted face, come
classical admonitions
of the finality of form
and the untrespassable regions
beyond it. I go
poaching there and come
back with news of
an owl's hoot, exploding
salmon and the profound eructations
from the flat nose of
a delicate duck.

Since I am your convert
and true believer, I have

to enlarge the admonitions
of your never averted face
to include these wild regions
where the lunacy of form
is normal and caricature
impossible. Am I bringing
your news to them or their news
to you? Am I envangelising
the duck or you? – For how can a man
breathe hymns to the Lord
with one lung and hymns to the devil
with the other?

July 1964

In this wild day

You wade through galloping grass
in this parish mythical
with Hebridean cuckoos and corn so alien
it pines for a fatter sunshine, a less
acid grip to its feet. Your raincoat
tries to go back home, but your mind,
hauling on a long purpose, pulls you,
thought over thought, to
the edge of the sea. There
you stand on a steep rock and throw
into the galloping water bottles and
tins – if they won't burn,
they'll drown. They'll rust
to a red web or glitter in the tangle
to the misunderstanding
of lobsters and congers. – But one
won't sink and, wearing itself askew,
drunkenly toddles off towards Harris.
You turn back home, with your coat
for spinnaker and the tide
of grass in your favour, to where I sit
in my snug ark, the smoke
from its streaming funnel racing

out of itself over
the slanted cornfield. From it I throw
used up ideas, empty feelings
to drown in another tide – except this one
that sidles and bobs and makes
its landfall on this
white shore.

August 1964

Interruption to a journey

The hare we had run over
bounced about the road
on the springing curve
of its spine.

Cornfields breathed in the darkness.
We were going through the darkness and
the breathing cornfields from one
important place to another.

We broke the hare's neck
and made that place, for a moment,
the most important place there was,
where a bowstring was cut
and a bow broken for ever
that had shot itself through so many
darknesses and cornfields.

It was left in that landscape.
It left us in another.

September 1964

Walking home exhausted

When I lay down by the roadside,
the water being white,
I could believe that
if I fell asleep
I wouldn't wake for seven years.

I didn't want to happen to me
what happened to Thomas the Rhymer –
especially as he awoke
with a tongue
that could never lie.

What would my friends say?
and how could I bear
the triumphant cries
of my enemies?

September 1964

The streets of Florence

Tired of these ordinary heads carrying
from somewhere else to somewhere or other
their ordinary ambitions and lusts and boredoms,
I turned aside into the Uffizi Gallery
and submerged myself in the throng
of undying presences, created once
in the minds of great painters and
continuously creating themselves ever since.

When I went out again
into the steep sunlight, I saw with astonishment
these undying presences had climbed down
from the walls and with an unconvincing
change of clothes were carrying
their extraordinary heads from one
great rendezvous to another.

I, then? What am I
a continuing creation of? What Hebridean
island and what century have I failed
to escape from in the dangerous journey
from my first great rendezvous to the one
I have still to keep?

October 1964

Above Inverkirkaig

I watch, across a loch
where seatrout are leaping,
Suilven and Cul Mor, my
mountains of mountains,
looming and pachydermatous in the thin light
of a clear half moon. Something swells
in my mind, in my self, as though
I were about to be enlarged,
to enclose informations and secrets
that lie just beyond me that I would utter
in one short, stupendous sentence, to the everlasting
benefit of mankind and landscapes and me –
a pregnant feeling that is, naturally, caused
by love.

I know, half moon-struck as I am,
the usual miscarriage will follow. I am beyond
the reach of miracles. And am glad of it,
thinking that, if this miracle were to happen
this time, it would be as if
Suilven should monstrously
move over to Cul Mor and after
coupling through human generations
drag himself back and sit
by his own lochside, indifferently
observing on the bogs of Assynt
a litter of tiny Suilvens, each one
the dead spit of his father.

October 1964

On a cloudy mountain

The shot stag runs through
more mists than one,
his lower jaw swinging loose
from burst hinges.

Let him run his fastest,
he will not outstrip
the slow death
that keeps pace with him.
For how many days
will the light darken before
his empty cage lies, growing green
on the green ground.

October 1964

Escapist

Sitting under the wolf's howl,
watching
a crepitation of violets
advancing on the shadowy ground,
I play my part
of the terrified, miraculously preserved
traveller in dark woods.
How can I dare
knock at the door of that hovel
where a woman screams in childbirth?
I turn aside from the axe-shine
and the man smelling of smoke
who strides ferociously by, re-assembling himself
from a cubism of sun-glints.
The hunting horn twangs, and horses
crash past the bramble covert
where I cower, pale and sweating. And
even the squirrel's claws
scratch on the delicate membrane
my brain beats under.

Within reach of my hand, the radio
waits in the silence
I have locked it in. On my walls
books stand, palms closed together –
I will not accept

176]

what they would offer. I sit
under the wolf's howl, miraculously
preserved in the fairytale
I am writing myself, watching
violets creeping on the shadowy ground
I will never be buried in.

October 1964

Linguist

If we lived in a world where bells
truly say 'ding-dong' and where 'moo'
is a rather neat thing
said by a cow,
I could believe you could believe
that these sounds I make in the air
and these shapes with which I blacken white paper
have some reference
to the thoughts in my mind
and the feelings in the thoughts.

As things are
if I were to gaze in your eyes and say
'bow-wow' or 'quack', you must take that to be
a despairing anthology of praises,
a concentration of all the opposites
of reticence, a capsule
of my meaning of meaning
that I can no more write down
than I could spell the sound of the sigh
I would then utter, before
dingdonging and mooing my way
through all the lexicons and languages
of imprecision.

October 1964

No consolation

I consoled myself for not being able to describe
water trickling down a wall or
a wall being trickled down by water
by reflecting that I can see
these two things are not the same thing:
which is more than a wall can do,
or water.
            – But how hard it is
to live at a remove
from a common wall, that keeps out and
keeps in, and from water, that
saves you and drowns you.

But when I went on to notice
that I could see the pair of them
as a trickling wall or as a wall
of water,
it became clear that I can describe only
my own inventions.
            – And how odd to suppose
you prove you love your wife
by continually committing adultery
with her.

                                        November 1964

Blind horse

He snuffles towards
pouches of water in the grass
and doesn't drink
when he finds them.

He twitches listlessly
at sappy grass stems and stands
stone still, his hanging head
caricatured with a scribble
of green whiskers.

Sometimes that head swings high,
ears cock – and he stares
down a long sound,
he stares and whinnies
for what never comes.

His eyes never close,
not in the heat of the day
when his leather lip droops and
he wears blinkers of flies.

At any time of the night
you hear him in his dark field
stamp the ground, stamp
the world down, waiting impatiently
for the light to break.

                              November 1964

Near midnight

I hear a bull blaring
from the sad shores of love.

Owls never haunt
the dark rides of this darkness,
so the one now calling over
the hayfield has the voice
of a prophet returned
from the wilderness.

What wilderness shall I
go into so that you will listen
when I return?

Under the few stars
terns are dipping through the air
towards the green islet
they rest on, quarrel on.
Though they seem half

179]

reptile, half angel, they
are closer to me
than you.
Their silence frightens me
less than yours. – I listen,
I listen, and hear only
reeds whispering their language and
a bull – sailor on shore
calling the sirens in.
And all this
is wilderness enough
for me.

                                    December 1964

Frogs

Frogs sit more solid
than anything sits. In mid-leap they are
parachutists falling
in a free fall. They die on roads
with arms across their chests and
heads high.

I love frogs that sit
like Buddha, that fall without
parachutes, that die
like Italian tenors.

Above all, I love them because,
pursued in water, they never
panic so much that they fail
to make stylish triangles
with their ballet dancer's
legs.

                                    December 1964

Looking down on Glen Canisp

The summer air is thick, is wads
that muffle the hill burn's voice
and stifle colours
to their cloudier selves – and
bright enough: the little loch
is the one clear pane
in a stained-glass window.

The scent of thyme and bog myrtle
is so thick
one listens for it, as though it might be
a drowsy honey-hum
in the heavy air.

Even the ravens
have sunk into the sandstone cliffs
of Suilven, that are dazed blue
and fuzz into the air around them –
as my mind does, till I hear
a thin far clatter and
look down to where two stags
canter across the ford, splashing up before them
antlers of water.

December 1964

Old poet

The alder tree
shrivelled by the salt wind
has lived so long
it has carried and sheltered
its own weight
of nests.

January 1965

181]

Sounds of the day

When a clatter came,
it was horses crossing the ford.
When the air creaked, it was
a lapwing seeing us off the premises
of its private marsh. A snuffling puff
ten yards from the boat was the tide blocking and
unblocking a hole in a rock.
When the black drums rolled, it was water
falling sixty feet into itself.

When the door
scraped shut, it was the end
of all the sounds there are.

You left me
beside the quietest fire in the world.

I thought I was hurt in my pride only,
forgetting that,
when you plunge your hand in freezing water,
you feel
a bangle of ice round your wrist
before the whole hand goes numb.

January 1965

Trio

That side of the road:
the red bull mowes his way
in a straight line, tearing,
with a sideswipe of his tongue,
ryegrass, coltsfoot, clover.

This side:
a nannygoat delicately, greedily,
nips two blades, one leaf, that nettletop –
no, this one.

182]

Bull grazes, goat browses,
I think to myself,
and both are lechers –
and I go off,
picking with my eyes seven
trees, two lochs and a
spectacular mountain.

March 1965*

Four o'clock blackbird

Just when it was possible to think
the darkness was less dark,
I heard a blackbird thoughtfully
saying what he thought
from a hawthorn tree I'm fond of.
He was slow, but precise. – How lucky
for him not to be restricted, like tits,
to a mechanical rote of notes played
with pianola exactness. And if he didn't have
the acrobatic aplomb of
the wise thrush that says everything twice over,
like Browning,
he was bronze to the thrush's silver
and, between night and day,
made a rich sound that said,
thoughtfully and unhurriedly,
from the heart of a hawthorn tree
I'm more fond of than ever,
that to be between
night and day is to be
between two richnesses and
in a third.

May 1965

Obituary

Writing the death notice
of a man who, in spite of being a politician,
had been his friend, he listed
the compliments and flatteries customary
on these paper tombstones. Naturally,
having a sense of style,
he kept the greatest compliment to the end –
He failed
to reach high office.

May 1965

Illumination: on the track by Loch Fewin

Suddenly the sun poured
through an arrow-slit in the clouds
and the great hall we walked in – its tapestries
of mountains and parquet of rich
bogland and water – blazed on the eye
like the Book of Kells.

For four days a cloud
had sat like a lid on the round
horizon. But now
we walked in a mediaeval manuscript –
doves flew over the thorn, the serpent
of wisdom whispered
in our skulls and our hands
were transparent with love.

May 1965

Humanism

When the glacier was defeated
in the siege of Suilven and limped off
to the East, it left behind it all that
burdened its retreat –
stones, the size of

sandgrains and haystacks:
abandoned loot of Glen Canisp.

What a human lie is this. What greed and what
arrogance, not to allow
a glacier to be a glacier –
to humanise into a metaphor
that long slither of ice – that was no more
a beaten army than it was a horde
of Cinderellas, each,
when her midnight sounded,
leaving behind her
a sandstone shoe.

I defend the glacier that
when it absorbs a man
preserves his image
intact.

September 1965

No choice

I think about you
in as many ways as rain comes.

(I am growing, as I get older,
to hate metaphors – their exactness
and their inadequacy.)

Sometimes these thoughts are
a moistness, hardly falling, than which
nothing is more gentle:
sometimes, a rattling shower, a
bustling Spring-cleaning of the mind:
sometimes, a drowning downpour.

I am growing, as I get older,
to hate metaphor,
to love gentleness,
to fear downpours.

November 1965

A difference

Trying to recall
the feel of pebbles underfoot
on the beach at Kirkaig, I
recall it. But my feet
are not hurt.

Or, remembering the well
at the Bay of the Lambs and its water
exploring
the length of my throat,
I remember it, but
remain thirsty.

Memory keeps from me
that trivial hurt, this
trivial pleasure.

What it does is not
trivial, when I
remember you –
my sore journey, my draught
of pure being.

January 1966

Between

To think that between
those stoniest of mountains, Foinaven and
Arkle, there lies a loch
that deserves a name like –
The Loch of the Corrie of the Green Waterfalls!

Today and tomorrow are
Foinaven and Arkle, are
the barest of days.
– But tonight
she will be with me whose name
outsings in my mind
all the waterfalls in Scotland.

January 1966

Foiled shepherd

I drive my little flock of beliefs
along a narrow road. They behave well
until we pass your house.

You are that parrot in Lairg
that had learned the language
whistled by shepherds. When
the Lamb Sales were on – what
confusion in the road! – what scattering,
what barking, what human execrations!

You parrot my language.
All you need now is to learn
its meaning. Then I, with my dogs
at heel, will saunter at ease
behind that flock, my mind
filled with their baaing, my face
grinning in their dust.

                                    February 1966

Brooklyn cop

Built like a gorilla but less timid,
thick-fleshed, steak-coloured, with two
hieroglyphs in his face that mean
trouble, he walks the sidewalk and the
thin tissue over violence. This morning,
when he said, 'See you, babe' to his wife,
he hoped it, he truly hoped it.
He is a gorilla
to whom 'Hiya, honey' is no cliché.

Should the tissue tear, should he plunge through
into violence, what clubbings, what
gunshots between Phoebe's Whamburger
and Louie's Place.

Who would be him, gorilla with a nightstick,

whose home is a place
he might, this time, never get back to?

And who would be who have to be
his victims?

April 1966

Circle Line

I sit on a hard seat and do not raise
my carton of weak beer to the green
Statue of Liberty whose back is turned
on Manhattan.

Negroes and whites, enfilading her
with cameras, will take her home
in proper reduction.

The guide, hobnobbing with gossip,
information, blue jokes and Reader's
Digest philosophy, keeps disappearing and
returning, slightly pinker, slightly
bluer.

He points to the apartments
of the La-di-dah, the playparks of
regular kids, the UN building and
the Hospital for the Insane. But nothing is
more shot alive by a broadside of
cameras than Frank
Sinatra's penthouse.

We reduce speed for Harlem River –
like troops closing ranks
where an ambush is possible –
then turn south down the Hudson, by
the Jersey Palisades, gawping at
the 'Queen Elizabeth', that tiny boat moored
to a skyscraper, and ignoring
the Statue of Liberty. We've seen her
already. We've had her.

April 1966

Tugboat poet

He calls in the dark, under
his Brooklyn Bridge of constellations,
stubbornly pushing against
the filthy tide his
useful cargo.

His crying wails through
any East Side, so sad it is
beautiful, so beautiful it is
sad.

And minds, wakeful in
midnight apartments, listen
and think of
marvellous voyages.

April 1966

Writers' conference, Long Island University

The moderator's spectacles twinkle in the light.
His brain twinkles in five languages.
Two speakers sit on each side of him, desperately
at ease. The microphone
sucks his words in and sprays them
out again over the dry
audience. All round and overhead, glitters
a poor man's Sistine Chapel
of gold scrolls and foiled trumpets, of
pumped-up Cupids and Muses, their blank eyes
unable to show
the astonishment they're unable to feel
at the languages of the world
crackling and sibilating around them
instead of
what they were used to – the revolving orbs
of Eddie Cantor, Sophie Tucker's
Guinness and velvet voice

– hoofers and clowns and galvanised
tap-dancers – all gone, all gone,
now fat in penthouses or mad
in flophouses or
silent at last under the hush-hush
language of grass.

The panel, tails feathering, give tongue after
an elusive quarry. But
no votes will be taken. No
resolution will be made. – That
will be left to the grass
that counts no votes but by which
a resolution will be passed that
no-one will contradict
in any language.

But the quarry will not
stop running. And the sweet vocables
will carry their human thoughts in pursuit of it
into territories where,
though the quarry always escapes,
new thoughts will meet them and new worlds
seem possible.

April 1966

Hotel room, 12th floor

This morning I watched from here
a helicopter skirting like a damaged insect
the Empire State Building, that
jumbo size dentist's drill, and landing
on the roof of the PanAm skyscraper.
But now midnight has come in
from foreign places. Its uncivilised darkness
is shot at by a million lit windows, all
ups and acrosses

But midnight is not
so easily defeated. I lie in bed, between
a radio and a television set, and hear
the wildest of warwhoops continually ululating through
the glittering canyons and gulches –
police cars and ambulances racing
to the broken bones, the harsh screaming
from coldwater flats, the blood
glazed on sidewalks.

The frontier is never
somewhere else. And no stockades
can keep the midnight out.

April 1966

Leaving the Museum of Modern Art

I went out from the unsheltered world of art
into the unsheltered world,
and there, by the door –
Picasso's Goat –
a shape of iron entered into by herds,
by every aspect of goatishness.
(What are you to say of a man
who can carve a smell, who
can make a goat-smell out of iron?)

This is the lie of art
telling its great truth:
a shape of iron, destructible and
created, being a revelation about life,
that is destructive and
indestructible.

From now on,
whatever of life passes
my understanding, I know more of it
than I did, being

191]

a professor of goats, a pedant
of goatishness.

April 1966

Last night in New York

A fortnight is long enough
to live on a roller-coaster.
Princes Street, Edinburgh, even in the most rushed
of rush hours, you'll be
a glade in a wood, I'll
foretell the weather, I'll be
a hick in the sticks.

The sun goes up on Edinburgh.
Manhattan goes up on the sun.
Her buildings overtop Arthur's Seat
and are out of date as soon as
a newspaper. Last year's artist is
a caveman. Tomorrow's best seller
has still to be born.

I plunge through constellations
and basements. My brain spins up there,
I pass it on its way down. I can't see
for the skyscraper in my eye, there's a traffic jam
in my ears. My hands are tacky
with steering my bolting self
through unlikelihoods and impossibilities.
Flags and circuses orbit
my head, I am haloed but not saintly –
poor Faust in 42nd Street.
The tugs in the East River butt
rafts of freight trucks through
my veins. I look at my watch
and its face is Times Square
glittering and crawling with invitations.

Two weeks on a roller-coaster
is long enough. I remember
all islands are not called Coney.
I think, Tomorrow my head will be
higher than my feet, my brain
will come home, I'll be able
to catch up on myself – and, tilting my halo,
I walk out into
exploding precincts and street-bursts.

April 1966

New England Theocritus

They boil it and boil it till
a thimbleful, neat, is
enough to swallow:

This is all right for maple syrup,
but not for me, not for you.

I will not reduce and concentrate
my experience of you. I will sip
for all the waking day
the natural juices of your sweet tree
under which I lie, a new man
in an old idyll, always satisfied,
always hungry.

With what an excess of moderation
will I fail to surfeit myself, while I watch
my friends and rivals waking from bouts
of passion into the terrible
hangover of love.

I sit, and sip, and carve
this poem, I hang it
in your branches.

April 1966*

Estuary

Saltings and eelgrass
and mud dimpling under the moon –
a place for curlews but not for me; a place
for dunlin, godwit, sandpiper, turnstone
but not for me.

The light is blue. The far away tide
shines like a fish in a cupboard.

I see the blues of your eyes.

Don't step on the little green crab.
Don't step on the mud hump, it will hold you
in a soft fist.

Your brow shines. The inside
of a mussel shell shines. I make
horrible correspondences.

Somewhere behind us
a clear river has died, its muscles
gone slack, its innumerable voices turned
into sounds of sucking and slithering.

Can we turn back? Let me take
your hand, cold as eelgrass, and look for
a meadow trimmed with fresh water, let me
turn the blues of your eyes away
from the moon dimpling in mud.

By correspondence then
your eyes will be clear, you will
sometimes look at me, you will laugh
at the lolloping hare or the hedgehog trundling by
like a mediaeval siege engine – at a world
of beginnings, at a world of possibly
desperate ends, but
a world of beginnings.

April 1966

Sleeping compartment

I don't like this, being carried sideways
through the night. I feel wrong and helpless – like
a timber broadside in a fast stream.

Such a way of moving may suit
that odd snake the sidewinder
in Arizona: but not me in Perthshire.

I feel at rightangles to everything,
a crossgrain in existence. – It scrapes
the top of my head and my footsoles.

To forget outside is no help either –
then I become a blockage
in the long gut of the train.

I try to think I'm an Alice in Wonderland
mountaineer bivouacked
on a ledge five feet high.

It's no good. I go sidelong.
I rock sideways ... I draw in my feet
to let Aviemore pass.

May 1966

Painting – 'The Blue Jar'

The blue jar jumps forward
thrust into the room
by the colours round about it.

I wonder,
since it's thrust forward,
what true thing lies
in the fictitious space
behind it.

I sink into my surroundings,
leaving in front of me a fictitious space
where I can be invented.

But the blue jar helplessly
presents itself. It holds out a truth
on a fiction. It keeps its place
by being out of it.

I admire the muscles of pigments
that can hold out a jar for years
without trembling.

May 1966

Power dive

He spent a fortune on architects and builders.
He signed tickertapes of cheques for furniture,
carpets, paintings, filmstar beds. He surrounded the house
with plantations and parterres, hahas and gazebos.
And in the right place, the properest place
at last he saw completed a swimmingpool
that glittered like ancient Rome.

It was just before he hit the water
in his first dive that he glimpsed
the triangular fin cutting the surface.

June 1966

Diplomat

The eagle's beak that looks
such a terrifying weapon of attack
is used only
to tear apart the flesh of cadavers.

What hurts is when
he shakes hands with you.

June 1966

Antique shop window

Spearsman of molasses, shepherdess
cut from a sugarblock, rings with
varicose stones – all
on a one-legged table perched
on a birdclaw.

And your face in the glass and
my face in the glass, and the real world
behind us translated before us
into dim images, there
– so that the spearsman crouches
on a bird-legged table in
a busy street and the shepherdess runs
through head after head after head
and who can tell
if your face is haunted by the world
or the world by your face?

Look left at the birds stitched
still in their singing, at the sword
half drawn from the scabbard – look left,
more left, to me, this side of the window,
a two-legged, man-legged cabinet
of antique feelings, all of them
genuine.

September 1966

Space travel

I lay like someone in a ballad
under a whinbush.
A petal the size of a goblin's helmet
in a child's book
dangled so near my eye
it seemed I could be the first man
to land on it.

197]

In a way that crumpled my face
I drew back my head to have
a clearer look, and did, and saw
creeping out of the golden helmet a red,
a malevolent, a Martian spider.

Before I came to earth
I heard something in my mind laugh
with the homicidal hilarity
of a laugh in a ballad.

January 1967

Now and for ever

I watch seven sails going in seven directions –
but all heeled over one way.
This satisfies
the dying Calvinist in me,
who is corrupt enough, anyway,
to observe that, if you can't escape
the wrath of God, you can't escape His pleasure
either.

(I remember this morning,
when a marmalade cat made a small rainbow of itself
whose crock of gold was
a rabbit in a bracken bush.
I walked away
from the thin screaming, I couldn't stand
the decorum of that death.)

I dribble through my fingers
what was a rock once
and in my little doomsday
look with unreturned love at a cloud,
at the sea, at a rock where
a cormorant, wings half spread, stands
like a man proving to his tailor
how badly his suit fits.

January 1967

Starlings

Can you keep it so,
cool tree, making a blue cage
for an obstreperous population? –
for a congregation of mediaeval scholars
quarrelling in several languages? –
for busybodies marketing
in the bazaar of green leaves? –
for clockwork fossils that can't be still even
when the Spring runs down?

No tree, no blue cage can contain
that restlessness. They whirr off
and sow themselves in a scattered handful
on the grass – and are
bustling monks
tilling their green precincts.

February 1967

Learning

Through these streets bright as hosannahs
I see Blake walking, listening through hosannahs
to notes of woe, to the shrieks and curses
my ear is deaf to.

In these crowds of people I see Hieronymus Bosch
skinning faces, undressing she-devils, observing
mouths choked with abortions – and to all of it
my eyes are blind.

In these crowds of people I see Breughel making
marvellous matter-of-fact notations of
unemphatic marvels – that woman, child, horse:
I see them too.

And through these streets walks Bach, giving order
to all hosannahs and adding to them, announcing

the tragedy of praise, the enrichments of grief – things
my ears are tuned to.

I walk, I see, I listen: enlarged a little
by deafness and hearing, seeing and blindness,
I begin to understand, I begin to reject
the bad lie of loneliness.

February 1967

Orgy

Thinking of painters, musicians, poets
who visited the world outside them and the world
inside them and brought back
their sweet discoveries, only to be devoured
by those they brought them to,
I remembered
a wood near Queensferry, where
a banquet of honeydew, that sweet exudation,
was spread on a million airy leaf-tables
in an avenue of lime trees.

Under the tables,
on the broad path below,
a million bees crawled and fell about,
blind drunk.
And a million ants
bit into their soft bellies
for the intoxicating liquor stored
in these tiny tuns – having discovered
that the innkeeper was the inn.

February 1967

Moment musical in Assynt

A mountain is a sort of music: theme
And counter theme displaced in air amongst
Their own variations.

Wagnerian Devil signed the Coigach score;
And God was Mozart when he wrote Cul Mor.

You climb a trio when you climb Cul Beag.
Stac Polly – there's a rondo in seven sharps,
Neat as a trivet.
And Quinag, rallentando in the haze,
Is one long tune extending phrase by phrase.

I listen with my eyes and see through that
Mellifluous din of shapes my masterpiece
Of masterpieces:
One sandstone chord that holds up time in space –
Sforzando Suilven reared on his ground bass.

February 1967

Rhu Mor

Gannets fall like the heads of tridents,
bombarding the green silk water
of Rhu Mor. A salt seabeast of a timber
pushes its long snout
up on the sand, where a seal,
struggling in the straitjacket of its own skin,
violently shuffles towards the frayed wave,
the spinning sandgrains, the
caves of green.

I sit in the dunes – the wind
has moulded the sand in pastry frills
and cornices: flights of grass
are stuck in it – their smooth shafts shiver
with trickling drops of light.

Space opens and from the heart of the matter
sheds a descending grace that makes
for a moment, that naked thing, Being,
a thing to understand.

I look out from it
at the grave and simple elements
gathered round a barrage of gannets
whose detonations
explode the green into white.

February 1967

Windy day in March

The grass swarms East. Cows' tails point
to their heads. Sheep stand, each
in a thick ripple of wool.

The wind whirls my thoughts away
and breeds more
and whirls them away, like the pigeons
I disturb – they tower out of the wood
in a fusillade of wingclaps and flicker off, high
over the ploughland.

Winter lies dead in the foxy ferns.
His bones are green
in the green morass. He grins up
through puddles.

A secret is waiting to be told.
In me a secret is waiting to be discovered.
when the wind drops and pigeons
fill their crops
with useful seeds.

I wait by the pool – its water
is a shuffle of broken crockery, and across it
a crooked branch swims
arm over arm.

March 1967*

Milne's Bar

Cigarette smoke floated
in an Eastern way
a yard above the slopped tables.

The solid man thought
nothing could hurt him
as long as he didn't show it –

a stoicism of a kind. I
was inclined to agree with him,
having had a classical education.

To prove it, he went on telling
of terrible things that had
happened to him –

so boringly, my mind
skipped away among the glasses
and floated, in an Eastern way,

a yard above the slopped
table; when it looked down,
the solid man

was crying into his own mouth.
I caught sight of myself
in a mirror

and stared, rather admiring
the look of suffering
in my middle-aged eyes.

March 1967

Crossing the Border

I sit with my back to the engine, watching
the landscape pouring away out of my eyes.
I think I know where I'm going and have
some choice in the matter.

203]

I think, too, that this was a country
of bog-trotters, moss-troopers,
fired ricks and roof-trees in the black night – glinting
on tossed horns and red blades.
I think of lives
bubbling into the harsh grass.

What difference now?
I sit with my back to the future, watching
time pouring away into the past. I sit, being helplessly
lugged backwards
through the Debatable Lands of history, listening
to the execrations, the scattered cries, the
falling of roof-trees
in the lamentable dark.

                                        March 1967

Aunt Julia

Aunt Julia spoke Gaelic
very loud and very fast.
I could not answer her –
I could not understand her.

She wore men's boots
when she wore any.
– I can see her strong foot,
stained with peat,
paddling with the treadle of the spinningwheel
while her right hand drew yarn
marvellously out of the air.

Hers was the only house
where I've lain at night
in the absolute darkness
of a box bed, listening to
crickets being friendly.

She was buckets
and water flouncing into them.
She was winds pouring wetly
round house-ends.
She was brown eggs, black skirts
and a keeper of threepennybits
in a teapot.

Aunt Julia spoke Gaelic
very loud and very fast.
By the time I had learned
a little, she lay
silenced in the absolute black
of a sandy grave
at Luskentyre.But I hear her still, welcoming me
with a seagull's voice
across a hundred yards
of peatscrapes and lazybeds
and getting angry, getting angry
with so many questions
unanswered.

March 1967

Uncle Roderick

His drifter swung in the night
from a mile of nets
between the Shiants and Harris.

My boy's eyes watched
the lights of the fishing fleet – fireflies
on the green field of the sea.

In the foc'sle he gave me a bowl
of tea, black, strong and bitter,
and a biscuit you hammered
in bits like a plate.

The fiery curtain came up
from the blackness, comma'd with corpses.

Round Rhu nan Cuideagan
he steered for home, a boy's god
in seaboots. He found his anchorage
as a bird its nest.

In the kitchen he dropped
his oilskins where he stood.

He was strong as the red bull.
He moved like a dancer.
He was a cran of songs.

March 1967

Country postman

Before he was drowned,
his drunk body bumping down the shallows
of the Ogle Burn, he had walked
fifteen miles every day
bringing celebrations and disasters
and what lies between them
to MacLarens and MacGregors
and MacKenzies.

Now he has no news to bring
of celebrations or disasters,
although, after one short journey,
he has reached
all the clans in the world.

March 1967

The Red Well, Harris

The Red Well has gone.
Thirty years ago I filled pails from it
with a flashing dipper and floated

a frond of bracken in each
so that no splash of water should escape
from its jolting prison.

Where that eye of water once
blinked from the ground
now stands a gray house
filled with voices.

The house is solid. But
nothing will keep the children
in its happy prison
from scattering abroad, till
the house at last stands empty –
one drained well
on top of another.

March 1967

Uncle Seumas

Mad on his small island
he scribbled by lamplight, fluttering down
great snowflakes of paper
on to the drift at his feet.

Fishermen dug his potato patch,
fetched stores from the pier, hung
on his door handle
small bombs of fish.

Behind barricades and shutters
he listened to them, his eyes
sore with terror. They prowled
in the darkness of his mind.

When men came and took him away,
mad king of his small island,
he left behind him his people
buried, dead, in the paperdrifts.

March 1967

Fog at dusk

Fogs move in drifts and where the drifting comes
Their cold webs change clear bushes into slums
Where branches blacken with an evil stain
From drops that could not ever have been rain.

The fog webs fatten the spiders' till they sag
As thick as cloths. I touch one – its cold rag
Becomes a filthy glove. Trees disappear
And come again, translating there to here.

A drift goes by. I walk out of the murk
And see, high overhead, the moon at work
Like Cinderella, though soon to be so proud,
In the cold kitchen of a sluttish cloud.

Hollows are cups of vapour. One, too full,
Spills over, slow as lava. The seapool
Is ghosted with false sails. A window's spark
Is a red eye that burns sore in the dark.

March 1967

Balances

Because I see the world poisoned
by cant and brutal self-seeking,
must I be silent about
the useless waterlily, the dunnock's nest
in the hedgeback?

Because I am fifty-six years old
must I love, if I love at all,
only ideas – not people, but only
the idea of people?

Because there is work to do, to steady
a world jarred off balance,
must a man meet only a fellow-worker
and never a man?

208]

There are more meanings than those
in text books of economics
and a part of the worst slum
is the moon rising over it
and eyes weeping and
mouths laughing.

March 1967

Truth for comfort

So much effect, and yet so much a cause –
Where things crowd close she is a space to be in:
She makes a marvel where a nowhere was.

Now she's not here I make this nowhere one
That's her effect and it becomes a marvel
To be more marvellous when her journey's done.

Ideas can perch on a nerve and sing.
I listen to their singing and discover
That she can share herself with everything.

This chair, this jug, this picture speak as her,
If in a muted way. Is that so crazy?
My singing mind says No, and I concur.

And is this lies for comfort? She won't know
(Who could not be the cause of lies), for comfort's
What I won't need, until she has to go.

April 1967

Small round loch

Lochan Dubh is too small
for any wind to lash it
into the vulgarity of crashing waves
and spit spray. In any storm
it finnicks amongst its reeds and pebbles
with inextinguishable preciosity – cunning

watchmaker of light and water.
I see a jewel here, a jewel there,
small emerald, chip of diamond, minuscule
sapphire, taking the strain
of light
swivelling on water:
delicate mechanism, measuring
a time
that has no escapement.

April 1967

Names and their things

You stood by a window in Amherst
pointing to names I knew
that became birds.
I stood with you
watching a familiar word
turn into a hickory tree.

So many names in my mind
are naked of their meanings –
scrod, Popocatapetl, rickshaw –
even freedom, even justice: but not
love, nor, any more,
grackle and chickadee
that flew into my mind
that summer morning
and perched there beside
a mourning dove.

May 1967

Intrusion

We sat by a Scottish stream
in Massachusetts.
A groundhog observed us,
its whiskered face peering
from a hole in the ground

like a cartoon from World War I
and through the still, bright air
flew birds whose names
I did not know.

Suddenly, in front of us,
thirty yards away,
a twenty foot limb
crashed from an elm tree.

Now, three weeks later,
in a Scottish house in Scotland,
I tell myself
it was one of a million
dramatic acts
in the world of nature's
perpetually symbolic play
that, if we had not been there,
would have taken place anyway.

But it disturbs me. I try
to see it as no other than
the Scottish water crimpling away
through America and
the watchful face peering
from its dugout across
the No Man's Land that lies
between me and everything.

May 1967

Old man thinking

Oars, held still, drop
on black water
tiny roulades
of waterdrops.
With their little sprinkling
they people
a big silence.

You who are long gone,
my thoughts of you are like that:
a delicate, clear population
in the big silence
where I rest on the oars and
my boat
hushes ashore.

May 1967

Song without music

I saw a hind (with time enough to stare).
I saw a trout flip up into the air.
I saw a flower whose name I wished I knew –
Outlined in white and shaded in with blue.

I heard a water sliding over stones.
I heard your voice in its sweet overtones.
I heard your voice, but saw you not at all,
Not even as ghost in the white waterfall.

June 1967

Old rose bush

In this salt air, the wild rose bush
is a tatter from the root up, is
a diagram from which
most lines have been erased.

With straight lines and obtuse
angles it explores
the three visible dimensions
and produces from the fourth
one rose.

It stands like a beggar
at the corner of the road –
skinny old seaman with
a parakeet on his shoulder.

July 1967

Mirror

My thoughts, poor abstracts, caress that richer one,
The idea of you. I sit in a cold sun
And there's their image, lamenting on its own –
Lubricious water wooing a cold stone.

July 1967

Names

In that shallow water
swim extraordinary little fish
with extraordinary names
they don't know they've been given –
rock goby, lumpsucker, father lasher.

I sit among sea lavender and see it. Easy
to point and say buckthorn,
tamarisk, purple rocket.
But they no more know these names
than I know who named them.

I know your name and who named you.
But you have selves as secret from me
as blenny or butterfish.
I sit by you and see you
with eyes ignorant as a glasswort
and I name you and name you
and wonder how it is
that the weight of your name, the most ponderable
thing I know, should raise up
my thoughts
from one shallow pool to
another where
we move always sideways to each other, like
a velever fiddler and a porcelain crab.

July 1967

Numismatist

I think of you
in gold coins.
My thoughts of you, each one,
is a gold coin –
I am their miser but
they belong to you.

You think of me
as this and that and
something else.
But see me now –
blackjawed mediaeval smalltime crook
shaking gold coins in a bag
for the pinch of rich dust
left in the bottom.

October 1967

Brechtian blues

Look at me – failed St Sebastian, vainly
summoning the arrows
that stand on their heads
in quivers everywhere.

– What have I done
to deserve this sort of peace?
I see suffering all around me.
What have I done that I
should be exempt from it?

Don't I sin too? Am I not
as proper a victim as anyone
for misfortune and injustice?

To be ignored is the worst.
– My luck to live in a time
when to be happy
is to have no neighbours.

October 1967

Visitor

Fire in the sky and a great tattered cloud being
Turner's *Fighting Téméraire*.

Three yards away, a reed warbler fires notes at me
from his soft peashooter.

I am a hump of history. That grassblade
is seeded with it.

A satisfaction with no morals includes even
the rabbit's squeal, the fish in the gull's beak – even me

who sit, peppered with pea-notes, in the world's art gallery
watching a full-rigged cloud

foundering in the West, in the red haze
of its own broadsides.

November 1967

Basking shark

To stub an oar on a rock where none should be,
To have it rise with a slounge out of the sea
Is a thing that happened once (too often) to me.

But not too often – though enough. I count as gain
That once I met, on a sea tin-tacked with rain,
That roomsized monster with a matchbox brain.

He displaced more than water. He shoggled me
Centuries back – this decadent townee
Shook on a wrong branch of his family tree.

Swish up the dirt and, when it settles, a spring
Is all the clearer. I saw me, in one fling,
Emerging from the slime of everything.

So who's the monster? The thought made me grow pale
For twenty seconds while, sail after sail,
The tall fin slid away and then the tail.

December 1967

Walking to Inveruplan

Glowing with answers in the aromatic dark,
I walk, so wise,
Under the final problem of lit skies.

I reach the bridge, where the road turns north to Stoer,
And there perch me
Under the final problem of a tree.

I'm in my Li Po mood. I've half a mind
To sit and drink
Until the moon, that's just arisen, should sink.

The whisky's good, it constellates. How wise
Can a man be,
I think, inside that final problem, me.

If you are short of answers, I've got them all
As clear as day ...
I blink at the moon and put the bottle away

And then walk on (for there are miles to go
And friends to meet)
Above the final problem of my feet.

December 1967

So many summers

Beside one loch, a hind's neat skeleton,
Beside another, a boat pulled high and dry:
Two neat geometries drawn in the weather:
Two things already dead and still to die.

I passed them every summer, rod in hand,
Skirting the bright blue or the spitting gray,
And, every summer, saw how the bleached timbers
Gaped wider and the neat ribs fell away.

Time adds one malice to another one –
Now you'd look very close before you knew
If it's the boat that ran, the hind went sailing.
So many summers, and I have lived them too.

December 1967

Whales

I saw a live whale once
only, disporting itself with what seemed
ungainly playfulness in the cold
waters of the Minch.

Dead ones – they lay anchored
in Ardhasaig bay,
skidded on by gulls, waiting
to be lugged by a fussy winch
on to the flensing platform.

What unimaginable leagues had they travelled,
shouldering aside great storms, sounding
to the dark stillness of the sea's foot,
absurd amongst ice-floes.

Now, through the thickest fog of all,
they were starting on a new stage
of their journey – whose end would be
hairbrushes, margarine, oil,
fertiliser, perfume – a sad
transmigration of bodies
for that peaceful, clownish monster, bucking
in a ten-thousand-mile carousel
round the Pole, a hundred-ton oildrop, sliding
through the harshest of waters and
tossing up over them
playful plumes.

December 1967

Old myth, new model

Because his girl
thought no more and no less of him
than of anybody else,
his love became a burden to him.
He couldn't get rid of it, he hated it.

Watch the gods when they seem
kind. For he came

to love the love he hated –
it was necessary for him, what
would he be without it?

And who doubts
Sisyphus, also, grew, in a horrible way,
to love his stone:
a double punishment.

From A Man in my Position (mostly 1967–68)

The root of it

On the rug by the fire
a stack of vocabulary rose up, confidently
piling adjectives and nouns and
tiny muscular verbs, storey by storey,
till they reached
almost to the ceiling. The word at the bottom
was love.

I rushed from the room. I
did not believe it. Feverishly
I turned over the pages of the dictionary
to find the blank spaces
they had left behind them – and there they were,
terrible as eyesockets.

What am I to do? What
am I to do? For I know
that tall stack would collapse,
every word would fly back and fill
those terrible spaces,
if I could snatch that word
from the bottom of the pile – if I could learn again
the meaning of love.

From A Man in my Position (mostly 1967–68)

No wizard, no witch

   Watch the sky clear:
I wave my hand – and clouds crowd grumbling up.

You want a rose? Why, yes –
I wave my hand and there's a wilderness.
I offer wine in my most splendid cup;
What reaches you? A mug of flattish beer.

You give me a stone –
It preens and sings in Yeats's Byzantium.
And when you say Goodnight
It turns to lyrics Shakespeare failed to write.
You gave me a garden (it's one chrysanthemum)
And your hand's a consort, with every flute a bone.

Not fair, not fair.
My brain cracks trying to please you, muttering
New and ancestral spells …
It's your transfiguring innocence that tells
A stone to be a bird – or, a stranger thing,
The actual air to be the actual air.

From A Man in my Position (mostly 1967–68)

Reclining Figure by Henry Moore: Botanic Gardens, Edinburgh

It was the place that it was in
And was in what the place was. So,
Its dinosaurish head poked out
Into the twentieth century.

It seemed as though it had been left,
Denying momentariness,
A glacial deposit, by
A geology of ancestors.

Yet it was, too, one mass of these
Douce citizens sprawled on the grass –
See them, ferocious ratepayers
Flirting with lovely dinosaurs.

From A Man in my Position (mostly 1967–68)

Descent from the Green Corrie

The climb's all right, it's the descent that kills you.
Knees become fists that don't know how to clench
And thighs are strings in parallel.
Gravity's still your enemy; it drills you
With your own backbone – its love is all to wrench
You down on screes or boggy asphodel

And the elation that for a moment fills you
Beside the misty cairn's that lesser thing
A memory of it. It's not
The punishing climb, it's the descent that kills you
However sweetly the valley thrushes sing
And shadows darken with the peace they've brought.

From *A Man in my Position* (mostly 1967–68)

Dancing minister

In a one-two-three
she waltzes by, big as a brigantine.

Her tug, with a red-hot smokestack,
is short of tonnage, is short of horsepower.

She has no visible means
of propulsion. She drifts
curvaceously on
invisible swirlings and eddies.

A passing tug hails them: 'Minister,
what would St Luke think of you now?'

The parson sweats. Theology
was nothing to this.

From *A Man in my Position* (mostly 1967–68)

An academic

You sit at your fat desk, starching
your brains; you're the tone-deaf man
in the orchestra, you're the frog
who wouldn't a-wooing go.

What a job is this, to measure
lightning with a footrule, the heart's
turbulence with a pair of callipers.
And what a magician, who can
dismantle Juliet, Ahab, Agammemnon
into a do-it-yourself kit of semantic gestures.

Tidiness is decent. Trains
have to reach their destinations.
But yours, that should be
clattering and singing,
through villages and landscapes, never
gets out of the shunting yards.

I'm a simple man – I believe
you were born, I believe it
against all the evidence.
I would like to give you
a present of weather, a
transfusion of pain.

From A Man in my Position (mostly 1967–68)

A man in Assynt

Glaciers, grinding West, gouged out
these valleys, rasping the brown sandstone,
and left, on the hard rock below – the
ruffled foreland –
this frieze of mountains, filed
on the blue air – Stac Polly,

Cul Beag, Cul Mor, Suilven,
Canisp – a frieze and
a litany.

Who owns this landscape?
Has owning anything to do with love?
For it and I have a love-affair, so nearly human
we even have quarrels. –
When I intrude too confidently
it rebuffs me with a wind like a hand
or puts in my way
a quaking bog or a loch
where no loch should be. Or I turn stonily
away, refusing to notice
the rouged rocks, the mascara
under a dripping ledge, even
the tossed, the stony limbs waiting.

I can't pretend
it gets sick for me in my absence,
though I get
sick for it. Yet I love it
with special gratitude, since
it sends me no letters, is never
jealous and, expecting nothing
from me, gets nothing but
cigarette packets and footprints.

Who owns this landscape? –
The millionaire who bought it or
the poacher staggering downhill in the early morning
with a deer on his back?

Who possesses this landscape? –
The man who bought it or
I who am possessed by it?

False questions, for

this landscape is
masterless
and intractable in any terms
that are human.
It is docile only to the weather
and its indefatigable lieutenants –
wind, water and frost.
The wind whets the high ridges
and stunts silver birches and alders.
Rain falling down meets
springs gushing up –
they gather and carry down to the Minch
tons of sour soil, making bald
the bony scalp of Cul Mor. And frost
thrusts his hand in cracks and, clenching his fist,
bursts open the sandstone plates,
the armour of Suilven;
he bleeds stories down chutes and screes,
smelling of gunpowder.

Or has it come to this,
that this dying landscape belongs
to the dead, the crofters and fighters
and fishermen whose larochs
sink into the bracken
by Loch Assynt and Loch Crocach? –
to men trampled under the hoofs of sheep
and driven by deer to
the ends of the earth – to men whose loyalty
was so great it accepted their own betrayal
by their own chiefs and whose descendants now
are kept in their place
by English businessmen and the indifference
of a remote and ignorant government.

Where have they gone, the people
who lived between here and
Quinag, that tall

huddle of anvils that puffs out
two ravens into the blue and
looks down on the lochs of Stoer
where trout idle among reeds and
waterlilies – take one of them home
and smell, in a flower
the sepulchral smell of water.

Beyond Fewin lies the Veyatie Burn – fine
crossing place for deer, they trot over
with frills of water flouncing
at their knees. That water rests in Fewin
beneath the sandstone hulk
of Suilven, not knowing what's to come –
the clattering horserush down
the Kirkaig gorge, the sixty-foot
Falls … There are twenty-one pools
on the Kirkaig … Since
before empires were possible
till now, when so many have died
in their own dust,
the Kirkaig Falls have been walking backwards –
twenty-one paces up their own stream.
Salmon lie
in each of the huge footprints.
You can try to catch them –
at a price.
The man whose generations of ancestors
fished this, their own river,
can catch them still –
at a price …

The salmon come from the sea. I watch
its waves thumping down their glossy arches in
a soup of sand, folding over from one
end of the bay to the other.
Sandpipers, ringed plover, turnstones
play tig with these waves that

pay no heed but laboriously get on with
playing their million-finger exercises on
the keyboard of the sand.

The salmon come from the sea. Men
go out on it. The *Valhalla*, the *Golden Emblem*
come in, smoking with gulls,
from the fishing grounds of the Minch
to lie, docile, by the Culag pier.
Beneath it the joppling water
shuffles its blues and greens till they almost
waver the burly baulks away.
From the tall bows ropes reach ashore
in languid arcs, till, through rings, round
bollards, they clot and
twist themselves in savage knots.
The boats lie still with a cargo
of fish and voyages.

Hard labour can relax.
The salty smell outside, which is made up
of brine and seaweed
and fish, reaches the pub door but
is refused admittance. Here,
men in huge jerseys drink small drinks.
The thick talk
of fishing and sheep is livened
by a witty crackle of gossip
and the bitter last tale
of local politics. At ten o'clock, the barman
will stop whistling a strathspey to shout
'Time, please!' and they
will noisily trail out, injecting a guff of alcohol
into the salty smell made up
of brine and seaweed
and fish, which stretches from the pub door
all the way to America.

Whom does the sea belong to?
Fat governments? Guillemots? Or men
who steal from it what they can
to support their dying acres?

Fish from the sea, for Glasgow, London,
Edinburgh. But the land, too, sells
itself; and from these places
come people tired of a new civilisation
to taste what's left
of an old one. They outnumber
the locals – a thing
too easy to do … In Lochinver,
Achmelvich, Clashnessie, Clachtoll
they exchange the tyranny of the clock
for the natural rhythm of day and
night and day and night and for
the natural decorum that binds together
the fishing grounds, crofting lands
and the rough sheepruns that hoist themselves
towards the hills. They meet the people
and are not rejected. In the sweating night
London and Edinburgh fall away
under the bouncing rhythms of *Strip the Willow*
and the *Gay Gordons*, and when the lights go out
and all the goodnights are spoken, they can hear
a drunk melodeon go without staggering
along the dark road.

But the night's not over. A twinkle of light
in Strathan, Brackloch, Inveruplan, shows
where the tales are going round, tall
as the mast of the *Valhalla*, and songs are sung
by keeper, shepherd and fisherman,
each tilting his Rembrandt face in the light
and banging the chorus round, till, with a shout
he takes up his dram and drinks it down.
The Gauger of Dalmore lives again

in verses. An old song
makes history alive again,
as a rickle of stones peoples the dark theatre
of the mind with a shouting crowd and,
in the middle, MacLeod of Assynt and
his greater prisoner – Montrose.

An old song. A rickle of stones. A
name on a map.
I read on a map a name whose Gaelic means
the Battlefield of the Big Men.
I think of yelling hosts, banners,
counterattacks, deployments. When I get there,
it's ten acres, ten small acres
of boggy ground.
I feel
I am looking through the same wrong end
of the same telescope
through which I look back through time
and see
Christ, Socrates, Dante – all the Big Men
picked out, on their few acres,
clear and tiny in
the misty landscape of history.

Up from that mist crowds
the present. This day has lain long,
has dozed late, till
the church bell jerks and, wagging madly
in its salty tower, sends its voice
clanking through the sabbath drowse.
And dark minds in black clothes gather like
bees to the hive, to share
the bitter honey of the Word, to submit
to the hard judgment of a God
my childhood God would have a difficulty
in recognising.
Ten yards from the sea's surge

they sing to Him beautiful praises
that surge like the sea,
in a bare stone box built
for the worship of the Creator
of all colours and between-colours, and of
all shapes, and of the holiness
of identity and of the purifying light-stream
of reason. The sound of that praise
escapes from the stone box
and takes its place in the ordinary communion
of all sounds, that are
Being expressing itself – as it does in its continuous,
its never-ending creation of leaves,
birds, waves, stone boxes – and beliefs,
the true and the false.

These shapes; these incarnations, have their own determined
identities, their own dark holiness, their
high absurdities. See how they make
a breadth and assemblage of animals,
a perpendicularity of creatures, from where,
three thousand feet up, two ravens go by
in their seedy, nonchalant way, down to
the burn-mouth where baby mussels
drink fresh water through their beards –
or down, down still, to where the masked conger eel
goes like a gangster through
the weedy slums at the sea's foot.

Greenshank, adder, wildcat, guillemot, seatrout,
fox and falcon – the list winds through
all the crooks and crannies of this landscape, all
the subtleties and shifts of its waters and
the prevarications of its air –
while roofs fall in, walls crumble, gables
die last of all, and man becomes,
in this most beautiful corner of the land,
one of the rare animals.

Up there, the scraping light
whittles the cloud edges till, like thin bone,
they're bright with their own opaque selves. Down here,
a skinny rosebush is an eccentric jug
of air. They make me,
somewhere between them,
a visiting eye,
an unrequited passion,
watching the tide glittering backward and making
its huge withdrawal from beaches
and kilted rocks. And the mind
behind the eye, within the passion,
remembers with certainty that the tide will return
and thinks, with hope, that that other ebb,
that sad withdrawal of people, may, too,
reverse itself and flood
the bays and the sheltered glens
with new generations replenishing the land
with its richest of riches and coming, at last,
into their own again.

From A Man in my Position (mostly 1967–68)

Drop scene

Fit for a pantomime, my familiar landscape,
Now tiny twigs are flocculent with snow
And walls are coped with it and fields stare white –
A good place for Bad Uncles to recite
Atrocious rhymes to the Princess and her beau.

Through this goosefeathery water real water
Runs inky black. It made a chuckling sound
But now it sobs under its breath, slipping
Beneath gold streaks of the moon. And no birds sing
Under a sky whose clouds have gone to ground.

That's where mine are. I watch their level whiteness
Comforting seeds that will make a new Spring day.

Yet though it's in its pretty winter time
My mind's made sad, too sad for pantomime,
By that one line of footprints going away.

January 1968

One of the many days

I never saw more frogs
than once at the back of Ben Dorain.
Joseph-coated, they ambled and jumped
in the sweet marsh grass
like coloured ideas.

The river ran glass in the sun.
I waded in the jocular water
of Loch Lyon. A parcel of hinds
gave the V-sign with their ears, then
ran off and off till they were
cantering crumbs. I watched
a whole long day
release its miracles.

But clearest of all I remember
the Joseph-coated frogs
amiably ambling or
jumping into the air – like
coloured ideas
tinily considering
the huge concept of Ben Dorain.

January 1968

Millstones

Old millstones
By skeleton mills
Are always buried
In jungles of nettles.

Or you find them
Where no mill was –
In corners of hayfields,
Slumped against barns.

But always they're buried
In lusty nettles.
This is one of
My many puzzles.

They look toilworn
But never exhausted,
Like old age pensioners
Who'll live to a hundred.

Throw them away
Into the past –
They boomerang back
Complete with history.

For round them gather
Ghosts of villages
And shouts and laughter
And creaking carts.

We ignore their garrulous
Sandstone chronicles
And leave them in peace
In their beds of nettles.

– They've earned the right
Of oldest inhabitants
To sprawl in hayfields,
To lounge against barns.

January 1968

World within world

When a thin cloud goes over
it drops a shadow on the bed of the rock pool
like a reflection of smoke.

It doesn't disturb
the glinting fish-needles, the bazaar jungles
of weed, the hermit crab's
preposterous claws.

But if I break the water surface
with a finger tip, what dartings
and scuttlings and tiny fountains
of sand. Gods are alright
if they stay in heaven.

I glance up, idiotically imagining
bright ripples on the blue and the tip
of a huge forefinger. – It's more difficult
than that. How escape
a god who disguises himself
as me being god observing
himself disguised as
a hermit crab, three whelks and
a pouting anemone?

                                    January 1968*

Boundaries

My summer thoughts, meek hinds, keep to their ground.
They graze and drowse and never think to roam
Beyond the pale of what they think is home –

A landscape with one fence, and that for deer.
Yet though it's seven feet high, and so seems fit,
In winter snows they walk right over it.

                                    January 1968

Structures

Stand in this shade and think of me as me –
The moon's a pedant of the present tense
And I'm recessions, my own short history.

I changed before you changed me, as you must
Be differences in this moment's mode:
Stars once were gases or exploding dust.

I'm no forever. My tomorrow's man,
Necrophilous of me, will all the same
Have bridged a crack that only I could span.

I'll grin with new jaws in your smiling face,
That dulcet resurrection, but not forget
The one I now see in this moment's place.

Don't tie me down in it. Recession has
Its gifts to give, though some of them to guess –
Being differences hard for logic, as

The great world leader was a schoolboy dunce,
A sandgrain was a hilltop and – look up –
That moon's blood orange was a cat's claw once.

January 1968

No end, no beginning

I
… And a moon fat as a butterball
Over the wet feathers of treetops;
Meadowsweet smelling of gray honey;
The sealoch bulged like a biceps
In a jersey sleeve of rocks …
When ever was there a beginning? –
Not of night and its furniture,
Its transcriptions, its cool décor;
Nor of thinking about it:
But when was there a beginning
Of this turbulent love

For a sea shaking with light
And lullabying ditchwater
And a young twig being grave
Against constellations – these –
And people, invisibly webbing
Countries and continents,
Weeping, laughing, being idle
And always, always
Moving from light to darkness and
To light: a furniture
Of what? – a transcription, a décor
Of Being, that hard abstract
Curled in the jelly of an eye
And webbed through constellations
And cities and deserts, and frayed
In the wet feathers of treetops.

   2

On the track to Fewin I met
heaped hills – a still-life of enormous apples:
and an owl swivelling his face like a plate
in a fir tree: and a grassgreen beetle
like a walking brooch.

All themselves and all likenesses.

Or I peer down from a sea rock
through the sidling glass, the salty light,
and see in that downward world green Samoas
and swaying Ceylons.

Resemblance makes kinships. Your face,
girl in my mind, is the heir
of all the beautiful women there have been.
I look and dazzle with the loveliness
of women I've never known.

And your hand is as cool as moonlight
and as gentle.

Such a web of likenesses. No matter
how many times removed, I am cousin
to volcanoes and leafbuds, and the heron
devouring a frog eats a bloodbrother of
suns and gravestones.

   3
When you, in your unimaginable self,
suddenly were there, shut boxes opened

and worlds flew out coloured like picture books
and full of heavy lethargies and gay dances:

when I met a tree, my old familiar, I knew
this was the first time I was meeting it;

and the birds in it singing – for the first time
I could crack the code of their jargon.

And the boredom and loneliness
in the lit rooms of monotonous streets became

terrible and pitiful – you made me a member
of the secret society of humanity.

The future that had been failing muscles,
sagging flesh, cindering eyes –

all mine, all only mine – swarmed in the air
and spread its new meaning back

into every yesterday. Flux, revolution
emerged into sense, into their own

explanations. I could understand them,
not wholly, but I could understand them

as I could know, not wholly, the meaning
of your still hand, quiet look, a way of walking

that takes you from the first garden to the future
where the apple hangs, still, on its dangerous tree.

4

The dinghy across the bay
Puts out two hands and swims
An elegant backstroke over
A depth full of images.

A gull swings round a rock,
Glides by. No feathers stir –
Dead still as a living fossil
In a geology of air.

I pick a round grassblade
And chew it. The sap breeds
A campfire, dark figures, a blackness
Full of dangerous woods.

And in that tree, that house,
That girl on the gray rocks,
That wave – in everything
A vigorous future kicks.

He'll be born, full of graves.
Greedy and angry. His screams
Will fill us with an ancient pity.
He'll lie helpless in our arms.

February 1968

To a poet, grown old

I saw that fire once in a falling place.
The flames raced up, the red place crumbled down.
There were two sorts of sounds: the flames were angry,
The walls were sad as they came frowning down.

You burn yourself with anger at yourself
For being an empty house, in a waste ground.
Yet crowds stand gaping – what a fiery flourish
Above that ruin on the fiery ground.

February 1968

In my mind

I go back ways to hurl rooftops
into that furze-blazing sunset.

I stare at water
frilling a stone, flexing a muscle.

Down sidestreets I sniff
cats in passages, old soup and

in one hot room
the fierce smell of hyacinths.

From the tops of spires
I lasso two counties in an eye-blink

and break my ears with a jukebox
in a frowsy cellar.

I am an honorary citizen
of these landscapes and a City Father

of this city. I walk
through its walls and burn

as traffic lights. It is all
lines on my hand.
But I turn away
from that terrible cul de sac.

I turn away from
the smiling house there

and the room in it
with green blinds drawn

and a bed with a bed lamp shedding
its kind light down

on a dead hand
and a book fallen from it.

February 1968

Give or take

I approximately approach you and arrive
approximately there. You make
a Pisgah of every place there is.

You tore up my past and scattered it,
still singing, on that dark stream.
You're filling me with new histories.

For you've created
a new neighbourhood for me to be in
where I stand, peeping from Pisgah.

Comical. But what's comical
in a mobile whose two parts
threaten to, but never kiss?

I would bang approximations together.
What destructions there might be – but what
sparks, what harmonious sonorities!

                                        February 1968

Wild oats

Every day I see from my window
pigeons, up on a roof ledge – the males
are wobbling gyroscopes of lust.

Last week a stranger joined them, a snowwhite
pouting fantail,
Mae West in the Women's Guild.
What becks, what croo-croos, what
demented pirouetting, what a lack
of moustaches to stroke.

The females – no need to be one of them
to know
exactly what they were thinking – pretended
she wasn't there
and went dowdily on with whatever
pigeons do when they're knitting.

February 1968

Mrs Grant

She was a wild one, clutching in a fist
(Made of green fingers once) whole crews of lost
Norwegian sailors drunk till half past four
And up at six each with a woodpecker
Inside his skull. She bred her blacktongued chows
And starved them, and the Jerseys, while the glass
Of gin was filled and filled. Pigeons and doves
Tumbled about the turrets; goats scavenged leaves
And rags and woodchips; on the lawn's half-ring
A jackboot peacock strutted, suffering
Its self-inflicted cries.
              One day she walked
Medusa-haired into the sea but hooked
Her dirty nails on life and back she splashed –
A picture Botticelli didn't paint.
Then drugs, of course, and fat policemen not
Knowing what to do, screams in the village street,
Coals on the carpet, dishes moulded blue
And lengthening notes from the RSPCA.
A Greek doom gathered round, the Furies whetted
Their ugly beaks and one by one alighted
On the rooftree ... What of her was seen last
Through the cracked windscreen of her blue Ford Eight
Was a bruised cheek, a wild and staring eye ...
Her house (it's true) was called Society.

March 1968

Green stain

A filth of leaves, she said, a froth, she said
Of sudsy flowers, and there's your mawkish Spring.
Oh, barebone tree, what has it done to you?
Black field, you're gone but for remembering.

I keep my winter where my heart should be.
– I'd rather bear it in its blackest moods
Than see those frilly leaves and blossoms make
A haberdashery of wholesome woods.

A mish-mash green, a sickly groping, such
A fumbling into light! How could they surpass
The icy shapes of darling winter hidden
In luckless trees and ill-starred meadow grass?

March 1968

Night fishing on the Willow Pool

The water with a stir in it
Shuffles its shadows. Past my feet
A long white snake swims upstream,
A snake of white and crumbling foam.

Its carrying eddy seems to cheat
The downward flow. And I, like it,
A long snake on a different stream,
Think to myself I do the same.

But it's no use. It tops the pool,
Bends round in a neck-breaking swirl
And, shattered into bits, becomes
The helpless headlong of all streams.

March 1968

Things in their elements

Ten thousand starlings in the air
Right-turn as one, as one go soaring.
A pear-shaped shoal of baby herring
In shallow water does the same.

Who gave them orders is your boss.
For when I watch your thousand graces
They move as one – not even two inches
Act as a tiny awkward squad.

The links of things! I cross the room
And influence tides; a hopping sparrow
Gives a small shog to the centre
Of gravity in Betelgeuse.

I move, he moves, they move – and, given
An eye that's sharp enough and subtle,
You'd notice how at every gesture
The earth stutters going through heaven.

But you're a friend of gravity,
With such accommodation (its nature's
Love) your sensitive, huge planet
Dozes on dreamlessly through space.

Not mine, though, I'm all earthquakes – they
Smash tall trees down and rebuild ruins.
My seismograph's gone crazy: proving
Your element is more than air.

April 1968

Venus fly-trap

Ridding my mind of cant
With one deft twist of my most deep convictions,
I find you are less animal than plant.

You suck the rank soil in
And flourish, on your native commonplaces,
The lively signal of a sense of sin.

I buzzed and landed, but,
Encroaching with my loving bumbling fumble,
Found the whole world go black. The trap was shut.

Now in your juices, I
Am helpless to give warning to my rivals
And, worse, have to digest them when they die.

And worst, since now I'm one
Of your true converts, what is all my labour? –
To flaunt your signals in the shocking sun.

May 1968

Cliff top, east coast

A trawler lounges North through a gorsebush
that blazes
between me and the horizon.

What horizon? I lay my head down
on the world
and there's a new one, the limit
of a jungle of grassblades.
On one of them, beautifully bent over
a foot from my face,
I watch a caterpillar
filing past.

Horizons are plenty.
I sit up, and there –

242]

seagulls tinily soaring
against huge brown cliffs –
guided snowflakes.

I remember the so many people
dying of horizons, dying of a surfeit
of moderation:
and I think – Girl,
I'll write you a poem
that praises you so well
it'll glow in the dark.

May 1968

A man in my position

Hear my words carefully.
Some are spoken
not by me, but
by a man in my position.

What right has he
to use my mouth? I hate him
when he touches you
the wrong way.

Yet he loves you also,
this appalling stranger
who makes windows of my eyes.
You see him looking out.

Until he dies
of my love for you
hear my words carefully –
for who is talking now?

May 1968

Gulls on a hill loch

They resent our arrival, they rise like big snowflakes
blown up in a swirl. They tilt and dive, make sudden
accelerations and effortless towerings, or float, dead still,
offering us
two stony eyes hung between angelic elbows.
They draw diagrams in the air and score them out,
they unravel the sense of pattern.

And all the time the crying, the cackling, the objurgations
in that impossible language! – some
like the cries a shell would make,
or a corkscrew singing in the morning,
or the leading contralto in a choir of tombstones,
or a shell-less egg, or a terrified slate,
or the hinges of a door in the Hospital for the Insane,
or a moonbeam mewing in its forest, or an icicle
arguing with an icicle.
But mostly they are mad, and defiant,
those Gothic scritches and yells and opulent
ululations, compulsively
tearing the air at the seams or yodelling
from a precipice of space.

When we leave, they land on the water,
shrugging and sipping, affronted, glad
to see the back of us, who go downhill
into a summer evening, observing such sanities
as hens – fat dowagers bowing and scraping –
eight swallows clothespegged on a telephone wire
and the village bull, as usual, pretending to be Jove.

July 1968

The unlikely

I dropped a bottle on a stone –
and the stone broke.
A friend (drunk) fell from the top box in the theatre
and landed in the second top one. Impossible.

We like the unlikely. It's good
that the boundaries of the normal should be widened.
It means – how many things there are still to be noticed!

A mistake in a laboratory –
and there's penicillin.
Throw a stone into a cave and what do you get?
The Dead Sea Scrolls.

We like the unlikely. The terrible thing is
we like it, too, when it's terrible.
When the quiet clerk poisons his family,
when the doctor says *Cancer*, when the tanks
clank on the innocent frontier,
inside the fear, the rage and the horror
a tiny approval smirks, ashamed of itself.

That tiny approval has murdered more people
than Genghis Khan. It widened the boundaries of the normal
with the explosion over Hiroshima.

That means – how many things there are still to be suffered!

September 1968

Message taken

On a day of almost no wind,
today,
I saw two leaves falling almost, not quite,
perpendicularly – which
seemed natural.

245]

When I got closer, I saw
the leaves on the tree were
slanted by that wind, were pointing
towards those that had fallen.

When I got closer than that, I saw
the leaves on the tree
were trembling.

And that seemed natural too.

October 1968

It's hopeless

To see you from three places at once –
ah, I'd like to do that.
Rushing around you doesn't help
though I exhaust myself doing it.

Those mystical mathematicians
don't help either. I listen
to their fifth dimensions, I try
to pick up a piece of bent light –

and there you are, with no legs,
no breasts, no voice. How can I
take a formula to the movies
or lie in bed fondling an equation?

If only you could stand
in a row of three! – But then, what torments
of indecision before I'd give one of you
that golden, that Freudian apple.

November 1968

Tree hung with fairy lights

It's not additions but extensions give
A thing its further self,
Changed from within:
Blossom's a sort of leaf, as nail is skin.

But decoration contradicts the tree.
I love you best (and know
It's love, not lust)
When clothed in nothing but your altered dust.

November 1968

Concerto

Miss pianist bows her lovely back
under the hail of notes
that she's returning, slightly damaged,
to Beethoven.

The audience puts on looks
of exquisite thoughtfulness. How lucky
to have horn-rimmed glasses
in the middle of your skull.

On the podium, the conductor
is a cobra half reared
from a basket. How stupid
not to know who's the charmer.

Beethoven knows nothing of such things
ever since he became
deafer
than deafness.

November 1968

247]

Old Edinburgh

Down the Canongate
down the Cowgate
go vermilion dreams
snake's tongues of bannerets
trumpets with words from their mouths
saying *Praise me, praise me.*

Up the Cowgate
up the Canongate
lice on the march
tar on the amputated stump
Hell speaking with the tongue of Heaven
a woman tied to the tail of a cart.

And history leans by a dark entry
with words from his mouth
that say *Pity me, pity me*
but never forgive.

November 1968

Spilled salt

A salt hill
is the size it is
because I'm the size I am.

Suilven (that mountain)
since it notices nothing
takes its size from me ...

That grief I suffered
when she died
was made to my measure.

I loved her, I mourned her
with all the love I had,
with all the grief I had.

248]

She whose look
gave me the size
I thought I was

became spilled salt;
for she
had stopped noticing.

I look at her image.
I hate it.
I sweep it away.

November 1968

Preening swan

On the green canal the swan
made a slow-motion
swan-storm of itself:
wings moved through wrong angles,
feathers stared, neck
forgot its bones
and a rotted figleaf of a foot
paddled in the air.

Then – one last shrugging ruffle
and everything fell into place,
into stillness, into a classic
hauteur. – The washerwoman
put on an aristocracy
as false as any other one
and, head high, stared at the ridiculous world
through invisible lorgnettes.

November 1968

Spring tide

So shrunk. So thin,
he sits by the fire
less a man
than a birdcage
in which wings still flutter
a little.

He seldom speaks. But sometimes
he remembers a thing
that happened in a sixty years ago
other world.

How he laughes with glee
when he tells how the butcher
anchored his dinghy, one Spring tide,
with a rope so short
it pulled the boat under.

It's the glee that hurts.
– Doesn't he realise
what he's saying?

November 1968

Sure proof

I can no more describe you
than I can put a thing for the first time
where it already is.

If I could make a ladder of light
or comb the hair of a dream girl with a real comb
or pour a table into a jug …

I'm not good at impossible things.
And that is why I'm sure
I will love you for my ever.

November 1968

Limits

So far as we know
a dropped jar smashes
without noticing it.

Trample a flower;
it dies with no malediction
Is the noise made by a star
as it burns like a heretic in space
a noise of agony?...

Three terrible things happened to me.
I'm here. I survived them.
I take this for granted, it's part
of my knowledge.

But what frightens me is
our knowledge goes,
so far as we know, only
so far as we know.

And I think, when molecules jump
from one figuration to another
they may not go hallelujahing into heaven
or howling into hell,
but
water becomes ice.

                                  November 1968

Lord of Creation

At my age, I find myself
making a mountainous landscape
of the bedclothes. A movement
of knee and foot
and there's Cul Mor and a hollow
filled with Loch Sionascaig.
I watch tiny sheep stringing along
a lower slope.

251]

Playing at God.

One day, when I go back to Assynt,
this could frighten me, this could make me
have to drive from my mind
a leg stretching out under ground, the collapse
of Cul Mor, the shedding
in every torrential direction
of Loch Sionascaig. But now
I cock up my left foot and create
Suilven. I watch myself
fishing from a rocky point.

– I think, *At my age!* – and
stretch out. My image vanishes.

God has destroyed himself again.

December 1968

Sparrow

He's no artist.
His taste in clothes is more
dowdy than gaudy.
And his nest – that blackbird, writing
pretty scrolls on the air with the gold nib of his beak,
would call it a slum.

To stalk solitary on lawns,
to sing solitary in midnight trees,
to glide solitary over gray Atlantics –
not for him: he'd rather
a punch-up in a gutter.

He carries what learning he has
lightly – it is, in fact, based only
on the usefulness whose result
is survival. A proletarian bird.
No scholar.

But when winter soft-shoes in
and these other birds –
ballet dancers, musicians, architects –
die in the snow
and freeze to branches,
watch him happily flying
on the O-levels and A-levels
of the air.

December 1968

Two focuses

Blind worm, lasciviously stroking yourself through
damp grass, do you think to escape
the springheeled thrush or the wren,
that fusspot in green hedges?

Brown water, you'll lose
that peat stain, your throat
will be choked with salt, you
will entertain monsters.

Red stag, you'll be an old rug rotting in the heather,
or a bullet
will drop the whole world away
from under your feet.
Such dooms, and nothing to tremble for them
but the one human figure in the landscape
who, because he trembles for them,
is the one intruder.

I tremble for them. But death shrinks back again
into the beautiful forms of his disguises.
And I see only that mountain, this stream,
this pool, clipped between rocks like an agate.
And death and history hide behind
a rowan branch that
drags and skips and drags and skips

on the brown glass of water – on it
spin Christmas roses of foam.

December 1968

I and my thoughts of you

Remember that old thorn bush
amazed by
its one flower

If I stood by it, would it be diminished
as an image must be when
it stands beside
what it's an image of?

December 1968

July day spectacular

I sit in the third row
of gray rocks upholstered
with lichen. Light pours
from the flies of heaven
on a thirty-mile stage set;
and there, by the footlights
of breaking water,
oystercatchers
put on their black-and-white minstrel show,
watched by a bandmaster pigeon
with built-in epaulettes.

December 1968

God in the grass

The basking adder
looks at the world
with a softly beaming eye
as though he had created it.

Coiled round himself

in a sabbath stillness
he approves of everything, he knows
it is all good.

In heavenly contemplation
he lets the world
bask in his look.

(...How is he to know
the cries, the sad crying
that he is deaf to?)

December 1968

One Easter Time

So many frogs croaked together
in that pond by Loch Earn
they made a tambourine of it.
The males mounted the females
and clutched them
with merciless wrestler's arms.
It's impossible to suppose
they know what a tadpole is.

When I returned
there was no sign they'd been there
except the tapioca globes and globules
in the greenish water.
They'd all gone,
hopping over the world,
gay-coloured troubadours
with no song in their throats.

Love is nothing like that,
I think, in my superior human way,
and go on, since my love
neither sleeps nor is frantic,
singing the little songs I can
all the year round.

December 1968*

Country dance

The room whirled and coloured
and figured itself with dancers.
Another gaiety seemed born of theirs
and flew as streamers
between their heads and the ceiling.

I gazed, coloured and figured,
down the tunnel of streamers –
and there, in the band, an old fiddler
sawing away in the privacy
of music. He bowed lefthanded and his right hand
was the wrong way round. Impossible.
But the jig bounced, the gracenotes
sparkled on the surface of the tune.
The odd man out, when it came to music,
was the odd man in.

There's a lesson here, I thought, climbing
into the pulpit I keep in my mind.
But before I'd said *Firstly brethren*, the tune
ended, the dancers parted, the old fiddler
took a cigarette from the pianist, stripped off
the paper and chewed the tobacco.

March 1969

Television studio

Through an undersea growth
of flexes and cables,
three four-eyed monsters
prowl stealthily to and fro.
I know they're looking for me.

One stays still.
– Cousteau'll be in that one.

Another, an angler fish,
reaches forward

a long antenna and dangles
a microphone before my face.

The three prowlers pause and
converge on me.
They stand in a terrible half-circle.

A green anemone lights up,
and from my mouth
learned bubbles emerge
as I give up the ghost
of what I had meant to say.

March 1969*

Below the Green Corrie

The mountains gathered round me
like bandits. Their leader
swaggered up close in the dark light,
full of threats, full of thunders.

But it was they who stood and delivered.
They gave me their money and their lives.
They filled me with mountains and thunders.
My life was enriched
with an infusion of theirs.

I clambered downhill through the ugly weather.
And when I turned to look goodbye
to those marvellous prowlers
a sunshaft had pierced the clouds
and their leader,
that swashbuckling mountain,
was wearing
a bandolier of light.

April 1969

Portrait

I draw you, so,
in the empty air before me.
The thin line goes unbrokenly
till it joins itself again and completes
the lineaments
of my ungratified desire.

May 1969

Bookworm

I open the second volume
of a rose
and find it says, word for word,
the same as the first one.

The waves of the sea
annoy me, they bore me;
why aren't they divided
in paragraphs?

I look at the night
and make nothing of it –
those black pages
with no print.

But I love the gothic script
of pinetrees and
on the pond the light's
fancy italics.

And the cherry tree's petals –
they make
a sweet lyric, I appreciate
their dying fall.

But it's strange, girl, how I come back
from the library of everything

to stare and stare at
the closed book of you.

When will you open to me
and show me the meaning of all
the hard words
in the lexicon of love?

May 1969

Last word

I don't want to speak to you
romantically.
I don't want to puff you up
with verbal inflations and gassy metaphors.
I want to describe you
with slide rules, callipers and the value of pi.

How clever of grasshoppers and cuckoos
to find their true final word
and keep to it. What an artist
is the corncrake, who makes a whole field
an orchestra of one note. How sensible the frog
who says nothing but *croak*.

But how can I find
that final true word if it lies
at the endless end of
the value of pi? And what use
are slide rules and callipers
for measuring the dimensions
of dimension.

May 1969

Incident

I look across the table and think
(fiery with love)
Ask me, go on, ask me

259]

to do something impossible,
something freakishly useless,
something unimaginable and inimitable
like making a finger break into blossom
or walking for half an hour in twenty minutes
or remembering tomorrow.

I will you to ask it.
But all you say is
Will you give me a cigarette, please?
And I smile and,
returning to the marvellous world
of possibility,
I give you one
with a hand that trembles
with a human trembling.

June 1969

The big tease

When the flood went down
Noah was glad
in his gloomy way
and gave thanks to the Lord.

When the ram
made its pitiful noise
in the thicket
Abraham gave thanks to the Lord also.

They thought big in those days.
– Anyone who carried a joke
so far
must be the Lord.

Even Ishmael
had to admit it.

September 1969

In a mist

The mountains fold and move.
I'm not quite lost. The thing that troubles me
Is that the easiest way out
Is not the one that's easiest to see.

I know just where you are.
But how to get there when lochs change their place
And the familiar track
Squirms like an adder into the heather bushes?

I curse my senses: and speak
Into the mist: Stay where you are, please stay –
I've got my compass yet.
It'll get me to you, if not by the easiest way.

December 1969

Confused heretic

The archangel Gabriel, whom I've never met,
Has meanings for me I don't understand
And yet
My heaven is here and my unpromised land.

I wish he and his plumy seraphs would
In all good faith keep their own myth and not
Intrude
On my clear clouds with thoughtless rays of thought.

See how they paradox me. I would give
Even that great power – the power to understand –
To live
Without being poked at by his scorching hand.

Gabriel has no navel. I stare at mine
To prove I have no wings ... What strange worlds share
Design
And the belief it proves that they are there.

Design's a sign? – of nothing other than
Its own existence. I turn to it and see,
To plan,
Night falling patly on that explicit tree.

The star in the East's on time. I turn and gaze
At the far Western sky – I see it plain –
Ablaze
With plumes of seraphic fire ... He's there again.

December 1969

Sunset ploughing

The ploughhorse leaning through the red haze
shuttles also a field without fences,
a gay one, mine. I keep it
inside my skull.

Close up:
his chest gleams, his head
hammers; dragonish steam
jets down from his nostrils.

Long shot:
on the field of my mind
reddening towards another sunset
he shuttles, across and back and across,
adding rib after rib
to that black corduroy.

January 1970

Among the talk and the laughter

Why does he fall silent?
Why does that terrible, sad look
tell he has gone away?

He has died too often.
And something has been said

262]

that makes him aware of the bodies
floating face downwards
in his mind.

March 1970

Words in nowhere

With you not here what have I not to say?
I beat my mind dazed on the space between us.
– I'd write you; but the words have gone away.

The words gone? No: they bulge so in my net
I can't haul them up from the great depth between us
No matter how the stretched ropes fray and fret.

And my mind, rejecting limits as it must do,
Mindlessly rages through the time between us
In search of the where and when that make up you.

Yet all this shows, when all's not said or done,
That what's between us is all that's between us –
Our single quarrel that proves that we have none.

June 1970

Mirror talk

In such falsities, she said,
I recognise your loving truth.
I hated her for it.

When you stay away, she said,
I forgive you, for I know
you're longing to come back.
I hated her for that, too.

When you hurt me, she said,
I know you're hurting not me
but the world.
Pretentious fool.

I can't leave her
for I secretly know
she knows she is lying.
This adds her hurt
to my guilt.

How can so helpless a thing as truth
survive
so many wounds?

June 1970

Flirt

Before he met her
he was a fiddle bow
without a fiddle.
Now he's a part
of her string quartet.

October 1970

Bluestocking

Anything I say
she judiciously considers with
quotations and references.
What weight is anything I say
When in the other scale she puts
Aristotle and Chomsky?

Such a length of learning!
I can no more approach her
than one bookend
can approach the other.

Even her tears,
I think savagely,
will drop from each eye in pairs,
quoting her nose.

264]

And yet she's pretty ...
If only I could bluepencil
this bluestocking
and get down to
the original script.

October 1970

Aesthetics

Words with Greek roots
and American blossoms
have taken over the pretty garden.

That speckled concept
swaying in the hot air
sucks the sap from the branches
it dangles from.

The ground rustles
with centipede nouns.
That soft green adjective devours
its leaf
with lateral jaws.

And the gardeners
hiss together as they walk
with dreadful sprays in their hands.

October 1970

Excuse

You make me a weather
that erodes time
and decorates its gulches and ledges
with childish flowers till it looks like
a slightly tipsy old lady
enjoying herself.

I play on space
like a concertina –
I stretch it and shrink it, playing
the tune of you.

When I think
that the mountain remains
and there's an end to the tune,
do you wonder I attack time
with increasing ferocity? Do you wonder
I play that tune
louder and louder?

Is that excessive?

Don't you know my family motto? –
Excess is not enough –
Though, being a reasonable man,
I sigh and
put up with it.

October 1970

Midnights

In any midnight blood bubbles
into ferocious flowers that eat the darkness and crawl
on the sleeper's skin. That safe chair
releases its ghost; it climbs the wall like a louse
and like a daddylonglegs hangs from the ceiling
by one toe. Hear how the pillow ferments.
See how the picture on the wall turns into some other
hanged thing, not dead yet. And the window,
that pale psychiatrist, stands watching it all
and coming to dreadful decisions.

And in any midnight blood runs through its narrow streets
shouting the marvellous news: the sleeper's mouth
smiles and his hand half closes to hold
the shape that means perfect. Green wavers of light

spill from the cornices like Spring, like happiness,
like the tenderest of new beginnings. The bed
stands sturdy, its solid block of space
fraternal with everything, holding the sleeper still
in his safest of selves.

And every morning is a landing
at a new airport, is a congregation and scattering of people,
in whose luggage
are undeclared midnights which they will exchange
secretly and without knowing it. A look
is an orchid, a word is a knife, a gesture
a lamentable crying in sunlight. And the midnights wait, each one
a fable of the past, each one
a rehearsal of the future.

October 1970

Battlefield near Inverness

Only dead bodies lie here,
for dreams are not to be buried.
You can't keep down with a stone
the stink of loyalty and honour
that still poison the air
with all the corpses they've made
since the air rotted at Culloden.

October 1970*

Old maps and new

There are spaces
where infringements are possible.
There are notices that say:
Trespassers will be welcome.

Pity leaks through the roof
of the Labour Exchange.
In the Leader's pocket,

267]

wrapped in the plans for the great offensive,
are sweets for the children
and a crumpled letter.

There are spaces still to be filled
before the map is completed –
though these days it's only
in the explored territories
that men write, sadly,
Here live monsters.

November 1970

Another incident

In the pass between
the four great bens of the Cairngorms
an ant
climbed down a pinetree.

One followed it, and another, till
an unceasing narrow procession
filed through the tangled grass.
In their path my tent opened
its huge cave.

I began by killing them.

When one stumbled across
the corpse of a brother
he raised him high in his jaws
and bustled off with him.

If, a million generations from now,
a descendant of mine returns here,
he'll find a procession of ants
filing on the plain
where the four great bens of the Cairngorms
once used to be.

February 1971

Centre of centres

To call the pier a centre
I sit in a centre –
of cloud-stuffs, water lispings, a huge
charge of light and men doing things on boats
that result in fish. Yet I am, too, a centre
of roundabouts and No Entries, libraries,
streets full of cafés and the prickly stink
of burnt petrol:
an imposition of two circles
from different geometries
where a coincident stream refuses to be
the street it's coincident with
and tenements offer no ledge
to twirling, laborious ravens.

Where's my binocular vision now?
I see like a bird or a fish,
a boat with one eye a bus with the other,
a crofter left a traffic warden right:
a supermarket ghosts up
from the shallows of Loch Fewin
and round the foot of Suilven
go red deer and taxis.

The *Golden Emblem* seethes in, sidles
and with a friendly nudge stables herself
beside the *Valhalla*. Round my head
she releases a flicker of names
that come out of geography but emerge, too,
from myth – Muckle Flugga, Taransay, Sule Skerry,
the Old Man of Hoy.
– Though I know
she's been no farther off than Coigach Point
she has ringed her nets in the imagination
as well as the Minch
and brings ashore a cargo
the fishbuyers won't bid for.

– So, with my other eye, from my other centre,
I look at Edinburgh's High Street and a film
starts unwinding, spool on spool,
of caddies and clan chiefs, lords
and layabouts – in a broad daylight's midnight
desperate men
pull themselves up the Castle Rock –
a scabbard clinks: whispers curse
the scaling ladder.

So where's my binocular vision again?
How many geometries are there
with how many circles
to be a centre of?
As though a man, alive in his imagination,
trips on this stone and stumbles
on the field of the Battle of the Braes or, walking
to Murrayfield, is one of a crowd
moving in silence
to the execution of Montrose.

I name myself, I name this place, I say
I am here; and the immediacies
of the flesh and of the reports
of its five senses (I welcome them)
make their customary
miraculous declarations, from which
all else falls away. The landscapes
and histories of memory
disappear in a yellow basket
rising from the hold of the *Golden Emblem* and swooping
ashore, towsy with fishtails
(gray haddock, falseface skate, flounders
with wrong eyes – they slide into the shallow boxes
with a slip, with a slither, watched by me
and by herring gulls and blackbacks that stroll
the fringe of the crowd like policemen,
like pickpockets).

Who would guess
the thorn in the rose tree, the scandalous life
of Professor Schmaltz, the grunt
of a puffin? Who could foretell
the wave that towers in humped high
over the others? The argument from design
has as many flaws in it as there are
unpredictables
in the design.

I think of a man who talks as if trees were
virtuosities of wood, as if water
were liquid mechanisms built for holding up
swans. He speaks as if winds were
recordings of a master wind and not
unexampled discourses, as if birds
were spools of song that
they unwind.

What sort of apprentice sorcerer is he
whose inventions
have got out of hand? – For he forgets
the intrusion of the comic (see that sun, strolling over,
lordly magnifico, with a wig of cloud
slipping over one ear) – and of the tragic:
that whimsical water
lullabying in the sun can clench its fist
on the timbers it cradles.

In mid-air a gull, peering down, bowed
between its wings,
unbows itself and cackles,
trips over the cackle and floats on;
and a baby boat
comically staggering across the bay
stops for a rest in the dead centre
of teeming unpredictables.

Grassblade, cathedral, hero –
strawberry jam pot – each
is a centre
of innumerable circles. I sit in mine,
enriched by geometries
that make a plenum of more
than the three dimensions.
I sit and stare at them
with a multiple eye.

February 1971

Memorial

Everywhere she dies. Everywhere I go she dies.
No sunrise, no city square, no lurking beautiful mountain
but has her death in it.
The silence of her dying sounds through
the carousel of language, it's a web
on which laughter stitches itself. How can my hand
clasp another's when between them
is that thick death, that intolerable distance?

She grieves for my grief. Dying, she tells me
that bird dives from the sun, that fish
leaps into it. No crocus is carved more gently
than the way her dying
shapes my mind. – But I hear, too,
the other words,
black words that make the sound
of soundlessness, that name the nowhere
she is continuously going into.

Ever since she died
she can't stop dying. She makes me
her elegy. I am a walking masterpiece,
a true fiction
of the ugliness of death.
I am her sad music.

March 1971

Between two nowheres

I have a small chaos in my house –
a thing easy to come by. I've not
tamed it, housetrained it.
No: I do my best
to enrage it, to cure it of a persisting small
infection of reason. I say to it
Come on, be chaotic! Make the door of my room open
on the door of my room. – That painting above the fireplace,
why shouldn't its birds fly off or land
on its own water, splashing the hearth tiles?
And me – why should I cross the room, why
shouldn't it cross me?

But all it can do
is push my spectacles under a cushion,
change dates in a letter, put an empty glass
in the chair I'm just sitting down in:
I reach for the book by my side
and it's been hi-jacked to the kitchen.

I say, Come on, you can do better than that!
Until I can get so lost in this room search-parties
have to be sent out for me, until I see what's behind me
more clearly than what's in front of me – until
you crack the sad articulations
in my mind,
how can I make something new, something crammed
with dangerous, beautiful possibilities –
something remarkable even if only for
its excess of normality?

We praise the good God for His creation
of the universe. – When are the hymns to be written
in praise of the unimaginable power of the Word
that first made the chaos that made
creation possible?

March 1971

After his death

for Hugh MacDiarmid

It turned out
that the bombs he had thrown
raised buildings:

that the acid he had sprayed
had painfully opened
the eyes of the blind.

Fishermen hauled
prizewinning fish
from the water he had polluted.

We sat with astonishment
enjoying the shade
of the vicious words he had planted.

The government decreed that
on the anniversary of his birth
the people should observe
two minutes pandemonium.

April 1971

Old man

He eats his past. The few days left to him
have no nourishment in them
till they've happened.
– How greedily he eats it –

stone bird on the castle gate
that began as a phoenix
and has been weathered
into a vulture.

May 1971

Marriage bed

The mountainy air going dry across the sea
Will come back in the morning
So soft and damp my hair will find new curls:
They won't cheat me to thinking I'm reborn.

Big moths, washed-blue, flutter their Kleenex wings
A foot above the grasses.
Their blunt gun-turret heads are masks of gold.
They shake like water bounced in a narrow glass.

A hundred yards away a corncrake keeps
Pressing the starter button –
The song won't fire. I wince to think what skulks
In my homely hayfield mind. (That's still uncut.)

In the white-blue fluttering appears a golden one.
She scarabs on a nettle.
White wings land on her and crawl underneath –
The future's coming ... I've years to squander yet.

June 1971

New tables

A mathematician who came to his senses
thought deeply
(putting his finger to his forehead,
putting his finger through his forehead)
and wrote:

One robust curse equals
two shrieks, four groans:
One hour with you
equals every convalescence:
One boy on a scooter equals
Concorde:
One Yes equals ten
commandments:

275]

One new life equals
a million old deaths:
Love equals
equal.

The world read this, stupefied
with admiration
and went on dying and laughing
and shedding
logarithms of tears.

June 1971

Caterpillar

He stands on the suckers under his tail,
stretches forward and puts down
his six legs. Then he brings up
the sucker under his tail, making
a beautiful loop.

That's his way of walking. He makes
a row of upside-down U's
along the rib of a leaf. He is as green
as it.

The ways of walking! – horse, camel,
snail, me, crab, rabbit –
all inventing a way of journeying
till they become like the green caterpillar
that now stands on his tail
on the very tip of the leaf and sways, sways
like a tiny charmed snake,
groping in empty space for a foothold
where none is, where there is no
foothold at all.

October 1971

Dumb blonde

Ever since someone said your body
was like the music of Mozart
it plays itself speechlessly through the air,
a divertimento
thinking it's a symphony.

October 1971

Grand-daughter visiting

She balances things – a brick upon a brick:
a ring in one hand, a spoon in the other:
and the two nine months she's lived.

Her home is warmed by the steady
glow of electric fires; but here
she holds a brick over another brick
to stare at the flames jumping
in the grate. With what concentration
she stares at them.

Soon she'll unbalance
that first nine months with nine years,
with nineteen years: her left hand won't know
what her right hand is doing; and who can guess
what fires she will stare at,
sitting in a scatter of forgotten toys?

October 1971*

Hogmanay

Murdo gave the cock meal
damped with whisky. It stood
on tiptoe, crowed eight times
and fell flat on its beak.

Later, Murdo, after the fifth verse
of *The Isle of Mull*,

fell, glass in hand,
flat on his back – doing in six hours
what the cock had done
in two minutes.

I was there. And now I see
the cock crowing with Murdo's face
and Murdo's wings flapping
as down he went.
It was a long way home.

November 1971

Private

Those who recognise my mask and recognise
my words – all to be found in the dictionary –
shall I scare them, bore them
with a truth? Shall I distort
the words to be found in the dictionary
in order to say what they mean
when they mean me?

How my friends would turn away
from the ugly sounds coming from my mouth.
How they would grieve for
that comfortable MacCaig whose
small predictions were predictable.
How they would wish back
the clean white bandages
that hid these ugly wounds.

December 1971

Prism

The whole forest is illustrations
in a book of botany.
But on the crest of a tree
a myth makes the moonlight glitter

on the carving of chairs, on printing presses,
on the miracle of ink.

The whole city
is a code in a foreign language.
But a fable glows on a street lamp
and someone draws a thread
towards the Minotaur, someone writes
in biblical ledgers
a forty-year wandering. Circe
draws a curtain aside.

A fairytale rustles in a dark room
and a girl weeps for what she has lost
and for what she will never have – she weeps
because rat is rat, Prince Prince,
and toad toad.

December 1971

July landing

The *Eilean Glas*, engine full ahead,
slavers through the sea, wolfishly
making for its lair
at Lochinver. It brushes aside
the sparkling splinters of water.

The day is wildernesses, all
desolate and lovely …
As monumental as a monument
a blonde sheltie drowsily stares
through filmstar eyelashes
at the road hemstitched on the skirt
of a mountain. Somewhere
a lamb laments
with the voice of desolation.

On the sand at Clashnessie
six sandpipers play tig

with the Minch, that
keeps casting up and withdrawing
a rinse of soiled lace infested
with sandgrains.

And round Stoer Point swirls
a typhoon of gulls and, under it, the *Eilean Glas*
grinning through the water
till it comes to rest at the pier
in a green seethe of watery
mushrooms and Catherine wheels
and the engine stops
with a clap of silence.

January 1972

Down and down

Therefore I fall
in a way that never misses the target
like all the marvellous fallers
Icarus Phaethon Lucifer.

The depth I fall into
is cruelly just light enough
for me to see it;
else how know I was falling?

I had only the usual
pride, the usual ambition.
Icarus Phaethon Lucifer,
I will be no legend.

When I reach the bottom
of bottomlessness, there will be
no broken wings beside me,
no chariot of the sun.

And no crystal battlements
will infinitely shine above me.

I will be left with only
the loneliness of falling.

January 1972

The white bird

The light comes back.
The light always comes back.

No need, I say to myself,
to creep into a nutshell –
that won't keep the light
from coming back.

The white bird
lay dead on my doorstep.
Was it a dove? I don't think so.
It lay there
like the sorrows of the world.

No need, I say to myself,
to make a cave and
hide in it. That won't keep the rain
from coming back, from
ending a dry season.

Scavengers took away
the white dove, if it was one.

No need, I say to myself,
to be glad of its beauty. That won't keep
the sorrows of the world
from coming back
pitiful and beautiful
like a white bird
that might be a dove.

February 1972

281]

Drop-out in Edinburgh

I steal nothing from you.
I am your incandescent heir.
You bequeath me my incandescence.

City of everywhere, broken necklace in the sun,
you are caves of guilt, you are pinnacles of jubilation.
Your music is a filigree of drumming.
You frown into the advent of heavenly hosts.
Your iron finger shatters sad suns –
they multiply in scatters, they swarm
on fizzing roofs. When the sea
breathes gray over you, you become
one lurking-place, one shifting of nowheres –
in it are warpipes and genteel pianos
and the sawing voices of lawyers. Your buildings
are broken memories, your streets
lost hopes – but you shrug off time, you set your face
against all that is not you.

I am your incandescent heir.
I am your morning side, I am your golden acre.
Your windows glitter me, the sheen
on your pigeons' breasts is me.
I glide through your dark streets like phosphorus.

March 1972

Drifting in a dinghy

Cloud, light, air, water and its depth –
a treble clef, on which
I am my monotonous single,
black breve
on a shining manuscript.

I think of grammar, I think of you.

– Subject, verb object in one,
your meaning is an everlasting
narrative of illuminations.
Yet I can no more analyse
the syntax of your going or parse
your parts of all speech
than I can explain why music
is a narrative of all illuminations except
yours, even though I can't tell
an organum from
a diminished clavichord.

I hum melodiously
in this abstraction of music,
thinking of grammar, thinking of you,
till a woodwind sighs from the west
and my black breve
goes sharp, goes flat, goes sharp.

March 1972

The Little Falls Pool

Giggle and thump –
the water does both at once.
The stone it creases over
smiles like a mandarin,
porcelained with water.
Upstream, a posse
of baby mergansers
squatters, eight squeaks in line,
across a sliding prairie of water.
It all makes happiness
seem easy.

There's a cloud
in the space between us.
Cruelty roams there,
cruelty and desolation.

There are sad minds
in the space between us
(and happiness, and happiness).
But where you are
and where I am
there is room only
for happiness natural as this water
creased over a stone. I watch
the eight fluff-balls running on its surface
with love, knowing they'll reach
the dark overhang
where their mother waits for them.

April 1972

Prospector

I go fossicking among
your laughing streams, panning
grits of gold. Insistent as a cuckoo
my knapping hammer clinks
in your peaceful valleys.
I walk among treasures.

I think
If only I could burrow down
layer by layer, fossil by fossil –

but then, then
I wonder
what horrible violence spewed up
that lava slope
in whose quiet valleys
I swish and swirl such gold
from these clear streams.

May 1972

Horoscope

I know there are words I don't understand
like apogee and azimuth.
I know there are diagrams that pretend to be
diagrams of the past and gossips
of the future.

It's my pretty Now I'm in love with
that won't stand still
to be measured. The past
has gone to a far country; and as for the future
there's no future in it.
But my pretty Now, I love her, I love her,
because she shows herself off to me
and will always be faithful.

May 1972

Woodsman

He felled one, and dreamed of no question.
Leaves shook and the wood was filled
with froggish exhalations.
He never thought of nests
arcing down, of desperate squirrels.

He felled another, and there was no answer.
He was the axe, he said *Thunk! thunk!*
He never dreamt
of indisputable ladies highstepping
from thickets or moonlighting in carriages
down the dark rides.

The space he made grew forward.
He was his own man, his dreamless self
on a lane of trashed branches.

285]

But ahead of him was a low building and in it
a woman with long nails and a smile
not nice to see. She waited for him
with a bad light in her eyes.

May 1972

Landscape and I

Landscape and I get on together well.
Though I'm the talkative one, still he can tell
His symptoms of being to me, the way a shell
Murmurs of oceans.

Loch Rannoch lapses dimpling in the sun.
Its hieroglyphs of light fade one by one
But re-create themselves, their message done,
For ever and ever.

That sprinkling lark jerked upward in the blue
Will daze to nowhere but leave himself in true
Translation – hear his song cascading through
His disappearance.

The hawk knows all about it, shaking there
An empty glove on steep chutes of the air
Till his yellow foot cramps on a squeal, to tear
Smooth fur, smooth feather.

This means, of course, Schiehallion in my mind
Is more than mountain. In it he leaves behind
A meaning, an idea, like a hind
Couched in a corrie.

So then I'll woo the mountain till I know
The meaning of the meaning, no less. Oh,
There's a Schiehallion anywhere you go.
The thing is, climb it.

May 1972

Blackbird in a sunset bush

Everything's in the sunset. Windows
flare in it, rooms blush.
Cars scatter everywhere – they make the city
one huge pintable. Life is opulent
as thunder.

Only the blackbird there
contemplates
what the sunset's in:
what makes a flower ponderous
and breathes a mountain away.

The gravity of beauty –
how thoughtfully, how pensively he puts it,
charcoal philosopher
in his blazing study.

June 1972

Back again, Lairg station

Into the seventh house of the stars
the train, caterpillaring between
green somewheres, huffed and
sighingly stopped. I, earth explorer,
stepped out, at my home station,
and faces I knew were not angels'
angelically greeted me. Hands gripped mine
with a forgotten hardness and I stood
saying nothing in different ways,
in a green somewhere, unable to bear
the fuschia hedge, the barrow wheels grinding
on grit, moved as by the finger of God
by the baggy trousers of the stationmaster,
by the stopped clock, by that most disobeyed
of orders, *Cross the line*
by the bridge only.

June 1972

Morning song

Morning, and something scratches
at the door of my mind.

Inside the door
you walk windy streets, you wash dishes,
you sit with astonishing books in your hand.
I want to praise your movements that are
so musical, so thrifty, and your stillness
that is so musical, so generous.
Though no birds sing, it's as if
birds were singing in the sweetest
of consort and it's your light
that fingers so gently
the brutal shapes and the delicate shapes
of the world. I want to tell you
how impossible it is
not to tell you how impossible
it is to tell you of the mornings
you make of this morning.

Something scratched
at the door of my mind.
I have let it in.
I make you a present of it.

June 1972

Lesson

He watches a fishbox, say,
or a languid rope
or a seagull at attention.
– What's the matter with a fishbox? So
he watches a fishbox.
He tries to see just what it is.
He counts the slats it's made of –
sides, top and bottom –

and reads, in neat black letters,
Return to Lochinver. He notices
sixpences of scales, gone grubby.
And then he's stuck.
He goes off knowing
he hasn't seen the fishbox at all.

Meantime the fishbox
waits till it's night. Then
like a pterodactyl it planes
through the darkness and flies into
the sleeper's mind. It opens
and crams the sleeper inside it.
And when the hammer hits
the first nail on the head,
he wakes with a scream, he knows
what a fishbox is, he knows
what a rope is, or a seagull standing
at its horrible attention.

                                    July 1972

Elemental you

As the rain makes
Blue gold-shines on the puddled mud at gates
And tinily trickles over small estates

And as the wind
Hullabaloos a tree against its will
To stop the nonsense of just standing still,

On any day
You, decorator and disturber, make
Me unexpected: my gray turns crimson lake,

My thoughts that are
Great liers on their backs get up and dance
And my face shines, though I lose countenance

289]

Being forced to agree
Mud can be trampled bright and – look at me!
I can dance too, if only like a tree.

September 1972

Return to Scalpay

The ferry wades across the kyle. I drive
The car ashore
On to a trim tarred road. A car on Scalpay?
Yes, and a road where never was one before.
The ferrymen's Gaelic wonders who I am
(Not knowing I know it), this man back from the dead,
Who takes the blue-black road (no traffic jam)
From by Craig Lexie over to Bay Head.

A man bows in the North wind, shaping up
His lazybeds,
And through the salt air vagrant peat smells waver
From houses where no house should be. The sheds
At the curing station have been newly tarred.
Aunt Julia's house has vanished. The Red Well
Has been bulldozed away. But sharp and hard
The church still stands, barring the road to Hell.

A chugging prawn boat slides round Cuddy Point
Where in a gale
I spread my batwing jacket and jumped farther
Than I've jumped since. There's where I used to sail
Boats looped from rushes. On the jetty there
I caught eels, cut their heads off and watched them slew
Slow through the water. Ah – Cape Finisterre
I called that point, to show how much I knew.

While Hamish sketches, a crofter tells me that
The Scalpay folk,
Though very intelligent, are not Spinozas …
We walk the Out End road (no need to invoke
That troublemaker, Memory, she's everywhere)

To Laggandoan, greeted all the way –
My city eyeballs prickle; it's hard to bear
With such affection and such gaiety.

Scalpay revisited? – more than Scalpay. I
Have no defence,
For half my thought and half my blood is Scalpay,
Against that pure, hardheaded innocence
That shows love without shame, weeps without shame,
Whose every thought is hospitality –
Edinburgh, Edinburgh, you're dark years away.

Scuttering snowflakes riddling the hard wind
Are almost spent
When we reach Johann's house. She fills the doorway,
Sixty years of size and astonishment,
Then laughs and cries and laughs, as she always did
And will (Easy glum, easy glow, a friend would say) …
Scones, oatcakes, herrings from under a bubbling lid.
Then she comes with us to put us on our way.

Hugging my arm in her stronger one, she says,
Fancy me
Walking this road beside my darling Norman!
And what is there to say? … We look back and see
Her monumental against the flying sky
And I am filled with love and praise and shame
Knowing that I have been, and knowing why,
Diminished and enlarged. Are they the same?

September 1972

Greenshank

His single note – one can't help calling it
piping, one can't help
calling it plaintive – slides droopingly down
no more than a semitone, but is filled
with an octave of loneliness, with the whole sad scale
of desolation.

He won't leave us. He keeps flying
fifty yards and perching
on a rock or a small hummock,
drawing attention to himself.
Then he calls and calls
and flies on again
in a flight
roundshouldered but dashing,
skulking yet bold.

Cuckoo, phoenix, nightingale,
you are no truer emblems
than this bird is.
He is the melancholy that flies
in the weathers of my mind,
He is the loneliness that calls to me there
in a semitone
of desolate octaves.

October 1972

Ringed plover by a water's edge

They sprint eight feet and –
stop. Like that. They
sprintayard (like that) and
stop.
They have no acceleration
and no brakes.
Top speed's their only one.

They're alive – put life
through a burning-glass, they're
its focus – but they share
the world of delicate clockwork.

In spasmodic
Indian file
they parallel the parallel ripples.

When they stop
they, suddenly,
are gravel.

October 1972

Birthdays

In the earliest light of a long day
three stags stepped out from the birch wood
at Achmelvich bridge
to graze on the sweet grass
by the burn.
A gentle apparition.

Stone by stone a dam was built,
a small dam, small stone by stone.
And the water backed up, flooding
that small field.

I'll never see it again.
It's drowned forever.
But still
in the latest light of a lucky day I see
horned heads come from the thickets
and three gentle beasts innocently pacing
by that implacable water.

October 1972

If

If your hand came, dead in the dead of night,
And touched my forehead, waking me to see
You standing dead there in the dead of night,
I who fear ghosts would have no fear at all.
I'd greet you with the tenderest hello
And you would smile, though sad. And then you'd go.

There would be nothing deathly in your death

For your love always was the laughing sort
That quickened life and would not die with death.
And when you'd gone, I would not want to weep –
That loving gaiety would still be there
Filling with its own peace the quickened air.

November 1972

In a whirl

The cross-migrations going on in my mind!
I'm dizzied blind
And blinded dizzy by those pantomime
And stroboscopic scene-shiftings. Old Time
Rattles his knees and, grinning fit to kill,
Jigs at all angles in the astounded air.
What can I do but stare
And carol won't you, will you, won't you, Will?

An Immanence is what I want, to be
That Unity,
That transcendental One I don't believe in.
How give it birth with no place to conceive in? –
My brain cells all are full: their prisoners lie,
Far too contented, on their bunks and grin
Even though I smuggle in
Files and ropeladders in the proper pie.

There was a time Time kept his printed place
In lower case.
But now he's boss and bully and off his head.
He's displaced place and promoted from the dead
His grandpa Chaos – it's terrifying to see
The douce Laws capering in hippy gear:
A jingbang where it's clear
(Good godless God!) that Immanence is me.

November 1972

The Pass of the Roaring

Such comfortless places comfort me.
Not my body but I am fed by these ravens
And I'm nourished by the drib-dab waters
That fingerling through the harsh deer grass.
The tall cliffs unstun my mind
Thank God for a place where no history passes.

Is this ghoulish? Is it the vampire me
Or grandfathers and greatgrandfathers
Specklessly flowing my veins that bury
A hummingbird tongue in these gulfs of space
And suck from limestone with delicate greed
A delicate vintage, the blood of grace?

Books vaporise in my lightning mind.
Pennies and pounds become a tribal
Memory. Hours assert their rightness,
Escaping like doves through their cotes of clocks
And lame philosophies founder in bogs
That stink of summer in the armpit rockfolds.

There's always a returning. A cottage glows
By a dim sea and there I'll slump by the fireside –
And another grace will gather, from human
Intercommunications, a grace
Not to be distinguished from the one that broods
In fingerling waters and gulfs of space.

From *The World's Room* (mostly 1972–73)

Pantheon

Are the gods odder
than a belief in them?

You're enough for me.

When I in my solitude
think of you – sometimes

what panic.
I seize your image
and you become
mist, zero, a full-face profile
or the flight of a bird
without the bird.
You commit in me
mindquakes,
my cockle boat bounces above
the swirl
of your delicate trident.
You bring me messages from ambrosial tables
and when I'm asleep
you let fall a drop
of boiling oil
on my defenceless dream

I, atheist, god-hater,
am tangled in your net
of runes and rigmaroles.
You make me your oddity.
– Girl, I beg you,
blow your nose,
scratch your head,
suffer a not too painful toothache.
Then I'll sit back and contemplate
with eyes blazing with reason
the earthly wisdom
of your immortal statistics.

From The World's Room (mostly 1972–73)

His son to Lacoön

You make a spectacular figure,
you'll be admired
by centuries of connoisseurs.
You, fool, who always pushed the truth too hard,
see what it has brought you to –

and Troy will fall anyway.

And what of me,
me, who was innocent of the truth,
and who will not live to enjoy
the blandishment of evil
for those hideous coils crushing
the ribs round my heart?

From The World's Room (mostly 1972–73)

Far gone in innocence

He sows seedpackets and throws away the seeds.
But what imaginary gardens flourish where
He takes the evening in his gaudy air.

He tells no lie but makes another truth
Of what is true and sees in a summer town
A snowstorm skimming tiny doilies down.

The odd thing is he goes clean through a face
And scans it from the inside. Real or fake,
He tells you what you are and no mistake.

He feels his way through life, like everyone,
But never falls; for nothing can eclipse
The suns he carries in his fingertips.

He has a fault, the fault true innocence
Can't know about, in its onesidedness:
He's full of love and yet is pitiless.

And so he's lonely: as though he always lives
In another month than ours and can make free
With every space but the one from you to me.

From The World's Room (mostly 1972–73)

Two into one

The thin sea breeze met a fat one coming
Down from a corrie. What a confusion
Of ideas and smells – mountain thyme
Growing in sea splashes and mackerel flirting
Round knolls of heather. It took no patience –

Girl who wasn't there – to invent true parallels
With you and me: my bladdery seawrack
And your moss campion: my watery slither
And your roe-deer delicate pacing: my yells
Blackbacking on barnacles – and you on a hillock

Golden plovering, sweetly sandpiping.
What a croft we'd be, with our own visitations!
It would swing like a bell, between sounds and shapes –
Its complete round voice would spread away, fading
Over holiday sabbaths of hills and oceans.

From The World's Room (mostly 1972–73)

Saying *Yes* is not enough

Of course I say Yes,
green bird in what branches?

Of course I agree, dusty branch
so still
in what singing?

The hole in my head
is willing, is shaped for
what can be poured into a full jug,
what lurks under the ice of zero.

Green bird, invent those branches,
my mind is hungry for them.
Dusty branch I have echoes lined up
for that singing.

When a dog runs away
I love that fuzzy film –
the innumerable shapes of dog
he trails behind him.

But the hole in my head
forms itself for
the dog he's running into.

Fulfilment is a sad word
since it helplessly means
its opposite – for I keep learning
what's left when you empty emptiness.

From The World's Room (mostly 1972–73)

Understanding

It was an evening, one of those evenings
when flutes play audibly and God's thrombosis
isn't too sore, and human fingers
touch human fingers in immortal braille.

And there was an O in my graph, though discursions
dangled from anywhere – from brambles or the pretty
armpits of lambs; and a stone was more
than just a thing for a vole to go round.

The praise is yours, girl: for you made
everything braille for my blind fingers.
Everything spoke you; for you are the word
to which all other words are a footnote.

It was an evening, one of the many
when your meaning was all the others'
and love and pity were the O in the graph
of the world's loneliness, of wars, and disasters.

January 1973

Wooden chair with arms

That chair, foursquare, sturdy as a fortress
Being invested by two year old Christopher
(He clambered up and through and on to)
Is as big in my mind as the hill Cul Mor.

Van Gogh might have painted it, solid
Essence of chair but this chair only,
An interjection into now and here
From where Van Gogh went when he was alone.

The authority of complete alonencss!
I sipped my whisky and watched Christopher
Laughing and jumping and landing unhurt
From a height that dwarfed the hill Cul Mor.

January 1973

Still going

Rock like a cargo boat wallowing through
The jopples of heather – and round its bow,
Look, a stag saunters, momentary seabeast,
Splashed with heather, its antlers foamy.

I won't give up being deceived by landscape's
Likenesses and incorrigible metaphors.
They swish long currents in my mind – fancy
A stagnant mind: a crystal of braincells.

And yet all movements so counterbalance
They spin and doze to such a stillness
That moon and leaf jampack together
And the sun's shone on by a glittering snail.

I have a feverish eye – the right one.
The other's icy. With which do I see
The still rock yawing on heathery tiderips,
The stag splashing towards his sea-nymphs?

January 1973

300]

Cheese and wine party

Strange, for instance, he said, *to suppose*
Animals differ from us in being chinless
Only, or having no calves to their legs.
I swirled my drink and thoughtfully said, *Yes*.

But structure, surely (she was structured all right)
Modifies modes till even the most formless
Becomes a kind of figurative abstract.
I thoughtfully swirled my drink and said, *Yes*.

As I told the Principal (the voice made nicks
On my brain's membrane) *Tony and Princess*
Margaret assured me I was right. Don't you …?
I swigged my drink and said, thoughtfully, *Yes*.

Outside, the Meadows lay (chinlessly) under
An abstraction of stars, figured and thoughtless.
Oh, mannerless planets, use your influence
To choke in my throat that bad word *Yes*.

January 1973

Gone are the days

Impossible to call a lamb a lambkin
or say eftsoons or spell you ladye.
My shining armour bleeds when it's scratched;
I blow the nose that's part of my visor.

When I go pricking o'er the plain
I say *Eightpence please* to the sad conductress.
The towering landscape you live in has printed
on its portcullis *Bed and breakfast*.

I don't regret it. There are wildernesses
enough in Rose Street or the Grassmarket
where dragons' breaths are methylated
and social workers trap the unwary.

301]

So don't expect me, lady with no e,
to look at a lamb and feel lambkin
or give me a down look because I bought
my greaves and cuisses at Marks and Spencers.

Pishtushery's out. But oh, how my heart swells
to see you perched, perjink, on a bar stool.
And though epics are shrunk to epigrams, let me
buy a love potion, a gin, a double.

February 1973

Two-year-old

Catherine in a blue pinafore
stands on a chair. Dishwashing's over.
She strokes a bottlebrush of clear water
around the sink and says, *Red.*

She dips the brush in the milk bottle
and strokes again and says, *Yellow.*
How carefully, how busily
she paints the sink with clear water.

I know she knows it's just her pleasure
to make two worlds of the one world.
There's nothing wrong with mottled porcelain –
but what's the matter with red and yellow?

She loads the brush, that little maestro,
and speaks with the same and such decision
I stare at the mottled porcelain –
her pinafore isn't half so blue.

February 1973

In everything

Once I was on a cliff, on a ledge of seapinks,
Contemplating nothing – it was a self-sufficient day
With not a neurotic nerve to zigzag in the blue air.

Was that happiness? (Yes.) I sat, still as a shell,
Over water, in space, amongst spiders in chinks.

But suddenly I was introduced to suddenness.
As though a train entered a room, a headlong pigeon
Cometed past me, and space opened in strips
Between pinions and tail feathers of the eagle after it –
It had seen me. What vans of brakes! What voluptuousness!

What a space in space, carved like an eagle,
It left behind it! Below me the green sea-water
Wishy-washed, the blind thing, and the corally seapinks
Nodded over my hand. How can there be a revelation
In a world so full it couldn't be more full?

The pigeon hurtled out of my life. And I don't remember
The eagle going away. But I'll never forget
The eagle-shaped space it left, stamped on the air.
Absence or presence? … It seems I'm on a ledge of seapinks
All the time, an observing, blank-puzzled cliff-hanger.

February 1973

Spendthrift

A sigh in the space I reserve for coins
To gleam bashfully of their fair future
Turned me into a cat at a mousehole
(I'm just rich enough to know I'm poor).

I'd miss even one of these bashful shiners.
Was one of them sick? Had a sneaking cutpurse
Keyholed in? What was needed –
A cool prescription? or clinking handcuffs?

No door ever opened so slowly
Or revealed less. There was nothing there.
How search for nothing in nothing? I did it
Then rushed out anywhere, nowhere, somewhere.

And anywhere, nowhere somewhere shone
With glints and gleamings, with round sparkles.
Flowers hung sixpences, trees were fires
Of pennies over the sovereign grass.

That's when I stopped being a miser.
I saw that beginnings have no end
And fell out of love with the ghostly future.
Today is Thursday. I'll go and spend it.

March 1973

The unlikely as usual

Green in the grass is a blade of grass
But you in my mind are a fiery cluster.
Milky the stars in the Milky Way –
In my dusty thoughts you're glinting gold dust.

Once I glimpsed in my thickety wood
A crimson unicorn. It snorted bluebells
And piaffered violets and like an angel
Vanished, leaving the air true.

On lucky days I visit that truth
And find you walking there, being gentle
With shades and toadstools and toadstool moss.
Each of these times is a lucky again.

A waterdrop is green in its wave
But you in any of the world's spaces
Deny likeness – and yet you make
The law of likeness a state of grace.

Unicorn, what were you in the shades
With your melting eyes and lifted forefoot?
You reached from myth and gave me a girl
Whose like was never in that wood before.

April 1973

Caterpillar going somewhere

Its green face looks as if
it were about to spit – pft.

It moves along a twig
by doing exercises, bend, stretch –

hard to imagine
a potbellied caterpillar.

It looks so active (hard to imagine it
in the lotus position)

and yet, and yet
it looks so melancholy.

Is it because it knows that
when it reaches a green leaf

its jaws will open sideways
instead of up and down? …

It's standing erect now – it turns
from side to side

like a retired sea-captain
scanning horizons.

                                        April 1973

Reversal

She showed me a polished pebble with a salmon fly
Painted on it. Local arts and crafts
Scrabble on beaches for an addled egg left
By a mountain, varnish it, make it domestic
And tart it up with a minuscule landscape,
An improbable flower or a salmon fly.

How tunes diminish when they become domestic.
Grace notes fall off, the lamentable, sour

Flat note climbs up that ruinous semitone
And there's the tune's ghost – a flabby ghost,
All its bonestructure gone. It tamely
Toddles the house, slippered, domestic.

Once in a peatbog I found – no ghost –
A blue hare's skeleton. It was its self,
Running dead still … Girl with the pebble,
I'll put you out in a wildness that'll tune
Bones and bones to glimmer back in you,
My homely nobody, my skin and ghost.

And seas will break on the pebble, the tune
Be restored to a state of gracenotes – for
Wildness is not wilderness. By the fire
I'll watch your true self moving dead still.
And you and I will, in that artful wildness,
Come into harmony out of tune.

May 1973

Stag in a neglected hayfield

He's not in his blazing red yet. His antlers
Are a foot that'll be a spreading yard.
The field was a hayfield: now a heifer
And two cows graze there and no dog barks.

That's the outward scene. The inner –
A mountain forgotten, a remembered man.
The deer will return to the hill: but stiller
Than the stone above them are the scything hands.

June 1973

Failed occasion

With words in my mouth I do my Demosthenes
Walk by the sea where little baby breakers
Two inches tall lisp and prattle:
With nothing in my mind I can't even do that.

A sunset flamingly retires. I feel
I'm a black smudge on a precious manuscript,
Not the exclamation mark I'd like to be.
– What's the use of mere elegant feelings?

Elegant? – sirens with raffish hair-do's.
Their singing's over. They unpick my bones.
I'm squandered. Sand is grit between the words
That ought to flute from me, liquid, birdlike.

It's that damned nothing. Lucky Demosthenes
With a thing to overcome. How overcome nothing? –
Good night to the sirens! I leave them combing
Their blue-rinse locks and go mooching home.

July 1973

One way journey

Warm clay in the stone wants to come back to me.
That Inchnadamph cliff is full of squeaking fossils.
The sun sinks back to helium. The sea
Boils before ice. Oh, the loud primevals!

There was a time, where I take short holidays,
Before man came shooting his morals
At what created him. I can praise
What never was tortured between true and false.

There was no sad mind to weep for cruelty
Before that mountain was belched into being.
Destruction could only create. What a day
When it made that mind, when it made suffering.

Time scuds full-sail towards a foundering
Not to be stopped by the links of Mozart
And space will be spaceless when Rembrandts cling
No more to its idea, to space free of hazard.

– And yet what starveling mind would surrender
A moment's love for a Time before crystals
Or step on a creeping concept? For there
New planets whirl in a space of fossils.

Spectres of spectra beyond imagining
Ghost an idea on, in a brain's doldrums.
Sad eyes will weep. – And voices will sing
With what unites triumphs and requiems.

July 1973

A.K.'s summer hut

It clamps itself to a rock, like a limpet,
And creeps up and down in a tide of people,
Hardly ever stranded in a tideless sabbath:
A pilgrimage place where all hymns are jubilant.

The starry revolutions around it,
The deer circling in new foundations
Of old worlds, the immortal noise
Of the river ghosted with salmon – these

Are a bloodstream it's a blood-drop in.
Such sharing. Such giving. See, at the window,
That silly chaffinch, practically talking Gaelic,
And the eiders domestic as farmyard ducks

And the lady gull yacking for her breakfast.
If I were a bethlehemish star I'd stand fixed
Over that roof, knowing there'd be born there
No wars, no tortures, no savage crucifixions.

But a rare, an extraordinary thing –
An exhilaration of peace, a sounding
Grace with trinities galore – if only
Those three collared doves in the rowan tree.

July 1973

Discouraging

Where anyway are answers? I think of that Greek
Drawing geometries in the sand. He thought he'd found some
Crouched like angelic toads in obtuse and acute angles
Or tangentially soaring off to touch other circles.
Happy fellow! He had more than one ground
For believing that find is a fruit of seek.

Walking in the umbrageous policies of my mind
I keep stepping in mantraps. (I'm only the tenant.
If ever I meet the owner I'll have some questions
To ask him.) The localest of explorations –
And I'm miraged, mosquitoed, shipwrecked, headhunted,
Boiled in a pot – something anyway unkind.

To question a microbe is to quiz
The supersuper universe. There seems no border
At all between things (except answer and question).
Poor Archimedes! He thought he was getting
Somewhere, when that soldier came by and a sword
Asked another question and cut short his.

November 1973

Small rain

The rain – it was a little rain – walked through the wood
   (a little wood)
Leaving behind unexpected decorations and delicacies
On the fox by the dyke, that was eating a salmon's head.
(The poacher who had hidden it wasn't going to be pleased.)

The rain whisperingly went on, past the cliff all Picasso'd
With profiles, blackening the Stoer peat stacks, silvering
Forty sheep's backs, half smudging out a buzzard.
It reached us. It passed us, totally unimpressed.

Not me. I looked at you, all cobwebby with seeds of water,
Changed from Summer to Spring. I had absolutely no way of saying

How vivid can be unemphatic, how bright can be brighter
Than brightness. You knew, though. You were smiling, and no
wonder.

December 1973

Bargain with a wren

If you give up that scolding,
Jenny, I won't tell you
what your other name is.

Have I no right to be
bucolic on a green bank?
Do I scutter about on it
screeching shrewishly at you?

I'm no weasel
to stick a needly face
in your nest's thumb-door …

Sweet day, so cool, so –

I warned you, feather-scrap! Jenny,
I warned you –

Troglodytes troglodytes!
Troglodytes troglodytes!

And what happens?

I give in, I retire, bowed under
a fusillade
of further and worse
vulgarities.

January 1974

Praise of a road

You won't let me forget you. You keep nudging me
With your hairpin bends or, without a *Next, please,*
Magic-lanterning another prodigious view
In my skull where I sit in the dark with my brains.

You turn up your nose above Loch Hope,
That effete low-lier where men sit comfy
In boats, casting for seatrout, and whisper
Up the hill, round the crag – there are the Crocachs.

You're an acrobat with a bulrushy spine,
Looping in air, turning to look at yourself
And faultlessly skidding on your own stones
Round improbable corners and arriving safe.

When the Crocachs have given me mist and trout
And clogs of peat, how I greet you and whirl
Down your half-scree zigzags, tumbling like a peewit
Through trembling evenings down to Loch Eriboll.

January 1974

Praise of a collie

She was a small dog, neat and fluid –
Even her conversation was tiny:
She greeted you with *bow*, never *bow-wow.*

Her sons stood monumentally over her
But did what she told them. Each grew grizzled
Till it seemed he was his own mother's grandfather.

Once, gathering sheep on a showery day,
I remarked how dry she was. Pollóchan said, 'Ah,
It would take a very accurate drop to hit Lassie.'

She sailed in the dinghy like a proper sea-dog.
Where's a burn? – she's first on the other side.

She flowed through fences like a piece of black wind.

But suddenly she was old and sick and crippled …
I grieved for Pollóchan when he took her a stroll
And put his gun to the back of her head.

January 1974

Praise of a boat

The *Bateau Ivre* and the *Marie Celeste*,
The *Flying Dutchman* hurdling latitudes –
You could make a list (sad ones like the *Lusitania*
And brave puffed-up ones like the *Mayflower*).

Mine's called *the boat*. It's a quiet, anonymous one
That needs my two arms to drag it through the water.
It takes me huge distances of a few miles
From its lair in Loch Roe to fishy Soya.

It prances on the spot in its watery stable.
It butts the running tide with a bull's head.
It skims downwind, planing like a shearwater.
In crossrips it's awkward as a piano.

And what a coffin it is for haddocks
And bomb-shaped lythe and tigerish mackerel –
Though it once met a basking shark with a bump
And sailed for a while looking over its shoulder.

When salmon are about it goes glib in the dark,
Whispering a net out over the sternsheets –
How it crabs the tide-rush, the cunning thing,
While arms plunge down for the wrestling silver.

Boat of no dreams, you open spaces
The mind can't think of till it's in them,
Where the world is easy and dangerous and
Who can distinguish saints and sinners?

Sometimes that space reaches out
Till I'm enclosed in it in stony Edinburgh
And I hear you like a barrel thumping on head waves
Or in still water gurgling like a baby.

January 1974

Praise of a thorn bush

You've taken your stand
between Christy MacLeod's house
and the farthest planet.

The ideal shape of a circle
means nothing to you: you're all
armpits and elbows
and scraggy fingers that hold so delicately
a few lucid roses. You are
an encyclopedia of angles.

At night you trap stars, and the moon
fills you with distances.
I arrange myself to put
one rose in the belt of Orion.

When the salt gales drag through you
you whip them with flowers
and I think –
Exclamations for you, little rose bush,
and a couple of fanfares.

January 1974

Grandchild

She stumbles upon every day
as though it were a four-leaf clover
ringed in a horseshoe.

The light is her luck – and its thickening
into chair, postman, poodle

with a ribbon round its neck.

She plays among godsends
and becomes one. Watch her being
a seal or a sleepy book.

Yet sometimes she wakes in the night
terrified, staring
at somewhere else.

She's learning that ancestors
refuse to be dead. Their resurrection
is her terror.

We soothe the little godsend
back to us
and pray, despairingly –

May the clover be
a true prophet. May her light be
without history.

January 1974

How I wonder what you are

They tell me, star-twinkle, you're an exploding belch,
A million years' example of space's bad manners.
Well, I walk by my green trees on the sappy Meadows
Banjaxed and bamboozled by the ways of understanding
That says of one truth it's *so* – or *such*.

Whose choice will I take? – the gingerly ultimatums
Of ferocious, long-brained scientists or the fragile
Singsong certainties of nursery rhymes? Can a cage
Hold a leopard and a badger? Or worse, a badger
That's a leopard? And it a swarm of atoms?

Gulls stand in the meadows – is each a fankle
Of something electric? … I give up, and see
A geology of overcoats, a drop-out, a wino

Gurgling from a bottle. When he belches, will he explode
Out of his mouth a tiny star-twinkle?

Thank God for sarcasms – they come in this case
From that twirling gull. Thank God for the simple
Certainty of trees getting on with their singsong.
And thank God for the comic – for the dog, here, last winter,
Standing still with a horn of snow on its nose.

February 1974*

To be a leaf

My 3 year old, after being a seal
and a daffodil and a frog
demanded – Glampa!
Be a leaf!

To hang nicely on a twig tip or snug
in a bosomly branch, to rockabye, to entertain
a star or two ...

A caterpillar loops in my mind, a goat snatches,
the wintry earth
draws my blood from me.

And the tree of my veins
is an aspen trembling.

I hold her, pulling out
the softest of thorns.

February 1974*

Stars and planets

Trees are cages for them: water holds its breath
To balance them without smudging on its delicate meniscus.
Children watch them playing in their heavenly playground;
Men use them to lug ships across oceans, through firths.

They seem so twinkle-still, but they never cease
Inventing new spaces and huge explosions
And migrating in mathematical tribes over
The steppes of space at their outrageous ease.

It's hard to think that the earth is one –
This poor sad bearer of wars and disasters
Rolls-Roycing round the sun with its load of gangsters,
Attended only by the loveless moon.

March 1974

University staff club

If a thing exists ... How I hate sentences,
Mr Professor, that begin with *if*.
Tilt your nose, Mr Professor, and sniff

The vinegar of existence with a wild rose growing in it,
Hear the ravishing harmony dunted with a drum thud.
Put a hand on your throat – that beating is blood,

Not a pussyfooting echo of remote subjunctives.
The name of a thing means one thing and
The thing means another: fanfare for the ampersand.

That joins and separates them with a third meaning.
Good ampersand: bad murderous if.
Tilt your nose, Mr Professor: there's a whiff

Of heretical impatience in your fantasies
That won't let the world be. Are you so wise
You can add one more to the world's impossibles?

March 1974

A sigh for simplicity

I like *so* and *therefore*: I like extensions.
It's one of my faults and a reason I'm afraid.

If only I could leave (where it's sunny and shady)
The physics of light to men of different passions.

If only I could see a hazelnut without thinking
Of monkish skullcaps. Does the fishing boat at the pier
Really rock like a bear? Is a mussel really *bearded?*
It's time I put the lady moon on my blacklist.

I groan, and think, If only I were Adam
To whom everything was exactly its own name –
Until one day the other appeared, the shameless
Demander of similes, the destroyer of Eden.

March 1974

See what you've done

I say comfortably
The core of the apple was sweet
and to hell with Eden
as I sway on my camel's back
through the eye
of that famous needle.

April 1974

Presents

I give you an emptiness,
I give you a plenitude.
Unwrap them carefully –
one's as fragile as the other –
and when you thank me
I'll pretend not to notice the doubt in your voice
when you say they're just what you wanted.

Put them on the table by your bed.
When you wake in the morning
they'll have gone through the door of sleep
into your head. Wherever you go

they'll go with you and
wherever you are you'll wonder,
smiling, about the fullness
you can't add to and the emptiness
that you can fill.

October 1974

Small lochs

He's obsessed with clocks, she with politics,
He with motor cars, she with amber and jet.
There's something to be obsessed with for all of us.
Mine is lochs, the smaller the better.

I look at the big ones – Loch Ness, Loch Lomond,
Loch Shin, Loch Tay – and I bow respectfully,
But they're too grand to be invited home.
How could I treat them in the way they'd expect?

But the Dog Loch runs in eights when I go walking.
The Cat Loch purrs on the windowsill. I wade
Along Princes Street through Loch na Barrack.
In smoky bars I tell them like beads.

And don't think it's just the big ones that are lordlily named.
I met one once and when I asked what she was called
The little thing said (without blushing, mind you)
The Loch of the Corrie of the Green Waterfalls.

I know they're just H_2O in a hollow.
Yet not much time passes without me thinking of them
Dandling lilies and talking sleepily
And standing huge mountains on their watery heads.

December 1974

Fishermen's pub

I leaned on the bar, not thinking, just noticing.
I read the labels thumbed on the bright bottles.
(To gallop on White Horse through Islay Mist!

To sail into Talisker on Windjammer Rum!)
Above my head the sick TV trembled
And by the dartboard a guitar was thrumming

Some out of place tune … Others have done this
Before me. Remember, in one of the Russias,
Alexander Blok drunk beyond his own mercy –

How he saw, through the smoke and the uproar,
His 'silken lady' come in and fire
The fire within him? I found myself staring

For mine, for that wild, miraculous presence
That would startle the world new with her forgivingness.
But nothing was there but sidling smokewreaths

And through the babble all I heard was,
(Sounding, too near, in my dreadful silence)
A foreign guitar, the death clack of dominoes.

January 1975

Three figures of Beethoven

Hawks could teach bullets a thing or two –
see one precisely repeating
the terrified unpredictable zigzags
of a mountain pipit.

And gannets and aeroplanes – can a plane
turn over and backwards and
slam stunningly into the sea – to re-emerge
with a ruffle and begin unwinding
the same long spool of flight?

These are swift and beautiful. But watch
the gull, the slow flier, the airy loiterer
that can pause, dead still,
curved on the air
like a hand on a breast.

February 1975

Bus stop

No bus, no bus … As though I'm a field
I'm cropped by boredoms, black bulls the lot of them …
My mind does a Houdini with time and space:
I'm casting a fly over far Loch Cama.

Behind me the cut-price shop says *Whisky
From £3.59*. I look in my cut-price
Mind, but what's for sale there? – old junk,
Cobwebbed and cranky, with parts missing.

I tread on a glowing fag-end, with such
Satisfaction I wonder what else I'm treading on
And don't want to know … I'm pulling a boat
That's not there up on grouchy shingle.

That girl's handbag's an untidy temple
Of icons, incense and cruel rituals.
Sweet priestess, sacrifice me … A newsboy
Gouts from his split face tortured vocables.

And I lift a wineglass – I'm a 1930s' actor
Tête-à-têting in a naughty nightclub,
And oh, seductively, leeringly, smile
At a 14 bus, at a taken-aback driver.

March 1975

Stonechat on Cul Beg

A flint-on-flint ticking – and there he is,
Trim and dandy – in square miles of bracken
And bogs and boulders a tiny work of art,
Bright as an illumination on a monkish parchment.

I queue up to watch him. He makes me a group
Of solemn connoisseurs trying to see the brushstrokes.
I want to thumb the air in their knowing way.
I murmur *Chinese black*, I murmur *alizarin*.

But the little picture with four flirts and a delicate
Up-swinging's landed on another boulder.
He gives me a stained-glass look and keeps
Chick-chacking at me. I suppose he's swearing.

You'd expect something like oboes or piccolos
(Though other birds, too, have pebbles in their throats –
And of them I love best the airy skylark
Twittering like marbles squeezed in your fist).

Cul Beg looks away – his show's been stolen.
And the up-staged loch would yawn if it could.
Only the benign sun in his fatherly way
Beams on his bright child throwing a tantrum.

March 1975

Beside a water

The night sat on the quay and I beside it,
Watching the slippery moon. The tide kept trying
To touch my feet. I thought *This is a proper night
For cicadas*. But Scottish grasshoppers were fast asleep.
That fitted the reconciliations that made the sky
Talk so lovingly, so gently to the deep mountain.

Someone, Medea, was crying in a Greek theatre
Shaped like a corrie. My hand clenched on the brooch

That was to blind Oedipus. Cuchulain, forgetting
His confounded nobility, scratched the side of his nose ...
It was nice to think of the lobsters down there in the ebb
Swimming backwards through the tangle, being orchidaceous.

(There are faults even in a fault. That comforts me. My sore lip
May prove I'm handsome. My first-class honours degree
In stupidity may mean I'm a sage. Is it too much to hope
I have a silence in me that never heard
Of words?) ... I noticed I was trying not to notice
A nudging seapink. I greeted it, across my border.

A moon-glance went by like Catullus on Loch Roe's
Hendecasyllabics. There was a Lesbia somewhere – as if
I needed to be told that. Mine was being orchidaceous
In her swimmingly way ... Claws and all, I wretchedly thought:
And concentrated on a ripple trying to turn a corner
On one foot, like Charlie Chaplin. It couldn't do it.

March 1975

Means test

I'd heard of a stony look. Was that one
You turned on me? Was I to be petrified?
But it seemed to me as beautiful as ever
And I walked from the house whistling into a sunset.

I took the look home and became uneasy.
I couldn't see it as other than limpid and shining.
Are you water? or diamond? I prefer things shifting
And lucid, not locked in a hard design.

I mustn't look at you with wrong eyes,
Inventing what I want to see. Turn to me now
And let me know if I'm a millionaire
Of water or a pauper of diamonds.

June 1975

Composers of music

Musicians, calling in your circles and phases,
helpless in their ruminant fire,
unable to speak anything
but the laws of miracles,
how can you fail to shed
your tremulous humanity? How can you carry
your spongebag heart, your tick-tocking brain
along those orbits where you go
without skidding – without dying
into the clusters of notes you explode
in the earth's dark mind?

– I regard you with joy and with envy
from my thicket of words.

July 1975

Summer evening in Assynt

The green of Elphin
in this particular light
is its particular green.
It might be worn
by a royal, pale girl
in a Celtic legend.

I look up
at the eagle idling over
from Kylesku.
I look away
at the shattering waterblink
of Loch Cama.

I look down at my feet
and there's a frog
so green, so beautiful
it might be waiting in a Celtic legend

323]

for the kind girl to come
with her gentle kiss:
for the spell to go backward.

August 1975

Lucifer falling

The black radiance
was Lucifer falling.
Space grieved for him
shuddering at its own guilt
and moons were never the same
after passing through
the gauze of his wings.
The crystal battlements shook
to hear him laughing;
and somewhere amid
the angelic jubilations
there was a small weeping,
forecast
of the time to come.

August 1975

Nothing too much

He draws one line,
two, three, four, five,
not knowing what he's doing
except that he's sending feathery invitations
to Apollo.

He draws the fifteenth line
and Apollo yawns and stretches
and saunters in.

At the fortieth line
Apollo cries *Stop*!

Twenty lines later
Apollo's asleep in the smooth web
of his certainties
and the artist is staring at
still another picture
he has choked to death.

Apollo stirs. He mutters
Artists! and sinks back
into the boring world
of perfection.

August 1975

Venus

Venus, that shrewd contradiction,
scatters coins of cardboard
that buy kingdoms and banquets.

Then she smiles her buttonhook smile –
thinking of all those crowned heads glittering
in the smoke of insurrections;
thinking of the proud exiles gathered
in the sad cafés of the world.

September 1975

Goddess of lust

Her coif, her coiffure,
Her watch-chain ankles
Make dizzy the air
In igloos and Insurance Offices.
Airports remember her,
Cafés wear her scent.

She saunters with mirrors
Through holy congregations –
She's everywhere: except

She has always just left
The million sad rooms
Where love lies weeping.

September 1975

Report

All the time water is steeplejacking
up the insides of flowerstems.
All the time stones buried in a field
float up to the surface.
All the time the lordliest mountain
goes on becoming a plain where houses will send
friendly smoke over the bellowing of cattle.

And a woman pours milk from a jug,
a doorhandle turns to let in happiness
and a doll spreadeagled on the floor says
I am the resurrection and the life.

And all the time
we won't let them alone –
eyes change what they look at,
ears never stop making their multiple translations
and the right hand refutes the meaning
of what the left hand is doing.

November 1975

Midnight encounter

Of all the roses on the rose bush
the head of one lolled over the fence,
a fiery bucolic seraph
contemplating the weather
in heavenly turnip fields.

What must have been a man
came from the house and, saying nothing,

326]

snipped off the rose
and gave it to me.

At home
I look at it and am not blinded,
I touch it and am not burned.

And I see what must have been a man
silently go back into his house
with a star by his side, a twinkle
of heavenly secateurs.

November 1975

1,800 feet up

The flower – it didn't know it –
was called dwarf cornel.
I found this out by enquiring.

Now I remember the name
but have forgotten the flower.

– The curse of literacy.

And the greed for knowing. –
I'll have to contour again
from the Loch of the Red Corrie
to the Loch of the Green Corrie
to find what doesn't know its name,
to find what doesn't even know
it's a flower.

Since I believe in correspondences
I shrink in my many weathers
from whoever is contouring immeasurable space
to find what I am like – this forgotten thing
he once gave a name to.

November 1975

Kingfisher

That kingfisher jewelling upstream
seems to leave a streak of itself behind it
in the bright air. The trees
are all the better for its passing.

It's not a mineral eater, though it looks it:
It doesn't nip nicks out of the edges
of rainbows. – It dives
into the burly water, then, perched
on a Japanese bough, gulps
into its own incandescence
a wisp of minnow, a warrior stickleback.
– Or it vanishes into its burrow, resplendent
Samurai, returning home
to his stinking slum.

November 1975

Close-ups of summer

That creepycrawly traversing the stone
six inches from my nose makes me a caveman
fanned by pterodactyls and roared at
by dinosaurs.

A butterfly dangles by, delicate
as a carrot leaf. If only it could write
its flowery memoirs. If only it could paint
the rich halls it has visited.

The weather doodles a faint cloud
on the blue
then pensively washes it out,
making the blue boastful.

There's something whirring
in the cat's mouth. It opens it

and a beetle flies out. The cat
is Amazement, in fur.

Hens sloven. But the cock
struts by – one can almost see
the tiny set of bagpipes
he's sure he's playing.

The sun's the same – pipemajoring
across space, where the invisible judges
sit, wrapped in their knowledge,
taking terrible notes.

November 1975

Unposted birthday card

I would like to give you
a thought like a precious stone
and precious stones a thought
couldn't think of.

When you see the lolling tongues
in the shadows, I would like to change them
to gentle candles whose grace
would reveal only yours.

I would like to place you
where the fact of the fairytale
and the fact of the syllogism
make one quiet room
with a fire burning.

I would like to give you
a whole succession of birthdays
that would add up only
to this one: that would be
without years.

December 1975

Ancestry

The ghosts I never saw
and don't believe in
won't go away.

They speak to me
but won't answer me.
When I whirl round
They're never there.

Should I be rural
and put out food for them?
– I'm not Homeric enough
to leave on the table
a bowl of blood.

And there's no need for that –
they drink mine.

December 1975

Down-to-earth heaven

Two harpsichords playing –
and there's a robust heaven:
no lackadaisical boredom of the infinite here,
no epicene angels being languid,
not a golden pavement in sight.
The logic of passion, made articulate,
invents fibres in the listening mind
that shape it from shapelessness.
A marriage is happening
in the holy precinct of reason – a consecration
of the elements of being – each
in its own distinction. They make it possible
to believe in the original Word that changed
being to becoming.

Cupola, half shell of white air,
vault of the idea of snowdrops,

white balance of forces,
you are the proper pureness to contain
this revelation of the ordinary
where the coloured windows let in
no light that's intrusive
and the corrupt mind is healed, for a time,
of its corruption –
in a shadowless place,
a place of benign voltages.

January 1976

Water

So that water might be
elephantine and pinpoint,
what an industry of air,
what transformations of heat.
And water goes off – it skulks
through the cracks in rocks,
jemmying them open:
or advances on parade, covering counties
with banners and bannerets. It trickles
nursery rhymes. It stuns a landscape
with its soft piledriver. It woos
planks ashore and liltingly
draws ships down
through its diminishing light.
A tree is its image, a bud
its cold candle flame, its amethyst,
its baby Lucifer and star of the morning.
The wastrel sun huffs off, but its light
is stored in ponds and lakes –
they beam in the dark, rustling
with the gentlest of frictions.

What mindlessness
in the buffeting of tides:
what revelation in a drizzling spray

with a round rainbow in it:
what lucidity
in the glass a woman hands
to a man.

January 1976

Waxwing

Waxwing, smart gentleman, gaudy bank manager
in your leafy bank, your swept-back crest
is the only thing about you that looks wind-blown.
Do you never face down-wind
or fly across the grain of a breeze?
Do you look with hauteur
when the grebe's crest frays sideways
and the lapwing's top-knot unravels?

I watch you choking down
plump, crimson berries – and the bank manager becomes
a lorry driver in a hurry
gobbling and gulping
in the wayside café of this branchy cotoneaster.

So many colours being busy at once!
Such a dandified gluttony!

You flirt to another branch:
and the wax-blob berry on your either side
winks among the clusters.

February 1976

Intrusion of the human

On the tiny sea, with an archipelago of two islands,
a breeze wanders aimlessly about,
snail-trailing over mucous water, depositing
small sighs on the sand.

A day for mermaids. A day for their inhuman eyes
and voices without vibrato. Shell mirrors
keep sinking from sight.

In the kingdom of fish whole parliaments are on the move
and guerrillas lurk
in the ruins and cellars of weed.

And in the history of light a peregrine
shoots from a sea cliff. Before its moment is over
a song will have ended, a flight
stalled in a zero of the air.

An implacable scenario – till
round the skulled headland a tiny sail
loafs into view. And everything
becomes its setting. Everything shrugs together
round a blue hull and a brown sail. Everything's changed
by the human voices carelessly travelling over
the responding water, through the translated kingdoms.

February 1976

Poems for Angus*

Notes on a winter journey, and a footnote

I

The snow's almost faultless. It bounces back
the sun's light but can do nothing with
those two stags, their cold noses, their yellow teeth.

2

On the loch's eye a cataract is forming.
Fistfuls of white make the telephone wires
loop after loop of snow buntings.

3

So few cars, they leave the snow snow.
I think of the horrible marzipan
in the streets of Edinburgh.

* The following twelve poems are presented in sequence, as in their original publication.

4

The hotel at Ullapool, that should be a bang of light,
is crepuscular. The bar is fireflied
with whisky glasses.

5

At Inchnadamph snow is falling. The windscreen wipers
squeak and I stare through
a segment of a circle. What more do I ever do? ...

6

(Seventeen miles to go. I didn't know it, but when
I got there a death waited for me – that segment
shut its fan: and a blinding winter closed in.)

April 1976

A. K. MacLeod

I went to the landscape I love best
and the man who was its meaning and added to it
met me at Ullapool.

The beautiful landscape was under snow
and was beautiful in a new way.

Next morning, the man who had greeted me
with the pleasure of pleasure
vomited blood
and died.

Crofters and fishermen and womenfolk, unable
to say any more, said,
'It's a grand day, it's a beautiful day.'

And I thought, 'Yes, it is.'
And I thought of him lying there,
the dead centre of it all.

March 1976

Highland funeral

Over the dead man's house, over his landscape
the frozen air was a scrawny psalm
I believed in, because it was pagan
as he was.

Into it the minister's voice
spread a pollution of bad beliefs.
The sanctimonious voice dwindled away
over the boring, beautiful sea.

The sea was boring, as grief is,
but beautiful, as grief is not.
Through grief's dark ugliness I saw that beauty
because he would have.

And that darkened the ugliness ... Can the dead
help? I say so. Because, a year later,
that sanctimonious voice is silent and the pagan
landscape is sacred in a new way.

January 1977

A month after his death

An accordion and a fiddle
fit nimbly together their different natures
with such bouncing wit it makes small
the darkness outside that goes straight up
for ever and ever.

Out there are the dregs of history. Out there
mindlessness lashes the sea against the sea-wall:
and a bird flies screaming over the roof.

We laugh and we sing, but we all know we're thinking
of the one who isn't here.

The laughter and the singing are paper flowers
laid on a wet grave in an empty darkness.
For we all know we're thinking
of the one who can't be here,
not even as a ghost smiling through the black window.

January 1978

Triple burden

I know I had my death in me
from the moment I yelled upside-down
in the world.

Now I have another death in me: yours.
Each is the image of the other.

To carry two deaths
is a burden for any man:
and it's a heavy knowledge that tells me
only the death I was born with
will destroy the other.

For a boat has sailed into
the sea of unknowing;
you are on board.

And somewhere another boat
rocks
by another pier.

It's waiting to take me
where I'll never know you again –
a voyage
beyond knowledge, beyond memory.

May 1977

Comforter

Thank God you don't tell me
to stop thinking of him –
that I'm grieving, not for him,
but for my loss
– for, though that's true,
my grief is also
his celebration of me.

February 1977

Praise of a man

He went through a company like a lamplighter –
see the dull minds, one after another,
begin to glow, to shed
a benificent light.

He went through a company like
a knifegrinder – see the dull minds
scattering sparks of themselves,
becoming razory, becoming useful.

He went through a company
as himself. But now he's one
of the multitudinous company of the dead
where are no individuals.

The benificent lights dim
but don't vanish. The razory edges
dull but still cut. He's gone: but you can see
his tracks still, in the snow of the world.

November 1977

From his house door

I say to myself, How he enriched my life.
And I say to myself, More than he have died,
he's not the only one.

I look at the estuary and see
a gravel bank and a glitter going through it
and the stealthy tide, black-masked,
drowning stone after stone.

June 1977

Angus's dog

Black collie, do you remember yourself?

Do you remember your name was Mephistopheles,
though (as if you were only a little devil)
everyone called you Meph?

You'd chase everything – sea gulls, motor cars,
jet planes. (It's said you once set off
after a lightning flash.) Half over a rock,
you followed the salmon fly arcing
through the bronze water. You loved everything
except rabbits – though
you grinned away under the bed
when your master came home
drink taken. How you'd lay your head
on a visitor's knee and look up, so soulfully,
like George Eliot playing Sarah Bernhardt.

… Black Meph, how can you remember yourself
in that blank no-time, no-place where
you can't even greet your master
though he's there too?

December 1977

Dead friend

How do I meet
a man who's no longer there?
How can I lament the loss
of a man who won't go away?

How can I be changed
by changelessness?

I stand in my gloomy field
like a Pictish carving
that keeps its meaning but is, too, weathered
into another one.

February 1977

In memoriam

On that stormy night
a top branch broke off
on the biggest tree in my garden.

It's still up there. Though its leaves
are withered black among the green
the living branches
won't let it fall.

November 1976

Defeat

What I think of him,
what I remember of him
are gifts I can't give
to anyone.

For all I can say of him
is no more
than a scribble in the margin
of a lost manuscript.

January 1978

End of Poems for Angus sequence

In all that whiteness

The air was on the point of creaking. Every overhang
was fanged with icicles. No bird stirred
on the white mountains.

In my head was a glass of wine, a ruby,
a poppy head in the wilderness.

The snow squeaked under my feet, the cold
clasped my two wrists.

But in my head was something that excused me
to the weather. I apologised to the air
that spidered on my face.

I was warm with the place I was going to
and the woman in it. They made
the one glowing thing in a winter landscape.
I walked through it, balancing
my lantern head.

April 1976

Miss Botticelli 1976

You'd never come ashore, cool Aphrodite,
on the frothy knuckles of waves. If you stood,
lasciviously still, on the most perfect scallop shell,
it would turn and dwindle you away.

For you're no landward lassie. You're the white enigma
of faking distances. Smoothly you wheel and turn
on meandering sea surfaces, still figure
of marble mists.

Yet across the bleakest haze
of a city bar, of a slip-slop café,
I suddenly see you looking at me
with a look I should drown in.
My glass wobbles down on the table

340]

like a landing helicopter. I take your hand
and you teach me beautiful things
about garbage cans and supermarkets
and the Poseidon policeman standing
where four currents meet.

April 1976

Fulfilled ambition

With too much leg and not enough wing
the daddylonglegs helicopters
about the room,
outer space to him, where the lamp
blazes like Saturn.

A while ago,
this stumbling brown fragility
was a monster guzzling in the potato patch.

Then he was full of purpose
(without knowing it).
How he munched and munched – and all to become
that endearing eccentric now hanging
by one toe from the ceiling.

I nurse him outside and toss him
into a night full of planets.

April 1976

The shifts of spring

The gean tree invisibly unwrinkles its leaves.
A fox lies among hundreds of green croziers
that will uncoil and be bracken. From between two stones
in the Bay of Stinking Fish an otter protrudes
its World War One face, before bonelessly slipping
into the seamless water.

My mind is full of shifting planes
like cards in a conjuror's hands. They make

341]

fans and concertinas and cascades
and sudden stills –
the ace of hearts: the five of clubs.
Am I changing in this weather
of transformation? I feel I'm a string
of trick shots in a film that's being made
without a camera.

I think of stolid summer
lying for miles on its fat haunches, hardly bothering
to reach up and pull down a cloud:
or winter, walking in its bones and greeting you
round any corner with its silly giggle:
or autumn, beautifully moping, pregnantly
self-obsessed.

But the cards slither and I'm staring at
the joker of spring. I steady myself. I take a straight look …
The fox has gone. But the gean tree's still working away
and the Old Bill otter's now peering across No-man's-land
from a dug-out camouflaged
with bladderwrack and blue bursts
of mussels.

April 1976

Notations of ten summer minutes

A boy skips flat stones out to sea – each does fine
till a small wave meets it head on and swallows it.
The boy will do the same.

The schoolmaster stands looking out of the window
with one Latin eye and one Greek one.
A boat rounds the point in Gaelic.

Out of the shop comes a stream
of Omo, Weetabix, BiSoDol tablets and a man
with a pocket shaped like a whisky bottle.

Lord V. walks by with the village in his pocket.
Angus walks by
spending the village into the air.

A melodeon is wheezing a clear-throated jig
on the deck of the *Arcadia*. On the shore hills Pan
cocks a hairy ear; and falls asleep again.

The ten minutes are up, except they aren't.
I leave the village, except I don't.
The jig fades to silence, except it doesn't.

April 1976

Heroes

The heroes of legend
and the heroes of history
met, by looking
in a mirror.

And the heroes of legend
capered with joy,
crying,
'We're real, we're real!'

And the heroes of history
wept with rage
and wanted
to smash the mirror.

But that would mean they'd cease
to exist. So they dried their eyes
and assumed once more
their insufferable poses.

April 1976

Survivors

The last wolf in Scotland
was killed two centuries ago.

I'd like to meet it.

I wouldn't ask
why it opened the throats of deer and
tore mountain hares to pieces.
I wouldn't ask why it howled
in the corries and put one paw
delicately in a mountain torrent.

– It would have nothing to ask me
except, 'Why am I
the last wolf in Scotland?'

I would know what it meant,
for I am the last of my race
as you are, and she, and he.

We would look strangely at each other
before it loped back to its death
and I again put one foot
dangerously into the twentieth century.

May 1976

Scale

The wind was howling with a Shakespearean howling.
Leaves scuttered by in a canto of Dante.
Aeschylus lit that watchfire on a glass crag.
– But what moved us most was the glimpse we had
Of pale Catullus stealing through sidestreets.

October 1976

No interims in history

Barbarians! growled Attila
as the pile of skulls mounted higher.
What fun! squealed Robespierre,
shaking the gloved hand of Monsieur Guillotin.
The sword of the Lord! roared Cromwell
while the church and the people in it
became a stack of fire.

It would be good to think
that Attila felt a headache coming on,
that Monsieur Guillotin fingered the crick in his neck,
that Cromwell had a grey taste on his tongue

– while, as now, the dove
flew wildly over the world
finding nowhere to land,
growing weaker and weaker.

October 1976

Folio

To think of Gertrude as a blonde
is difficult – but peep round the arras
and see her writhing whitely on a bed
with her honest, stodgy brother-in-law.

Fortinbras is being brave somewhere
and Rosencrantz and Guildenstern are being sick
into the North Sea.

Leatherworkers are tooling and engraving
and housewives are wishing it was
the children's bedtime and that their husbands
won't come home too drunk. Lovers
look in vain for the famous cliffs.

Ophelia is troubled about her low blood count
but forces herself to go off
to her flower-arrangement class.

Shakespeare's mind, which hasn't been invented yet,
will translate all this
into gothic glooms and ghosts and garrulities. It'll omit
the leatherworkers and the housewives;
but prodigious sentences will batman on battlements
and poisonous ideas will seep through interminable corridors
to where Hamlet sits in a buzz of flies,
pretending, for Shakespeare's sake, to be fat.

November 1976

Intruder in a set scene

The way the water goes is blink blink blink.
That heap of trash was once
a swan's throne. The swans now lean their chests
against the waves that spill on Benbecula.
On the towpath a little girl
peers over the handle of the pram she's pushing.
Her mother follows her, reading a letter.

Everything is winter, everything
is a letter from another place, measuring
absence. Everything laments
the swan, drifting and dazzling on a western sealoch.

– But the little girl, five years of self-importance,
walks in her own season, not noticing
the stop-go's of water, the mouldering swan-throne,
the tears turning cold in the eyes of her mother.

November 1976

Back from holiday

Did you have good weather? they say –
meaning, *Did the sun shine? was it warm?*
could you see the tops of the mountains?

And I thought of the sea
scraped white by the wind, and the clouds
stampeding on their high prairies.

And I thought
of the ugly face of Socrates –
made beautiful by the grave illuminations
of the ideas behind it.

November 1976

Consequences

What you've done to me
by way of enlargements and illuminations
puzzled me till I thought of
what a kettle and an apple
did to James Watt and Sir Isaac Newton.

If you say (smilingly), 'Ah,
but you're neither of these gentlemen,'
I can only reply (weakly), 'Nor are you
an apple or a kettle.'

What I know is, you've enlightened
my sense of gravity and raised in me
such a head of steam I'm filled
with new inventions.

My lazy bones that slept in the sun
bustle about
in an industrious revolution.
– Will you accept

my sudden discoveries, whose patent number
(they've all got the same one)
is in the telephone directory?

December 1976

Being offered a Time Machine

Chat with Bonny Prince Charlie? – he'd stare at me
with wet, tartan eyes and
help himself to another swig.

Buddha? I'd be the goose
that couldn't say Bo-tree. And anyway
I can't sit in my own lap.

I could speak to Socrates, but
I'm scared of being made a fool of – my blush
would floodlight the Parthenon.

If I liked being picked up with tweezers
I could talk to Goethe;
but I don't.

Now Napoleon on Elba: we could sympathise with each other
about exile. – But in no time
I'd be recruiting cavalry.

Nero would play a tune, and I'm musical.
I'd finish up among the lampreys.

And Bach: his genius is so formidable
he'd terrify me – he'd teach me
the true meaning of fugue.

… It's too difficult. I'll curl up in my Timex
and be scared enough there, watching
the frightening present becoming
the frightening past.

December 1976

Connoisseur

The rain makes a drumming on the roof
and a splish-splash on the road.
Nothing makes one sound only.

That cloud is a camel, a weasel, a whale.
Hamlet was right. Nothing
has only one appearance.

I collect
Your laughter, your talk, your weeping.
I collect your hundred of semblances.

I store you in the cabinet of my mind
I'm a connoisseur, in love with the value only
of priceless things.

Though my eyes blur, I look at these treasures.
Though my hands tremble, I touch them.
Though my heart grieves, I love them.

And a seed falls from a tree and
in its lowly cabinet sets about
creating forests.

                                        February 1977

Adrift

More like a raft than a boat
the world I sail on.

I say I'm not troubled – I accept
the powerful hospitality of the tides.

But I write little communications and float them off
to anywhere.

Some are Ophelias witless and singing
among the foam flowers.

349]

But others are Orpheus lamenting
a harbour, a house there, and a girl in it.

February 1977

Tighnuilt – the House of the Small Stream

for Charlie Ross

In a corner of Kirkaig,
in a wild landscape, he created
a garden, a small Eden
of fruit trees, flowers and regimental
vegetables. Such labour. Such love.

It's still there, though he is not.
To remember him is to put that garden
in another place. It shines
in the desolate landscape of loss –
a small Eden, of use and of beauty.

I visit him there
between the mountains and the sea.
We sit by a small stream
that will never run dry.

February 1977

Request

What I'd like for my birthday
is a box of telepathy,
a bottle of clairvoyance
and a gift of tongues.

Then I wouldn't need
to sit hunched up in my memory
staring at a screen of images
and listening to a voice
I can't converse with –

and anything I'd say
would need no translation.

– Everything would shrink
to the biggest thing of all,
the immediacy of meaning –
but with one language still to use,
the language of touch, the speechless
vocabulary of hands.

March 1977

Rowan berry

I'm at ease in my crimson cluster.
The tree blazes
with clusters of cousins –
my cluster's the main one and I
am the important berry in it.

Tomorrow, or tomorrow's tomorrow,
a flock of fieldfares
will gobble our whole generation.

I'm not troubled. My seed
will be shamelessly dropped
somewhere. And in the next years
after next year, I'll be a tree
swaying and swinging
with a genealogy of berries. I'll be
that fine thing, an ancestor.
I'll spread out my branches
for the guzzling fieldfares.

April 1977

Highland games

They sit on the heather slopes
and stand six deep round the rope ring.
Keepers and shepherds in their best plus-fours
who live mountains apart
exchange gossip and tall stories.
Women hand out sandwiches,
rock prams and exchange
small stories and gossip.
The Chieftain leans his English accent
on a five-foot crook and feels
one of the natives.

The rope ring is full
of strenuous metaphors.
Eight runners shoulder each other
eight times round it – a mile
against the clock that will kill them.

Little girls breasted only with medals translate
a tune that will outlast them
with formalised legs and
antler arms. High jumpers
come down to earth and,
in the centre
a waddling 'heavy' tries to throw
the tree of life in one straight line.

Thank God for the bar, thank God
for the Games Night Dance – even though they end
in the long walk home
with people no longer here – with exiles and deaths –
your nearest companions.

May 1977

Cormorants nesting

In this nest, newly hatched ones. Little creatures,
you're not the prettiest things in the world.

In that one, three others, each a foot long,
are one smudge of dark, downy feathers.

Bend close to that egg and you'll hear,
astonishingly, a *peep-peep* inside it. Little creature,
you're not the wisest thing in the world.

Heraldic fathers and mothers
take off and slide down a slope in the air
to the safe sea

where five seals lucently regard us. One submerges
and swims off,
its ankles tied together.

June 1977

Cock before dawn

Those dabbing hens I ferociously love
sag on their perches, half deflated.
I'll have none of it. I'm regimental. A plumbline
goes from my head to my toes. I burnish
the dark with my breast.

Lucifer's my blood brother. When I spread my wings
I'm crystal battlements and thunderbolts. I tread the earth
by pretending not to.

The West and the East are measured from me ...
It's time I crowed. The sun will be waiting.

June 1977

Thinned turnips

The ones we left lay flat on the ground.
Soft rain, sun, soft rain and they're up and sturdy.

Is that what you think you do, death and the god of war,
crouching along between the rows?

As if you left only
the best among us. As if your grasping hands
threw only the trash
on the rotting heap in the corner.

June 1977

Off Coigeach Point

Flat sea, thin mist
and a seal singing.
– And the world's an old man in his corner
telling a folktale.

Haddock goggle up, are
swung aboard. Gray as the sea mist.
They drown in air.

In the fishbox they
have nothing to do with death. They've become
a fine-line drawing
in the art gallery
of the world.

We make for home.

Near Soya
Seven seals oilily slide off a skerry
into the silky gray. Norman tells me
if he puts the engine into reverse
they turn
a back somersault.

And he does.
And they do.

June 1977*

354]

Ineducable me

I don't learn much, I'm a man
of no improvements. My nose still snuffs the air
in an amateurish way. My profoundest ideas
were once toys on the floor, I love them, I've licked
most of the paint off. A whisky glass
is a rattle I don't shake. When I love
a person, a place, an object, I don't see
what there is to argue about.

I learned words, I learned words: but half of them
died for lack of exercise. And the ones I use
often look at me
with a look that whispers, *Liar.*

How I admire the eider duck that dives
with a neat loop and no splash and the gannet that suddenly
harpoons the sea. – I'm a guillemot
that still dives
in the first way it thought of: poke your head under
and fly down.

                                                  June 1977

Report to the clan

His skin is in tatters, his face
is shiny, his feet have no toes!
He never climbs trees! – He burns things
before he eats them!
Run, brothers, run
from this visitor from the past!

This was said by
the first ape that saw Darwin.

                                                  August 1977

Me as traveller

The toy yacht and the clockwork liner
were bad prophets. I was to be
a bold rover? I was to carry the globe
in a stringbag of voyages?

Happy the man, I mutter,
who's had no need to travel
anywhere. I crisscross the glebe
of small Scotland and settle for
one small part of it.

America, Italy, Canada, I rested on you
briefly as a butterfly and returned
to suck the honey of Assynt
and want no more, though that honey
has three bitternesses in it, three deaths
more foreign to me
than the other side of space.

                                        September 1977

Classical translation

Venus, familiar name, means
thinking of you.

I love Venus and she smiles on me
with no condescension.

She comes to me like eyes, like hair,
like breasts. She comes like laughter
and sad weeping.

The other gods move off – spluttering Mars,
manic Neptune, even Pluto – even,
to my grief, friendly Apollo.

But wise Minerva stays near.
She whispers to me the meaning
of eyes and hair and breasts. She tells me
how your laughter and your weeping
are the children of Venus
and are not to be separated.

September 1977

A day and us

The day laid out for inspection
a tower, two dogs, a path by a hulking river
over which the sun stole leaves
from a painting by Pissarro.

The day wasn't in business.
It said without saying it,
They're there: take them or leave them.

We did both. And now
one of the rooms in my mind
is a boutique with huge trinkets of trees
(that blackbird!), a swathe of sea,
a sky-high goblet of clear air and
the many other things. I spread
my oriental hands and say,
None for sale. I rub
my hands together and say,
None for sale, not one of them for sale.

That room is a replica
of a room in your mind. Though you're there
and I'm here, let's look together
at a line of crags, a cannon and
the hurtling river with the ferryboat
crocodiled on the far bank.

November 1977*

Cupid

Zen archer, plump
with your cloudy flesh,
master of disguises and sly deceiver
of house detectives

– we all know your mother
was Venus. But you keep very quiet
about your father – slippery Mercury, god
of debit and credit and inventor
of double-entry book-keeping.

When you loosed that arrow
my heart is inflamed with, see how you juggled
the rate of exchange. Fat Cupid,
I jingle my fat profits and with them
buy little presents for the lady
who, wounded by you,
gave them to me in the first place.

November 1977

Ends and means

The club of Hercules
wept all the time –
it didn't want
to hurt anything.

Cuchulain's spear
cursed the magic
that forced it to be
infallible.

The brain of Nero
couldn't sleep for thinking
of the ideas that Ego
formed from it.

And what about
the men in armies,
the so many men
in so many armies?

November 1977

Fisherman

Look at my hands –
pickled like vegetables. Look at the secret crystals
in my knee joints and shoulders. My eyelids' rims
are drawn in blood, I stare at horizons
through eyes bleached with salt other than theirs.

I step ashore on to a lurching world.
I go to a bed between waves that sails me
into the dogfish nightmare, the horror film
of crabs.

Yet somewhere mermaids, whom I don't believe in,
are supple with their combs, are supply singing,
and (though I don't believe it) the halcyon nests
bluely in a blue miracle.

Tomorrow I'll go out again – the god of the sea,
who doesn't exist, has strayed my wits –
to sail over treasures and under treasures,
and when I come back my bunched hands
will be full of things no one will see –
that the loud auctioneer
could sell to nobody.

November 1977

Real life Christmas card

Robin, I watch you. You are perfect robin –
except, shouldn't you be perched on a spade handle?

Robin, you watch me. Am I perfect man – except,
shouldn't I have a trap in my pocket, a gun in my hand?

I, too, am in my winter plumage, not unlike yours,
except, the red is in my breast, not on it.

You sing your robin song, I my man song. They're different,
but they mean the same: winter, territory, greed.

Will we survive, bold eyes, to pick
the seeds in the ground, the seeds in my mind?

The snow man thinks so. Look at his silly smile
slushily spilling down the scarf I gave him.

December 1977

Little Boy Blue

Are you dreaming of the big city,
of movies and bus stops and supermarkets?
Or of some girl in swirly petticoats
crossing another field with a milking pail in her hand?

Or have you been listening to the news
on the telly? – are you taking
industrial action?

Whatever way, blow your horn for me.
For my sheep are in the meadow, my cows
are trampling the brave corn flat –
and I watch them with indifference.

You look from under your feathery hat
at me dozing under a haystack
and slowly, deliciously
close your nursery eyes that rhyme with mine.

January 1978

Sea change

I think of Lycidas drowned
in Milton's mind.
How elegantly he died. How languorously
he moved
in those baroque currents. No doubt
sea nymphs wavered round him
in melodious welcome.

And I think of Roddy drowned
off Cape Wrath, gulping
fistfuls of salt, eyes bursting, limbs thrashing
the ponderous green. – No elegance here,
nor in the silent welcome
of conger and dogfish and crab.

January 1978

Equilibrist

I see an adder and, a yard away,
a butterfly being gorgeous. I switch the radio
from tortures in foreign prisons
to a sonata of Schubert (that foreigner).
I crawl from the swamp of nightmare into
a glittering rainfall, a swathing of sunlight.

Noticing you can do nothing about.
It's the balancing that shakes my mind.

What my friends don't notice
is the weight of joy in my right hand
and the weight of sadness in my left.
All they see is MacCaig being upright,
easy-oasy and jocose.

I had a difficulty in being friendly
to the Lord, who gave us these burdens,

so I returned him to other people
and totter without help
among his careless inventions.

February 1978

Two friends

The last word this one spoke
was my name. The last word
that one spoke
was my name.

My two friends
had never met. But when they said
that last word
they spoke to each other.

I am proud to have given them a language
of one word, a narrow space
in which, without knowing it,
they met each other at last.

February 1978

The Kirk

Petitions pour into the Big House.
Haven't the people learned yet that God
is an absentee landlord?

In some Bahamas in the sky
he basks in his own sun,
reaching down through the clouds only
for the price of suffering with which to pay
a pittance to his estate workers.
In their mournful robes they patch fences
and board up the windows smashed
by theological vandals.

When he's not feeling too good, the Lord,
lounging by his infinite swimming pool, thinks
The sins of the fathers will be visited upon the children
and thanks God
that he is his own ancestor.

February 1978

Puffin

Where the small burn
spreads into the sea loch
I found the mad, clever clown's beak
of a puffin.

How many times
had it whirled into its burrow
with a six-fold whisker
of tiny fishes?
How many times
had it grunted love
to its parrot-faced lover?

I clack my own beak
by my own burrow
to feel how many little fishes
I've whiskered home, and
I grunt and grunt
before whirling off again
into the huge sea spaces.

February 1978

Earwig

You have more nicknames
than legs – some so strange, clipshears,
you'd think people give nicknames
to your nicknames.

Lord God, Saviour, Father,
your nicknames are
ingratiating flatteries.

Devil, Auld Nick, Clootie,
your nicknames
are shuddering familiarities.

I watch you, hornie-goloch,
trekking blindly across
the Gobi Desert of the floor.

Nickname the floor Life:
that's what I trek across.

But nobody ever
nicknamed me. I feel deprived.
Shall I call myself Earwig
and trek manfully on, seeking
the crumb of comfort,
the sighing, shining oasis?

February 1978

Thorns

It's usual to dislike them.
Yet what's more friendly?
What says all the time
Stay here. Don't go away?

You prune roses for the roses' sake.
They say *Glory and honour*
as they die in a blue jug.

Their incantation is no less true
than the thorn's message
– that round, red bead
on your startled thumb.

February 1978

Journeys

Travelling's fine – the stars tell me that,
and waves, and wind, and trees in the wind
tugging to go farther than their feet will let them.
Poor feet, clogged with the world.

Travelling's fine – when she's at the end of it,
or mountains breathing their vivid Esperanto,
or ideas flashing from
their always receding headlands.

There are other bad journeys, to a bitter place
I can't get to – yet. I lean towards it,
tugging to get there, and thank God
I'm clogged with the world. It grips me,
I hold it.

December 1978

Toad

Stop looking like a purse. How could a purse
squeeze under the rickety door and sit,
full of satisfaction, in a man's house?

You clamber towards me on your four corners –
right hand, left foot, left hand, right foot.

I love you for being a toad,
for crawling like a Japanese wrestler,
and for not being frightened.

I put you in my purse hand, not shutting it,
and set you down outside directly under
every star.

A jewel in your head? Toad,
you've put one in mine,
a tiny radiance in a dark place.

December 1978

Impatience

From its distance
the tower clock clucks twelve times
like a hen the size of Ben Nevis.

How to go on? I can no more
reach the end of this hour
than a snail can jump over a straw.

(Along the canal four young men scull
their needle of a boat, drawing a thread behind them
on the seamless garment of the water.)

I'm happy and unhappy. In my head
there's a lark singing
in a bogful of mist.

(That hawthorn smell
is a hospital room
with a man dying in it.)

Ends and beginnings –
they're seamless too.
For the tower clock
clears its throat of a dozen pigeons
and clucks
once.

I see her coming, and walk towards her
out of this trash of metaphor
into the simplicity
that explains everything.

                                        December 1978

Bird of which feather?

All very well for hens,
sauntering about their pedestrian precincts.

But what of the ptarmigan surfacing through the snow
with a cropful of heather tips – to be mugged
by an eagle?

Or the linnet
dodging through the mountain traffic of hawks and falcons
and being arrested by a merlin
for flying too slow?

Or the tern
whose engine begins to fail
on his one-way street
from Cape Town to Stromness? ...

And me? – I scuffle in the pedestrian precinct
of my mind ... but is it safe? If so, why
do I keep peering into the shadowy doorways
for the white glint, the brown glare
of an elegant fox?

December 1978

Memorials

Everywhere place names
jut up from history, carved
1314, 1066, 1939. Or last summer.

Each holds up in exhausted arms
a battle, a birth, a martyrdom. Or last summer.

The sad ones have no tears left. The happy ones
are filled with a music no one understands any more.

Last summer is beautiful and sad:
a full-rigged ship in a bottle.

I put it there. Now it sails only
in a dream of history,
tiny, ornamental and useless.

December 1978

Winter garden

The dunnock in the hedge – is he fearful
or fastidious? His eyes are fixed on the bird table
where five free-for-all sparrows
peck in a shower bath of crumbs.

A mouse zigzags
among the frozen raspberry canes,
going nowhere elaborately.

Three apple trees look as if they'd get on rehearsing
as Macbeth's witches
if they had the energy.

And, only seven hours old,
the day begins to die.

– The sparrows have gone, telling everybody, and the dunnock
is giving us all
a lesson in table manners.

December 1978*

The way it goes

Reality isn't what it used to be,
I mutter gloomily
when I feel like Cortez on his peak in Darien
and then remember it wasn't Cortez at all
and feel more like him than ever.

January 1979

Genealogy

The countless generations
that have gone to produce – me.

Was the man right who said
an oak tree is just an elaborate way
of making an acorn?

368]

But it's an acorn,
not a stone.

I say this to console myself
in my barren moods, aware
of the leafy generations above me
accepting the sun and giving it to the world
in fertile translation.

January 1979*

Rag and bone

That sun ray has raced to us
at those millions of miles an hour.
But when it reaches the floor of the room
it creeps slower than a philosopher,
it makes a bright puddle
that alters like an amoeba,
it climbs the door
as though it were afraid it would fall.

In a few minutes it'll make this page
an assaulting dazzle. I'll pull a curtain
sideways. I'll snip
a few yards off those millions of miles
and, tailor of the universe, sit quietly
stitching my few ragged days together.

January 1979

Blue tit on a string of peanuts

A cubic inch of some stars
weighs a hundred tons – Blue tit,
who could measure the power
of your tiny spark of energy? Your hair-thin legs
(one north-east, one due west) support
a scrap of volcano, four inches
of hurricane: and, seeing me, you make the sound

of a grain of sawdust being sawn
by the minutest of saws.

February 1979

A man I know

That cold man with bad poems to his discredit
stands, swirling his beer round and round,
among his friends but not with them.

I imagine him in a tropical forest
clambering hugely from tree to tree,
throwing silence down like a shadow.

Or he sits in a library: and a thousand books
whisper together, trying to make out
his small print.

It's necessary to suppose that inside him
there's a suffering fire,
if only because it sometimes splutters
as lockjawed poems,
illegible messages from loneliness,
the smudged fingerprints of desperation.

March 1979*

Writing a letter

With what colours will I daub
the meaning of these words? I hesitate over
the palette of everything, wondering
which is the gayest, which is on the point
of exploding with joy.

And gray, the shy one, tries
not to be noticed. It bows its head,
smiling quietly to itself. Already it knows
I'll brush it, so gently,
over my gaudy meanings. They'll come to you
like a little girl in a plain frock

coming to tea. Knees together, hands in her lap,
she'll say *Please*, and I'll wait anxiously
for the small voice also to say *Thank you*.

March 1979

Spring day

That green alone
proves the foolishness of King Midas.
Spring wears no ass's ears. Its gold
will be buried and come up again
as snowdrops and tender grass blades.

A blackbird on a roof top
is warblingly meditating
on the philosophical concept
of being a blackbird.

And outrageous energies
swarm on the gean tree;
they bend their backs and slowly haul out
the first, the second bud.

April 1979

Autobiographical note

The Calton Jail, it used to be.
When I was a boy
a man was hanged there at eight in the morning.

In its place now – St Andrew's House,
a papermaking mill of Civil Servants,
an ants' nest of bureaucrats.

My long shanks, pelmeted with short trousers,
storked me into the school opposite
where my long head under its plume of hair
sucked in words and choked
on mathematics.

From a classroom
I looked over a smoky valley and a royal palace
to a long curving cliff: Samson's Ribs.
Now, today, I stand by Nelson's Monument
regarding the ants' nest of bureaucrats.
They don't interest me.

It's best to turn round and watch the ships
sliding on the Firth of Forth. I don't know
where they've come from or where they're going to.

And that makes me think again
of the man, the lost traveller,
who years ago was hanged there at eight in the morning.

April 1979*

Jumping toad

Under the broad flat stone
was a metropolis of ants. By its edge
a toad sat, looking benign and grandmotherly –
it only needed specs.

Suddenly it floppily jumped,
little amateur – and swallowed
an ant that had left its home town.

The toad caught my eye with a look that said
You didn't think I had it in me, did you?

And I, dumbfounded, went off
whistling *Knees up, Mother Brown.*

August 1979

A true pleasure

Many's the stag I've seen running
behind his horizontal nose.

And cod, rubber-lipped, shabbily mottled
as though they'd lain too long in a dusty corner
of an antique shop at the bottom of the sea.

And sparrows that bustle and squabble
even when they're doing nothing –
each one a critic, and his own publisher.

I give them no pleasure.
But they give me a true pleasure
I can't explain, because it's without
superiority or humility.

See me smiling? I'm thinking of
the many grasshoppers I've seen
each crouched between the two triangles
of its own legs.

September 1979

Penelope

I thought they needed no Women's Lib.
in your day. And yet, there you are,
stuck with a lot of drunks
and your knitting and all that laundry:
unable even to slip out to the Mysteries.

Never mind. A dog is dying on a dunghill
and there's a boat in the bay.

He'll soon be home and you'll live happily
ever after, as long as you don't listen to him
muttering in his sleep
names you never heard of,
names like Calypso, names like Nausicaa.

October 1979

Balances (1979)

I like almost imperceptibles, near still lifes –
a limpet sloping full-tilt down a rock:
thunder mooching among mountains, trailing
delicate diminuendos: a mushroom
hoisting a paving slab on its darning-egg head:

and the brooch on her dress
rising so quietly, so quietly falling.

Don't judge me by that: I like suddennesses too –
fistfuls, platefuls, ewers of snow slithered
from a larch tree: the far away Chinese music
of gorse pods popping: a tower bell stunning
the black air of a black night with one dazing blow:

and a key turning in the door of a quiet house
when I didn't know she was coming.

November 1979*

Enough

I don't want to shuffle in a Greek Theatre
chanting powerful platitudes
while Nemesis, off-stage, gouges and stabs.

Or twangle a harp in an Irish castle
while the drunken louts, the great heroes,
quarrel over chess or lie with a snake-brained woman.

I don't want to be one of those who paused
between the walls of the Red Sea and thought with longing
of Egypt and the simmering fleshpots.

Enough for me to watch a new ice age
grind down the high tops of Scotland, the harbours
without a boat, the frozen minds
without a song.

November 1979

Hard division

No battle in the thrush – grenade of song
in the tangled gean-tree.

No politics in the newt – fat-legged saurian
in its lascivious jungle.

Morality? The gannet angles down its Concorde head
and crash dives into the mackerel host.

A free world, a world without hypocrisy, without masks.

Cramped with humanity, I envy them.

And I watch the concept *freedom*, that quick-change artist,
put on still another disguise:
and I think, without comfort –
the gentle worm is sinuous as a lawyer
but pleads no special cases.

November 1979

To create what?

Something small, like a new grass blade,
or a word like *love* with the lies
taken out of it, or a key
that would unlock the doors I myself made.

No hurricane, no revolution, no room
where a sane scientist
broods on the insanity he created.

Something small, like a gesture
as full of surrender
as the handful of earth thrown down on a coffin
or as marvellous
as the migration of swallows.

November 1979

375]

Helpless collector

Events come
bringing me presents –
more, as has been said, than the sands of the sea,
more, as has been said oftener, than the stars in the sky.

There's no refusal.

I'm the lucky possessor
of the ones that please me. I try to be
only the caretaker
of the ones I hate.

They won't let me.

I put the crooked mask
behind the delicate jar
and it moves to the front.

World of a Difference (about 1980)

Recipe

You have to be stubborn.
You have to turn away
from meditation, from ideologies,
from the tombstone face
of the Royal Bank of Scotland.

You have to keep stubbornly saying
This is bread, though it's in a sunset,
this is a sunset with bread in it.
This is a woman, she doesn't live
in a book or an imagination.
Hello, water, you must say, *Hello, good water*.

You have to touch wood, but not for luck.
You have to listen to that matter of pitches and crescendos
without thinking Beethoven is speaking
only to you.

And you must learn there are words
with no meaning, words like *consolation*,
words like *goodbye*.

January 1980

Circe

The strange wanderers – I was so good to them.
I disencumbered them
of their heavy embellishments, of their burdensome lies
and restored them to their truths. Pig was pig,
wolf was wolf, snake was snake.

But the gods, those bad civilisers,
came between me and Odysseus,
who sailed off with his companions, corrupt
with history, and left me desolate
for the one I loved, for the false image
of the one I'll never know.

January 1980

Also

You try to help, and what happens?
You hurt also.

You hoist a sail on a boat
and one day, gusted sideways,
the boat is scattered in timbers
round a slavering rock.
You put violets in water, and what happens?
They lose all their scent.

And you give absence and loneliness and fear
when you give love – that full sail,
that sweet water.

January 1980

Rewards and furies

In a ship hardly bigger than this room,
with a mind narrower than this pen,
with a library of one book
and that book with one word in it,
Columbus sailed and sailed and arrived.

The poor soul didn't know where.
Still, he succeeded:
Indians were massacred, railways
opened up wheatfields, jails and asylums,
and skyscrapers walked around
with atom bombs slung at their hips.

I hope Columbus didn't believe
in his own ghost. How could it rest
through these hundreds of years?
How could it stare into the future
at his monstrous descendants
ignorantly sailing, ignorantly arriving?

January 1980

Godot

I feel miserable, acting
their uncomprehending parts.
Don't they know they're waiting
for who's already there?

There I am, in their minds,
in their boots,
in the footlights: and worse,
in their incomprehension.

I can't even go
and sit in the audience,
since I'm there too.

I'm trapped. It seems
there's nothing to do
but wait
for something to happen.

February 1980

Family of long-tailed tits

Their twittering isn't avant-garde
or confessional or aleatory.
It doesn't quote other birds
or utter manifestos telling them
how to sing.

It's congruent with their way of flying,
for that, too,
is a sweetest, softest twittering
to the eye.

The clumsy, clever human
bumbles about in the space
between his actions and his words.
No congruence there.

He listens with envy
while their song flirts
from one twig of silence
to another one.

February 1980

Zeno, and his like

When Achilles, furious
for having let himself get mixed up
in such a ridiculous affair,
passed the tortoise with his first stride,
he left behind, also,
stupid philosophy, that's been muttering
And yet ... nevertheless ... all the same ...
ever since.

February 1980

Down and out

In a quarter of the city
where the streets try not to be noticed
Hope – in her old-fashioned clothes,
with her neglected hair-do –
pushes a pram.

Children try to play
but don't know how to.
Men with slack faces
lean on walls.

Hope trudges on, unnoticed
by everyone – except one old woman
who coos and gurgles over the pram
and the doll in it staring
at the nothing in nowhere
with manic blue eyes.

                                        February 1980

Queen of Scots

Mary was depressed.
She hadn't combed her red hair yet.
She hadn't touched her frightful Scottish breakfast.
Her lady-in-waiting, another Mary,
had told Rizzio Her Majesty wasn't at home,
a lie so obvious it was another way
of telling the truth.

Mary was depressed.
She wanted real life and here she was
acting in a real play, with real blood in it.

And she thought of the years to come
and of the frightful plays that would be written
about the play she was in.

380]

She said something in French
and with her royal foot she kicked
the spaniel that was gazing at her
with exophthalmic adoration.

February 1980

Go away, Ariel

Heartless, musical Ariel,
does everyone prefer Caliban to you,
as I do?

Supersonic Ariel, go zip round the world
or curl up in a cowslip's bell.
I'd rather be visited by Caliban.

As I am, I am. I chat with him
helplessly spilling out of an armchair,
scaly on the carpet.

I'm teaching him to smoke. It soothes him
when he blubbers about Miranda and
goes on about his mother.

Phone a bat, Ariel. Leave us
to have a good cry – to stare at each other
with recognition and loathing.

February 1980

Sad tale

When her life broke into smithereens
she wept north, south, east and west,
she cried for help into pillows,
through letterboxes – and past the stars
where, she remembered, someone was supposed to live
who looked after
even sparrows and lilies.

Her friends were sleepless,
comforting her and giving the advice
she pleaded for: till, exhausted,
they started discovering
urgent reasons for asking her to go.

And everywhere God's sparrows died
in their different ways. And she, a ghost already,
haunted her own loneliness
in a body where beauty had been, like the lilies
that rotted in the fine raiment God had given them.

March 1980*

Daedalus

He made a mousetrap
and his PRO man
called it a labyrinth.

It was to catch a mouse –
the local papers
called it a minotaur.

In the film they made of it
Theseus and Ariadne
got bit parts.

But the spectators loved them
(projections of themselves)
and called them stars.

Then Daedalus made his mistake.
He forced his son
to follow in daddy's wing-beats.

Icarus rebelled and fell
through the generation gap
into mythology.

In his way he won – his name
is on the map,
which is more than his father's is.

March 1980

19th floor nightmare, New York

The party had been a drunken one
so she sleeps a deep sleep
on the 19th floor
of the Mandragora Hotel.

And she dreams, she dreams
of bodiless horrors
and horrible bodies.
She can't breathe, her arms
are made of lead.

But when a fur-gloved hand
lands on her face, she wakes
at the end of a scream.
Lordy, Lordy, she says,
Just a dream, just a nightmare.

Trembling she gets up
and goes to the window.
Trembling, she pulls open the curtains
and looks out, straight
into the left eye of King Kong.

March 1980

Bruce and that spider – the truth

The spider tried again.
It was too stupid to learn from experience.

It swung like a black watch on a silver thread
before Bruce's face.

As swung watches do, it began
to hypnotise him.

Bruce shook his Norman head and muttered,
Damn, the brute, I'm getting out of here.

And, being too stupid to learn from experience,
he fought the Battle of Bannockburn. And won.

Moral? Experience teaches
that it doesn't.

April 1980

Creations

While he was writing
with furiously bent brows
and blots and vacant starings –
the children tiptoeing, the wife
laying with a trembling hand
a cup on a saucer with the noise
of the *Titanic* striking the iceberg –
while he was writing the third strophe of his
Lymphatic Ode on the Backwardness of Progress,
a spider in the garden hut
climbed his own telephone wire to his corner
and contemplated, with no racing pulse,
with no complacent grin on his horror-comic face,
the most perfect, the most beautiful,
the most deadly web
in the entire garden.

And night fell and owls invented
tunnels in the air to hoot in
and with a shiver a queen rose bowed
to an ecstatic crowd
of flag-waving grasses.

April 1980*

384]

Biblical discoveries

That the wind does not blow where it listeth;
that the still small voice speaks in thunderclaps;
that Balaam's ass knew a thing or two, both of them wrong;
that when you put Satan behind you, he gives you a push;
that compassion is no parachute for a sparrow
and winds are bad-tempered to shorn lambs;
that the seven wise virgins were stingy bores
and that, when the flood came, the MacNeils of Barra
had a boat of their own.

Such discoveries are helpful, for what do they mean?
– Write your own testament and start
building that boat.

April 1980*

View with no prospect

Though I'm in sunlight
a dangling shower drifts across the hill called
Durlain and across the eagle's nest on it.
Below, the Loch of the Thicket of the Fawns
tickles with the slight drops. Once, here, in one forenoon
I met and killed four adders. Fool.

My head's full of landscapes and their creatures.
My head's full of a handful of people, a few alive
as the lizard basking on that stone, a few
dead as the stone.

I wish I could wish those adders alive again.

But: thank God I don't get tired of ghosts.
Their tobacco smoke slowly writhes up and away.
Voices laugh. Heads nod wisely. And a collie stares
at nothing at all, and sees it, teaching me to do the same.

April 1980*

How to cover the ground

One autumn, a jobbing gardener and I
dug over a lady's suburban garden.
When we finished, he looked at the dark clods
and said, with satisfaction,
That's the way I like to see it –
none o'they bloody floo'ers.

A fundamentalist. His view, not mine;
for I still ignorantly cherish
my flibbertigibbet fripperies
that elaborately hide
the ground I came from
and, in due season, will return to.

April 1980

The first of them

The snake weeps below the tree.
He has been hated for so long.

Even Adam and Eve
were no sooner past that fiery sword
than they began to abuse him.

And the things that have been said about him
ever since – by parents to children,
by priests and lawmakers.

Poor snake. He crawls on his belly
dropping amber tears in the dust and whining
I was only obeying orders.

May 1980

The dolphin to Arion

I'm always happy to give a lift
to hitchhikers, Arion,
and I'm perfectly willing

to take you where you're going
if only, for God's sake, you stop
playing that damn lyre.

May 1980

City fog

The flagpole's kinky all the way up
and above the black canal tall towers
shimmy slowly
in their filthy seven veils.

Moses never thought of this
when he chatted with the Lord
on that funny mountain.

The light from the fruitshop window
tries to cross the road and can't.
The apples and bananas and grapefruit
have a TV look.

None of this bothered Aaron
drunkenly prancing with his chums
round his pretty golden calf.
(It was only the size of a kettle.)

Everything's baffled. Even the Tollcross clock
looks glum, as if it knew
five past ten might as well be
ten past five.

Meanwhile Moses keeps coming down
that mountain and Aaron
kicks higher, shouts louder and slobbers
down his bristly Jewish chin.

And all this in Edinburgh, where I dance
in my foggy way
round a tiny golden calf, ignoring

the thunder up there and the manic old man
clutching broken stones to his skinny bosom.

June 1980

In that other world

They sit at their long table
in a room so long it's a tunnel,
in a tunnel with a green roof
on which sometimes a flower nods
as if to remind them of something.

They talk about everything
except Death, but they don't listen
to each other. They talk, staring
straight in front of them.
And they tremble.

The only time they notice each other
is when Death sweeps past them
with his keys clinking and a long pen
in his hand.

Then they look shyly at each other
for a moment before staring ahead
and talking, talking, trying to remember
what a flower is,
trying to remember
why they are here.

June 1980

Local dance

In a corner of the village hall
five children sit behind their big round eyes.

Below the trashy decorations their elders dance,
thumping and Bruegelish. In the band
Ian Shimag, staring into another world,
spiders his fingers up and down

his Lazarus accordeon. And the night outside
goes away.

Wee Mary in the corner gets up and starts
dancing alone. The night inside her
goes away and she performs
dulcet rituals in a language of arms and legs
in the world Ian Shimag was staring at. And the stamping fishermen

and their bouncing ladies, capering by,
look at her with affection, remembering
when the night inside them used to go away
so long ago.

September 1980*

Clio

Socrates was never more right
than when the hemlock set about killing him
from the feet up: he was, himself,
what his irony had always been.

His judges, who had never understood irony,
went on drinking with their handsome boys
and pretty slave girls,
went on trying to corner the market
in wheat and olive oil.

The Muse of history, yawning with boredom,
judges the judges and finds them guilty.
Poor Clio. She has long since failed to be amused
by irony, truth, lies, murder
and suicide.

Sighing, she licks her finger
and wearily
turns over another page.

September 1980

Neanderthal man

If we met, I reckon I'd be
the one to be frightened,
seeing in you
what civilisation has failed to destroy
in me.

I'd rush back to my libraries,
my knives and forks,
my barbers and musicians,
leaving you twirling your club
and stupidly looking for
the spoor of the future
you think has escaped you.

September 1980

To explain you

I look for the answer, the one simple answer
among the so many,
that would explain you to me. I can't find it.

Am I a fool? Am I looking in the wrong places?
Am I expecting to find the Trojan horse
in a Rose Street boutique
or the sword of the Lord and of Gideon
under the sofa, behind the bookcase?

No, I know where to look. But the haystack
is so big and the needle I'm looking for
is the one on whose point all those angels danced
so many centuries ago.

September 1980

Gamekeeper's widow

She opens the door as if she has a right to.
She sits among the furniture as though
she were alien to it, or it to her.

Except, his gun on the wall, his crooks, his telescope
speak to her from an immeasurable distance
and she hears every word they say.

Outside, the garden he had created
is slowly dying back
to the wilderness it came from.

Like me, she thinks: and rises and goes
into the kitchen, glancing at the useless telescope,
lightly touching the brutal gun.

                              October 1980*

Old man in his chair

I am told (by me) to leave the fire
and go out into the wind and rain
like a starving hunter to bring back food
to the cave of my mind.

But my bow is broken, my arrows
without flight-feathers.

I feed on memories, a thin diet.
Their waves tumble over each other,
their creatures move learnedly
in a sad nowhere at all.

Death is a playboy, and a cruel one.

… I look at the fire, at the dresser,
at the garish calendar.

I savour them … Keep the door shut.
There's food here in plenty.
It'll last till the coming of the playboy king,
capering and giggling yet again
at his one bad joke.

October 1980

Two skulls

MacDiarmid found a pigeon's skull
on the bright shore turf of a Hebridean island.

I found the skull of a dogfish
on the sand at Cleethorpes.

His: the skull of a twirler and staller,
a rocketer, a headlong grace, symbol of peace.

Mine: hooverer of the sea's floor, sneak thief
of herrings from nets, corpse-eater, emblem of nightmare.

After death the one is as beautiful as the other
(but not to a pigeon, not to a dogfish).

I hate death, the skull-maker, because he proves
that destroying and making happen together.

He'll be no friend of mine, as long as I'm still
a feathery pigeon or a scrapeskin dogfish.

– I mean a man, whose skull contains
ideas death never thought of.

They'll cheat him, for they'll lodge in another skull
– or become nothing, that comfortable absolute.

October 1980

Bullfinch on guard in a hawthorn tree

Halberdier bullfinch
sticks out his chest
in a royal court of mayflowers.

Still enough for spies. Quiet enough for assassinations.

How imagine the mazy corridors unravelled
by ambassadors and cardinals?

The gentle sun cobwebs brightly
his black cap, his crimson breastplate.

Can a dream dream? Is there a Beauty sleeping
in a tiny chamber of leaves and small twigs?

He sees me and – duty calls – utters
his feeble, creaking, trisyllabic, piping song.

December 1980

Starling on a green lawn

He makes such a business of going somewhere
he's like a hopping with a bird in it.

The somewhere's an any place, which he recognises at once.
His track is zig – zag zig zag – zag.

He angles himself to the sun and his blackness
becomes something fallen from a stained-glass window.

He's a guy King, a guy Prince, though his only royal habit
is to walk with his hands clasped behind his back.

Now he's flown up like a mad glove on to a fence post.
He squinnies at the world and draws a cork from a bottle.

December 1980

Walking alone

The moon makes this one the sort of night
where everything's delicate except the blunt shadows.

I'm unaware of walking – Pollóchan's house
meets me and passes me.

Thoughts come to me, but only from outside …
You're far away. And the distance is sighing.

Everything so wavers towards nothingness
I think I can't think of you.

– Here's the gate. It stands
in a blunt shadow.

There's a cushion of moss on the wall top
and out of it grows one trembling grass.

I go in: and sleep. And my sleep is
a cushion of moss where a dream trembles.

December 1980

Encounter with a weasel

You poke your head from a window
in the dry stone dyke
and chatter at me.

I look at you and feel superior
(you're hardly bigger than my finger)
and friendly
(you're no longer than my hand).

You disappear.
I walk twelve steps –
and there you are again,
scolding me from another window
in your ramshackle tenement.

Silly weasel. I'm one thing
into whose neck
you won't sink the needles
you have for teeth.

You won't remember me
but I'll remember you,
minute sniper
in a huge, blue, June day.

December 1980*

John Brown and Queen Victoria

He smooths his kilt, strokes
his Dundreary whiskers
and stares gloomily
at the hills behind Balmoral.
It's a tricky business
shuttling between
Your Majesty and *Vicky*.

The hills behind Balmoral
stare gloomily back at him.
They're practising purple
for the Queen's watercolours.

There are mobs there, of things like
grouse and deer. She
and her ghastly friends
will deal with them.

How familiar dare he be today?
Is she going to be *Your Majesty* or *Vicky*?

It's a tricky business, he thinks,
and smooths his kilt
that's two inches too long.

Buckingham Palace! – he wishes
he were there, away from
clarsachs and midgy picnics
and these damn sniggering gillies.

December 1980

Invasion of bees

Between the ceiling and the roof
whole fields were humming.

Or, add to one bee a thousand others and it becomes
a dynamo.

A man was fetched from Helmsdale.
He carried a vicious brass pump.

It switched off that dynamo, it reaped
whole fields and heather slopes.

And a summer inside a summer
died, leaving a useless crop.

I have a summer inside my summer.
I cherish it. It's flowery and heathery.

Terrified, I dream of a man from Helmsdale
walking towards me, a sack in his hand.

December 1980

Old couple in a bar

They sit without speaking, looking straight ahead.
They've said it all before, they've seen it all before.
They're content.

They sit without moving: Ozymandias and Sphinx.

He says something! – and she answers, smiling,
and taps him flirtatiously on the arm:
Daphnis and Chloe: with Edinburgh accents.

December 1980

396]

Yes

You must say *Yes*, said the Commissioner
and the Gauleiter and the Priest and
their wet-lipped toadies.

They said it to the writer burying his poems,
to the woman going mad in a pink suburb,
they said it to the firing squad.

They said it to technology,
to philosophy, to stubborn science.

They even said it to the child
walking hand in hand with his mother.

And God trembled
like a man caught
with the imprint of the gun butt
still on his palm.

December 1980

Below the Clisham, Isle of Harris: after many years

On the mountain pass to Maraig
I met an old woman
darker but only just
than the bad weather we were in.

She was leading a cow by a rope
all the way round the mountain
to Tarbert.

She spoke to me in a misty voice,
glad to rest, glad to exercise
her crippled, beautiful English.

Then they trudged on, tiny
in a murky space
between the cloud of the Clisham
and a tumbledown burn.

And I suddenly was back home again
as though she were her people's history
and I one of her descendants.

December 1980

Hermes-Mercury

Hermes was a bad god, a shifty fellow,
a liar, a thief, a teller of the future
(with dice, of course), a musician,
herald and messenger of the gods.

No wonder mercury was called after Mercury.
No wonder the Romans gave him that name:
the Trader, the Business Man.

How he must have laughed when the Romans
raised a statue to him
– god of commerce, god of profit and loss –
in the Street called Sober Street
where no shops were allowed, no pubs.

No wonder he was the conveyor of dreams.
Garden of Bliss, Vision of Hell – what did he care?
Yet I admire him. He was a survivor.

What a god, to survive among
those other gods and goddesses, those arrogant,
selfish, high-living turncoats and lechers –
too stupid to notice they were only
the blind dupes of Fate.

… Fate must have loved him, the black sheep,
the con man, the wide boy of Olympus.

December 1980

Two thieves

At the Place for Pulling up Boats
(one word in Gaelic) the tide is full.
It seeps over the grass, stealthy as a robber.
Which it is.

– For old Flora tells me
that fifty yards stretch of gravel, now under water,
was, in her granny's time, a smooth green sward
where the Duke of Sutherland
turned his coach and four.

What an image of richness, a tiny pageantry
in this small dying place
whose every house is now lived in
by the sad widow of a fine strong man.

There were fine strong men in the Duke's time.
He drove them to the shore, he drove them
to Canada. He gave no friendly thought to them
as he turned his coach and four
on the sweet green sward
by the Place for Pulling up Boats
where no boats are.

                                        December 1980

Two thoughts of MacDiarmid in a quiet place

He helped me to understand
the swimming of words – slippery adjectives
with their pilot fish nouns, muscular verbs
glinting in the shallows –
or swordfishing through a blue wave.

He gave me the meaning of words
like *pantile*, like *corrieneuchin'*. He wooed them
from their lair in the dictionary.

Now, where a pantile branch hangs its S
over this gossiping stream that I've heard so often
corrieneuchin' a' the nicht,
I gaze down into a pool, and a trout
moves from the bright shallows,
as MacDiarmid did,
into a depth where my eyes see nothing.

January 1981

Pibroch: The Harp Tree

Pibroch, I make you a man
who could shake hands with Bach
and talk with him over a glass
of Rhenish wine.

You would walk in, with your sack
of images that are brightly dark and darkly bright,
and Bach, emerging from a labyrinthine fugue,
would greet you with warmth and pleasure. He'd pour
the Rhenish wine.

There'd be grave wings beating
in that room and happy silences
smiling to each other.

When you left, you'd return
to your crystal land of bogs and coloured rocks,
and Bach
would stretch his elbows sideways
like wings and fold them again and go back into
the labyrinth where he's never lost,
seeking, like you, the minotaur
that will crouch beside him
with his heavy horns,
with his beautiful, golden eyes.

January 1981

Courage

Courage looks down in the mouth.
He's as handsome as ever – he has the gift
of everlasting youth.

It's not that he's not admired
in his fine armour with its historic dents
or in hospitals where the flowers
are no less vivid than his wounds:

or that he's not wanted, in slums
and trawlers and choking rooms
in each of which sits
an old woman waiting to be visited.

And he gets paid – with banners
and banner headlines and ugly medals
and cups of tea with the Queen.

The job's not the same, he thinks.
It used to produce happiness and peace
at least some of the time. But now,
he thinks, more and more he's a destroyer,
a scavenger, a poisoner of sweet wells.

The telephone rings. He answers and,
making his mouth smile, making his eyes
flash as they used to,
he prances gloomily out into a world
he's been destroying, without knowing it,
for centuries of centuries.

January 1981*

Between us

There's no wall here –
not even a grating, not even a fence.

401]

I'm speaking of the space between us.

We don't collect fireflies
in a jar, or press leaves of dulse
in *A Book of British Shore Plants*.

We don't record the dipper
saying *clink clink* on a bubbly stone
or film a vole
moseying through the damp grass.

We don't take these things home.
They're there, in the space between us,
the beautiful things without sadness,
the sad things with their pitiful beauty.

As they are in you also
and in me also.

For we live there too,
in the space between us
which is not to be measured
by those bad things, miles,
and those worse things, hours.

January 1981

Cheerful pagan

Make do with what you have
was written in invisible ink
on his Birth Certificate.

He'll cut string with a match flame
and start a car with a paper-clip.
A bed's head is a gate. He'll carry water
in his hat.

His holy life has no religion.
He makes do with objects and people.

He's bedraggled as a saint,
with a go-to-heaven hat
and go-to-hell boots.

He's happy as an otter
lying on its back in Kirkaig Bay,
eating a fish
and using its chest for a table.

January 1981

Bell heather

People make songs about your big cousin
Extravagantly sprawled over mountain after mountain
They tear him up and he goes off to England
On the bumpers of cars, on shiny radiators.

But you're more beautiful and you blossom first,
In square feet and raggedy circles.
Your blue travels a hundred yards
That are a main road for bees.

If I were an adder, I'd choose you
For my royal palace. My sliding tongue
Would savour the thin scent
Of your boudoirs and banqueting halls.

A modest immodesty is a good thing,
Little blaze of blue on a rock face.
I'll try it myself. Will the bees come,
The wild bees, with their white noses?

January 1981

Meeting a goddess, maybe

I left a house in the middle of the city
and there on a tree was an owl
like a stub of wood pretending to be
the Goddess of Wisdom.

403]

Sparrows and blackbirds
made Scotch noises at it.
They skirled and screiched and skelloched.
Sore throats for them, you'd think.

The owl paid no heed whatever
as though to prove
it was a stub of wood or
the Goddess of Wisdom.

I spoke to it, but it paid
no heed whatever again, not even
when I addressed it in the local lingo.
Hoolet, I said, *hoolet*.

Only because it wasn't there
when I returned am I sure
it wasn't a stub of wood; though of course
it may well have been the other.

January 1981*

Pine trees

Enter the dignified wood.
The pine needles will give you
a cloak of inaudibility.

And you'll hear nothing yourself
unless a maverick gust of wind
drags a line of surf
through the tree tops.

A still from a war photograph –
staunch trees support their wounded comrades.

How can you bear it –
the turbulence in your mind surrounded
with such a silence?

404]

But the grave silence wins.
It enters your mind and destroys time there,
It drapes your mind with green veils.

And you smile when you hear
a voice of the silence, the sweet twittering song
of a siskin, that flies batlike (but brilliant)
between the melancholy banners.

January 1981*

Gin trap

In the wide bogland a hoodie crow,
six feet from the trap that had maimed him,
tries to stand, tries to fly.

In the rags of his feathers, with mad eyes,
he surges about in the heather. Sometimes
his frantic voice adds its ugliness
to the terror and the pain.

Little Lear, you have no Cordelia
to lament for, no steepdown gulfs
of liquid fire to burn you away
into a cindery darkness.

Your friends will come, your hoodie companions,
with their dreadful requiems – or
a gliding fox will tear you apart
with his flashing, beautiful smile.

January 1981

Camera man

Six rods are dapping for sea trout
On Loch Baddagyle. Their blowlines each make
A bosomy downwind curve. Six bushy flies
Ballet dance on the sunstruck water.

405]

– See that boulder? In its toupee of heather
There's a wild cat watching me. Two topazes with ears.
… I tilt up and pan along my trail of mountains
From Ben More Coigach all the way to Quinag.

An old ewe brings me down to the earth
She stamps her forefoot on. I look at her implacable
Whisky and soda eyes. She knows all a sheep
Needs to know: she's a black-stockinged bluestocking.

And a spinnaker line has straightened. The water
Explodes and shoots a sea trout into the air,
While five bushy flies still dance on the moving glitter,
Little water nymphs in their dangerous tutus.

February 1981

In folds of fire

In folds of fire – there's a fine-sounding phrase.
The reality
is different …

Creatures bolt in panic
in front of the roaring tidal wave
of a blazing forest.

Or love burns its candle and into it
jump the biggest of men
and the tallest of women.

Like Shadrach, Meshach and Abednego
they stroll
in the sexual flame.

In folds of fire. – What a mean
and narrow sound for what encloses
a candle flame and a fiery forest.

February 1981

A sort of physics

A tattery rosebush at a road corner
makes jubilant
a surly morning.
– And the song you begin to sing is cut short
by the dulled eye of a dead bird.

Archimedes was right. Give him a lever long enough
and he'd lift the world.

Even a moment, that weak and childish thing
that never grows out of childhood,
can tilt the world squint
with a lever as long as a wild rose petal,
as powerful
as the eye of a dead bird.

Archimedes was right, because his truths
contained others. He looked out from his one
into the weights and measures
of passion and hate and grief
where men spend lifetimes making
botched circles and trying to lift
immovable ounces.

(Though sometimes Rembrandt appears, or
Sophocles, or Mozart, and the uplifted world
sings a new song, a sad one and a merry one,
in the charnel house of space.)

                                        February 1981

Trapped

Man, frantic with admiration
for the gray mess inside his skull,
invented the wheel, which turned into
a bicycle and a fighter plane.

He invented hygiene, which turned into
interesting new diseases.

He invented an afterlife and can't wait
to go into it.

He invented Philosophy
that turned into philosophies:
dwarfish things.

If only he were more like the stars,
conventionally exploding into life
and out of it, with no arguments
about abortion and euthanasia.

– Look, a new thought has appeared
in the brain of Professor Cedilla.
He doesn't know it, but it's shaped
like a boomerang and it knows
where it's going.

February 1981

Portrait bust

That's forcing it, he thought,
and kneaded the clay back into
its shapeless shape.

Then he patted it, pulled it,
pared shavings off it.
His eyes ping-ponged
between it and his model.

No good … No good … It's not *him*.

And he pummelled the clay again
into its original shapelessness
and thought to himself
That's better. That's more like it
and started spoiling it again.

March 1981

Escapism

The Plough, infatuated with the Pole Star,
stands on one stilt to get a better view.

My mind stands on tiptoe, trying to get a better view
of things I only remember.

Weeks ago the Plough was aimed like a cleaver
at the skull of St George's Church.

My mind turned its back, trying not to remember
things I'd rather forget.

Do I put the Pole Star in a frame? Do I make
a picture of it? Do I live among pictures?

I have my own griefs, some of them the world's.
They hurt me, they damage me, they make me a better man.

I'll think of them, I say. But no. I turn away and watch
the sun looking down on a raven, purpling its beak.

It puts a painterly dot
in each eye.

                                                        April 1981

One more

That's it, said the stag
and buckled his front legs and fell over.

The stalker went up on a jet of exaltation
and sank down again.

That's it, he thought, watching
a hind leg give its last kick.

And premonitions bumped like gun shots
among the corries.

409]

But nothing cared, nothing cared at all,
except the man and the stag.

The small burn gabbled by and in the Red Corrie
another stag mounted a hind among the small flowers.

And the minutes filed by, all anonymous,
each with a gralloching knife in its belt.

April 1981

From where I sit

In any mist
I do not feel at home –
in the mist of the First Cause,
the fog of numbers,
the Chanel miasma
of Ergo and Q.E.D.

By my fire
Perhaps and Maybe
smoke cigarettes and get drunk
sipping pints of impossibility.

They are me
talking to myself,
while outside stalk
the gross idiocies of metres and kilograms,
and a priestly face
glares through the window, bellowing
the exact temperature of hell
and the statistics of eternity.

May 1981

Theologian

He tried to balance
the theory of predestination
on top of the theory of free will.
It kept tumbling down.

So he tried to balance
the theory of free will
on top of the theory of predestination.

He spent all day doing this.
But neither would stay on top.

In the evening he played another game.
He made a model of Justice
with her famous scales
and delicately put predestination
in one pan
and free will in the other.

They balanced.

He was disgusted. He growled
There's no justice in the world.

How could he know that Justice
was winking at him
behind her blindfold?

May 1981

In Hades

The shades drank from the ditch of blood
and talked with Aeneas.
He was not only pious, he was clever
and knew how to change their bat-squeaks
to brave baritones.

One of them said nothing. He stood
at the fringe of the crowd, looking sadder and sadder.

When Aeneas went off to found an empire –
he was not only pious, he was stupid –
they rounded on him –
Where are your manners?
Is there no friendliness in Hell?

And he moved away into the darkest
of the dark shadows. He'd had enough
of blood, he'd had enough of empires.
He was content to be in the one place
whose hospitality was unlimited
and would last forever.

May 1981

Gentle trap

I put my mind out there
like a bird table. On it I lay
a few crumbs of love, a grain or two
of admiration and one wriggling wish
asking to be noticed.

It works. See –
a thrush, two greenfinches
and a dunnock.
I'm pleased, but not satisfied.
What do you do to bring down
an eagle, a Great Auk,
a lammergeier?

Once a flash outside
made me rush to the window.
A phoenix! I thought.
But nothing was there
but one wriggling wish
waiting to be noticed
and a pretty thrush
wiping its nose on a fence post.

May 1981

Landscape outside and in

My rough ground lies under,
my scrub trees rise over
a tangle of grass half drowned

in a dazing wash of bluebells.
Four things, making a perpendicularity.

Beside them the loch water provides
the horizontal. It itches
with waterboatmen
and dimples with trout.

On top of all, on the high branches
I'm divided into birds, all singing.
How often do all my selves
sing together?..

You pick up a piece of wood,
a watersculpture; and we go to the car
and make for home.

We've left behind the bluebells
and the water. But all my selves
are still singing. They make no sound
but you hear their every note.

May 1981*

Summer idyll

Under a ferocious snowfall
of gulls and fulmars
a corner of the bay is simmering
with herring fry.

Into them slice
Assyrian hosts
of mackerel.

Sweet day, so cool, so calm, so bright ...

Three porpoises pronounce
three puffs and cavalry charge
into the Assyrians.

413]

Clouds lisp across the sky in a trance of silence.

Farther out, a commando of killer whales
grin and leap.
They're setting their ambush
for the cavalry.

And in the gentle West
a ladylike sunset
swoons
on the chaise-longue
of the Hebrides.

June 1981

A man I agreed with

He knew better than to admire a chair
and say *What does it mean?*

He loved everything that accepted
the unfailing hospitality of his five senses.
He would say *Hello, caterpillar* or
So long, Loch Fewin.

He wanted to know
how they came to be what they are:
But he never insulted them by saying
Caterpillar, Loch Fewin, what do you mean?

In this respect he was like God,
though he was godless. – He knew the difference
between *What does it mean to me?*
and *What does it mean?*

That's why he said, half smiling,
Of course, God, like me,
is an atheist.

June 1981

Woodcocks and philosophers

The woodcock I startled yesterday
clattered off through the birch trees
without starting to philosophise
and write a book about it.

That's his way.
And that's how he survives.
It amazes me that loafing philosophers
Don't all die young.

Unless, of course, when reality
saunters by, they crash off
through book after book, without reading
one blessed word.

                                        June 1981

On a beach

There's something I want to forget,
though I forget what it is.

… My mind niggles and grits
like the sand under my feet.

I used to know things I didn't know.
Not any more. Now I don't know
even the things I know, though I think I do.

… Little waves slide up the beach and slide back,
lisping all the way. The moon
is their memory. In my head
there's no moon.

What I don't know I don't even think I know.
That was Socrates, conceited man.

I'm trying to remember
what I've remembered to forget.

Twenty yards away, a seal's head
looks at me
steadfastly
then tucks itself
under the surface, leaving
no ripple.

July 1981

Running bull

All his weight's forward.
He looks like a big black hunchback
with a small black boy running behind him.

Put an invisible sixpence on the ground –
he'll turn on it.
So don't, if he's facing away from you.
People scatter. I scatter too.

Sometimes he stops
and looks redly around, wondering
which new direction
to hurtle at.

Donald saunters towards him.
The bull glowers at him
from between his knees.

And his fire goes out! … He puts on a nonchalance
and swaggers towards the byre, followed
by sauntering Orpheus.

July 1981

Characteristics

My American friends,
who claim Scottish ancestry,
have been touring Scotland.
In ten days they visited
eleven castles. I smiled –

How American.
They said they preferred
the ruined ones. I smiled again.
How Scottish.

September 1981

My last word on frogs

People have said to me, *You seem to like frogs.*
They keep jumping into your poems.

I do. I love the way they sit,
compact as a cat and as indifferent
to everything but style, like a lady remembering
to keep her knees together. And I love
the elegant way they jump and
the inelegant way they land.
So human.

I feel so close to them
I must be froggish myself.
I look in the mirror expecting to see
a fairytale Prince.

But no. It's just sprawling me,
croaking away
and swivelling my eyes around
for the stealthy heron and his stabbing beak.

September 1981

From my window

Outside, there are gardens full of trees
that have not yet fruited and a silence
waiting to grow apples of music
and clustering berries of words.

If I could sweep away those clouds
a moon would stare at me,
uncomprehending, meaningless and lonely.

A truck goes by. In the noise it makes
there's a mutilated shape
struggling to become
a cousin of Beethoven, a sweet child
of Mozart.

A group of teenagers turns the corner.
Raucous voices. Dyed hair.
Tribal badges.

I stare down at them, like the moon,
uncomprehending, meaningless and lonely.

What visions are waiting to be born
in their sad eyes?
What loving gesture weeps for itself
in the ugly angles of their arms?

October 1981

Dreams

The farmers are walking about
in their soggy fields. Inside their heads
a pleasant sun shines on crops without weeds.

In a house across the road a young man
plays a piano, aware of Bach and Bartók
listening indulgently to his blundering counterpoint.

And the dog asleep in a doorway twitches
his forepaws. He's chasing
the fattest hare in Midlothian.

Dreams fly everywhere. They creep
into minds whose owners have slammed them shut.
That boy's lungs are full of them.

Sometimes they come true and the world stares
at a new great painting or a body by the wayside
with chopped off hands.

The dreams of sleep dissolve when the window whitens
and the dreams of daylight swarm in with a passport to heaven
in one hand and a passport to hell in the other.

And sweet berries grow over the graves
of all of us or a white stone marks the place
which is the end of dreams, and of hell, and of heaven.

October 1981

Legends

The kingfisher flies out to sea
and breeds in a special doldrum
created for it by the god of the winds.

The phoenix dies in her blazing nest
and, fluffing the ashes aside, rises again, all feathers,
in the suddenly glittering air.

That's what they thought
in the good old days.

Now it's men who do it. They go out
into the storms and wildernesses of thought
and create a ring of peace: where they breed
their own ferocious likenesses.

And others, crouched in a public place,
put fire to themselves. They burn,
and from their ashes rise
a miasma of horror, a stink of pity,
a semblance of the whole world.

Will the day come when they too
will be only legends that men will tell
to each other, saying
That's what they thought.
In those terrible times
that's what they thought.

October 1981

A matter of scale

My troubles and griefs
may seem ordinary to you, my friend,
but they make me a Lilliputian
in a world of Gullivers.

I try to avoid
their huge feet. When one of them
picks me up
I hold onto him
so as not to be blown away
by the wild stink of his breath.
While somewhere something
tosses the world in its hand,
judging its weight,
wandering if it's worth keeping.

October 1981

Foggy night

We put the tea things on the table
and turn on the TV for the News.
I look at the brown teapot, almost expecting it
to cluck.

Night is heavy on the city.
The lights struggle and on the Firth of Forth
a foghorn is suffering.

But space, good space, does not desert us.
In it the clock's voice plods on the mantelpiece
and a petal falls on the table.

The line of its fall is a fence
between the millions of years that have gone
and the millions to come.

October 1981

Ugly waking

My early morning bird, sweet blackbird, starts
his early morning song. His note
never trembles.

And light begins to creep
along wires and shamelessly
to peer into windows.

I stir as though freed from ropes
and my morning thought begins
to speak in my head.

How its voice trembles.
How it flinches from the window
and won't look out.

I lie in a wretched darkness with no song in it
and with new ropes on me
made of light.

October 1981

The sea of sleep

Some float gently ashore. They lie
with their shoulders on the sand
till the sea ebbs.

Others splash violently through the shallows
and collapse panting
at high water mark.

I, king dolphin of the sea of sleep,
leap ashore – rising in air as dolphin,
landing as man.

I visit the huts of the natives
and eat their strange foods, and
keep looking out to sea

where this lumpish man was frolicsome
in a school of dreams – black hoops, submerging, then
slithering up into the light and scattering it.

October 1981

Portobello waterfront

It's acquired a French look – parasols
and bikinis and beach balls and
surf boarding and bullying speedboats.

When I was a boy, it was proletarian Scotch –
cloth caps, donkeys, Fun City,
the Salvation Army, beery faces
snoring under the *Daily Record*.

I'd like to make a gesture. Dare I paddle
with my trousers rolled up to the knee
and my shoes hanging round my neck?

I watch a birdwatcher. He steals
a gull from the air and imprisons it
in his binoculars, as I do
 with the year 1920.

– And I see my father
six feet two of him; St. Vitus dancing
along the cakewalk;
and into my mouth steals the taste
of sand and icecream and salty fingers.

October 1981*

Every day

What's that cart that nobody sees
grinding along the shore road?

Whose is the horse that pulls it, the white horse
that bares its yellow teeth to the wind?

They turn, unnoticed by anyone,
into the field of slanted stones.

My friends meet me. They lift me from the cart and,
the greetings over, we go smiling underground.

November 1981

On the Lairg to Lochinver bus

I travel West, a smudged figure
among people in four rows
divided in two.

The driver chain smokes. I know him.
Inside his bald head are microfilms
of poaching stags, loose women
and half bottles at Brackloch.

A young tourist (Scandinavian?)
stares at a map while the true facts
slide by the window.

We're apt to do that.

I've a map of tomorrow.
When I get there
I'll look round anxiously to see
if it's out of date.

If the broken gate is mended,
if old Flora is still alive,
if the tide still comes in
and goes out.

November 1981*

423]

Pastoral

The road folds itself half round a tree
and sets off at a new angle, seeming
pleased with the change.

It's not much of a road. It's been made
more by carts than men.

It bumps its nose against Lachie's house
and stops there
in the blue scent a peat fire makes,
in the cosy noises the brown hens make.

The cock, in the amazing uniform
of a wildly foreign Field Marshal,
scans two worlds through his monoculars.

– No enemy in sight … The Field Marshal becomes
a Pioneer Corps private in drag
and half-heartedly scratches the scratches
on the homely ground.

November 1981

Found guilty

To this day, poor swimmer as I am,
it grieves me
that I watched the little sandpiper drown.

When I passed the nest
shoulder high on a bank of Loch Lurgain
the young ones cheeped-cheeped out of it
to flop in the heather twenty yards away.

Except that one. It flew over the water,
lower and lower, then tried to fly in the water:
and drowned.

I've watched friends, strong fliers among mountains,
who flew lower and lower
and drowned in the uncaring water
they had soared above.

Little sandpiper, you left me
accused of what
I have no defence against.

Friends, I ask your forgiveness.
I ask for something
I don't deserve. And I ask for it
too late.

December 1981

Six schoolgirls

I met them for half a day
(we were making a TV programme)
in my familiar room. We talked
about poetry and were taken out
for an extravagant lunch. Such ice-cream!

I've thought of them since
with such relish of their likenesses
and differences it adds up
to affection.

It'll be strange when the TV flickers
and steadies and there they are, successfully
hiding their shyness.

Will I recognise in them
(so composed, so informed, so subtle)
those gossiping youngsters devouring
such soups and steaks? Such ice-cream?

December 1981

425]

Gentle saboteur

Slowly, slowly the new morning
has set fire to the darkness. I wake
in the harmless flames.

And slowly the room emerges
into where I am … As she does,
she whom I inhabit.

When I leave her, she'll say
Put your coat on. It's cold outside.
It's always cold outside
when I leave her
whom I inhabit.

But think of the new mornings she brings
at any time of the day
and at any time of the night.

I wake in those harmless flames
that burn away the darkness outside
and the darkness inside.

March 1982*

A new age

Before the barbarians came –
Dante tried to describe it
in all those cantos. Hieronymus Bosch tried to paint it
but he, even he, fell short of the truth.
And Goya …

When the barbarians came, things were better.
They even let us wear our clothes
when we went into the gas chambers.
And what gratitude we felt
when they killed the mothers before
they killed their babies and when they blew off

426]

the head of the Holy Prelate
without gouging his eyes out first.

How could we express our thankfulness
when the mass graves were filled
only with the dead?

We even revived the art of prayer. *O Lord*, we prayed,
we thank Thee for Thy present mercies,
we thank Thee for leading us forth
from the dark ages of civilisation.

April 1982

Philosophy

She manages
to trampoline and walk tightropes
in her own mind, does philosophy,
that turner of outsides
into insides.

Not many people love her. They turn aside
into the gipsy's tent or watch
acrobats being boneless.

Philosophy doesn't mind. At home
she turns them all
into a pack of concepts, shuffles it,
cuts it and every time
turns up the Joker.

All the same, it's something to see
the dowdy old lady in her long skirts
mincing along a tightrope
two inches above the ground and waving
a gaudy parasol to prove
how difficult it is.

May 1982

427]

Where we are

In the middle, inaudibly
a yellow flower dies giving birth to a yellow flower.

And the ghost of water climbs high into the air
to make a drop of water and another.

In the fireplace light cries *Let me out!*
and the coals eat themselves to free their prisoner.

Night blackens itself and we say, *A star!*
(The star climbs into us, into our darkness.)

And death smiles ruefully, thinking
how little he is understood.

May 1982

Beach scene

Transparency of shadow
under mushroomy sun-hats.

Five empty deck chairs – a blown-up still
from a Dance of the Insects.

The grown-ups have a hazy nowhere
inside their heads
where sometimes drift
the ghosts of cities.

A five-year-old loads
a tiny wheelbarrow with sand,
the reddest wheelbarrow between here
and William Carlos Williams.

And the water, forgetting wrecks,
waltzes a sea waltz on the sand –
it counts *One* coming in
and *Twothreefourfivesixseveneight* going out.

May 1982

Man in the crowd

Barenaked Emperor, I hate you for this:
you've converted me to a belief in deception,
for I hate the cruel robes you're not wearing
less than I hate you.

June 1982

Seen in the city

In the garden you walk the way
a tall flower would walk
in the music of Debussy.

The trees are fat now and heavy with blossom.
How slender you are
in their beautiful, podgy circle.

You call to your dog
who's bursting through the undergrowth
like a small black tank
on a tropical island.
He's filling himself with smells.

(A butterfly, crazy with wings,
is trying to go in every direction
at once.)

You stand still and the little dog
trundles flat out across the grass
to your feet. He sits down, panting,
and puts to shame the brightest flower in the garden
with two inches of tongue.

July 1982

No end to them

I said, Never again will I write
about love, or frogs, or absence
or the heart-stopping intrusion
of steep-down, steep-up mountains.

Satisfied, I sat down and was overwhelmed
with sheet lightnings of revelations
of new things, of absolutely new things.

Twitching with joy, I scribbled for days
– about what?
About love and frogs and absence …
etcetera.

Oh, William Blake and your grain of sand,
what a consolation you are to me.
I'll scuttle happily in my matchbox labyrinth
seeking no way out,
meeting my small marvels round every corner
till I meet the last one
swaying his heavy horns
in that shadowy dead end.

July 1982

Of you

When the little devil panic,
begins to grin and jump about
in my heart, in my brain, in my muscles,
I find the path I had lost
in the mountainy mist.

I'm writing of you.

When the pain that will kill me
is about to be unbearable,
a cool hand

puts a tablet on my tongue and the pain
dwindles away and vanishes.

I'm writing of you.

There are fires to be suffered,
the blaze of cruelty, the smoulder
of inextinguishable longing – even
the gentle candle flame of peace
that burns too.

I suffer them. I survive.

I'm writing of you.

September 1982*

Autumn

Wanting to go,
all the leaves want to go
though they have achieved
their kingly robes.

Weary of colours,
they think of black earth,
they think of
white snow.

Stealthily, delicately
as a safebreaker
they unlock themselves
from branches.

And from their royal towers
they sift silently down
to become part of
the proletariat of mud.

September 1982

Neighbour

His car sits outside the house.
It never goes anywhere. Is it
a pet?

When he goes for his morning paper
he makes a perfect right-angle
at the corner.

What does he do at home? Sit at attention?
Or does he stay in the lobby
like a hatstand?

Does his wife know she married
a diagram? That she goes to bed
with a faded blueprint?

When I meet him
he greets me with a smile
he must have bought somewhere.

His eyes are two teaspoons
that have been emptied
for the last time.

September 1982

Compare and contrast

The great thinker died
after forty years of poking about
with his little torch
in the dark forest of ideas,
in the bright glare of perception,
leaving a legacy of fourteen books
to the world
where a hen disappeared
into six acres of tall oats

and sauntered unerringly
to the nest with five eggs in it.

January 1983

Double journey

Move along! the driver shouts.
Move along there!

All day I've been doing that.
All my life I've been doing that.

Somewhere about me I have
the traveller's permit
given to me by my mother.

The bus halts. Some people get off.
I'll never see them again.

Some people get on.
I move along
to make room for them.

The place I know I'm going to
approaches. I move along again,
towards the exit.

January 1983*

Gray wagtail

It must be summer – you're wearing
your black gorget
above your sulphury shirt front.

You dip and dip and go on dipping
your tail, then shuttlecock up
(death of a fly)
and parachute down again

433]

on to your watery stone.
It's necklaced with bubbles.

No gossip you. You're too busy
dip-dip-dipping your tail – ah,
you're off
in four looping, airy bounds,
hurdling nothing,
to another watery stone
that wears a Beau Brummel jabot of foam
at its throat.

But you put it to shame, little dude.
You're the eight-inch spectacular
in the summery river's
fashion show.

March 1983

By the graveyard, Luskentyre

From behind the wall death sends out messages
That all mean the same, that are easy to understand.

But who can interpret the blue-green waves
That never stop talking, shouting, wheedling?

Messages everywhere. Scholars, I plead with you,
Where are your dictionaries of the wind, the grasses?

Four larks are singing in a showering sprinkle
Their bright testaments: in a foreign language.

And always the beach is oghamed and cuneiformed
By knot and dunlin and country-dancing sandpipers.

– There's Donnie's lugsail. He's off to the lobsters.
The mast tilts to the north, the boat sails west.

A dictionary of him? – Can you imagine it? –
A volume thick as the height of the Clisham,

A volume big as the whole of Harris,
A volume beyond the wit of scholars.

October 1983

Her illness

For this once I force myself
to write down the word *light*.
So many times in the last cloudy months
I've tried to and my mouth
said *dark*.

For the waters of Babylon
sound in my friendly river, my harp
hangs in a familiar tree.

I used not to care
that there never were unicorns
and that a phoenix was only
a metaphor on fire.
I knew that, but I loved them.

But truth has been stripped of its flesh,
its eyes, its gentle hands.
It reaches out an arm and lays
five cold bones on my knee.
It never stops smiling
with a changed smile.

April 1984

May morning

In their new sprigged frocks
the trees, the flower plots, the hedgerows
are flirting
with the whole May morning.

The morning – I'd like to call it jocund,
but that word died long ago.

Birds have collected all their notes
and pour them out
recklessly, carefully, one at a time,
over the housewifely roofs
and grenadier street lamps asleep at attention.

Something stirs in me. It used to be called happiness.

There are things not to be denied. – I walk,
happy, in a jocund morning. I think,
resurrection has a meaning after all
outside those black, those terrible covers.

April 1984*

Big Top

In the circus so many things
don't happen. When last did anyone fall
from those flying trapezes? When last
was the sword-swallower carried off
on a stretcher? And always the elephants
toddle off holding each other's tails.

Such expertise, such perfection
can't compare with the show going on outside,
where a man bleeds
on his bed of nails,
the high wire's always breaking
and only the clowns keep time
with the Universe going *oompah oompah*
over the broken tiger cage,
the fire exploding in a corner
and the crowds panicking towards exits
that aren't there.

April 1984

Backward look

Call up for my contemplation
the black longships with their snakish heads
sliding into a Shetland bay:
– and their murderous, witty crews
whose speech was as laconic
as their swords and battleaxes.

Or Troy and highminded Hector
scaring his baby with his nodding, noble plume
– and the wooden horse, stolid outside the walls,
pregnant with flames and screaming women.

Or ugly Socrates, monolith-still
in the middle of the battle, brooding
on his beautiful, improbable abstractions:
see his hand, without a tremor,
raise the glass of hemlock to his truthful lips.

Or Luther, hammering those famous nails
into the Cathedral door
– and into the minds of men, driving them to scurry
with the Lord's book in their hands
to torture chambers and battlefields.

Or Captain Cook or Livingstone or Columbus
bringing to unknown countries
the goodies of civilisation,
every one sweet, every one poisonous.

History frightens me. It reminds me
of me and you
and everyone else.

If only I come to be, in its long story,
a word with brackets round it,
a word drowned in a footnote,
a word
whose meaning has been forgotten.

May 1984

Highland barbecue

Darkness has come
snuffing the candles of distance,
binding the legs of the tall ash trees,
with black bandages.

By the Red Rock Pool
the youngsters of the village
have their barbecue going and near it
a bonfire of logs
and broken fishboxes. The flames jig
to the jigging of Jimac's accordion.

From a distance it looks like
a tiny, mediaeval hell – all that red,
those figures in the flicker.

But come close. It's a heavenly glebe
of charred sausages and laughter,
of young seraphs licking their fingers
and adding to the jewel heap
of praise-the-Lord
Coca-Cola tins.

They pay no heed, in their short-lived holiness,
to the gull over the bay
– rejected spirit
lamenting in the desolation
of the outer darkness.

May 1984

On the north side of Suilven

The three-inch-wide streamlet
trickles over its own fingers
down the sandstone slabs
of my favourite mountain.

438]

Like the Amazon it'll reach the sea.
Like the Volga
it'll forget its own language there.

Its water goes down my throat
with a glassy coldness,
like something suddenly remembered.

I drink
its freezing vocabulary
and half understand the purity
of all beginnings.

May 1984

Old Highland woman

She sits all day by the fire.
How long is it since she opened the door
and stepped outside, confusing
the scuffling hens and the collie
dreaming of sheep?
Her walking days are over.

She has come here through centuries
of Gaelic labour and loves
and rainy funerals. Her people
are assembled in her bones.
She's their summation. *Before her time*
has almost no meaning.

When neighbours call
she laughs a wicked cackle
with love in it, as she listens
to the sly bristle of gossip,
relishing the life in it,
relishing the malice, with her hands
lying in her lap like holy psalms
that once had a meaning for her, that once

439]

were noble with tunes
she used to sing long ago.

May 1984

The dear green place

I quarter my little field.
It stretches from the fall of Troy
to this minute, but it's not cramped
in my skull.

Its natives, all artists, make shapes
out of words and sounds and colours
and anything solid. They have a basilisk eye
for clocks and calendars.

Not an eagle, me, but
an ancient sparrowhawk
dowdily perched on fenceposts
in any century.

Still, I pop up over the hedges
in a dashing way, looking to surprise
a mousy philosopher
or a scuttling poet.

The pleasing thing is
when I've devoured a warbling musician
and fly off, I hear him behind me
still practising Op.4 No.6.

This country makes a fool of ecology
and an ass of conservation.
It's a land death has forgotten to visit
and I am not one of his angels.

May 1984

At the Loch of the Pass of the Swans

I dangle my feet in the cool loch water.
A thousand journeys, a century of miles
crinkle to the crimson flower beside me.

Where is the mist that wrapped itself round
the threshing machine last autumn?
Where's the blackface lamb I pulled from a peat bog?

Where are the places my father knew
and the storm waves roaring in the caves of Scarp,
frightening my little girl mother?

Escape from my history – to the campfires
of Huns and Goths, to the monks picking
hazel nuts and berries on sunny Iona.

I play with time and distance,
a game less cruel than the one
they play with me, the one they will win.

Let them. For this moment they've shrunk
to the crimson flower beside me
and two feet, corpse-white, in the smiling water.

May 1984*

Inside and out

In my head there's a book being written
about loneliness, who stares in a mirror
in her homeless home, watching
her limp hands, her frantic eyes.

Walking through buds and blossoms,
poor Spring, my Spring, is weeping. She sits by the pond
not heeding the swan sculptures. She leans
her head on the night's shoulder and weeps.

Take her to the window, someone. Make her see how
true Spring – gay in her finery, in a world smirking
in the latest fashion – goes smiling down the road
where even Time, at that corner, stands dressed to kill.

Is happiness to be found only in a world
of no mirrors? – where eyes look out only and relish
the cloud tumbling high over the ears
of the milkman's horse sticking up through its battered hat?

June 1984

Sealubber

Far on any ocean, with horizons
always the same distance away,
there's an Odysseus, a big bold fellow
made of bronze or a scruffy gray one
with a chewed moustache.
They know where they're going
even if there's no harbour there to creep into.
Do I envy them their hard way
with dissatisfactions and boredoms, their exchange
of the paradox of friends and of lovers
for the loneliness they're in love with?

I nid-nod in my rocking harbour.
It has a welter of waves in it
that no-one can see, that has
terror enough. And I sail
on the never-ending voyage
to where I am already, dizzy
with beautiful Troys and
dangerous Circes and dark journeys
to the land of the shades.

July 1984

Everywhere at Loch Roe

The brown dinghy labours round the point
like a damaged insect – only two legs left.

I stand on a rock
that's shrugged in a gray coat of barnacles.
The sea keeps slapping it.

The slaps measure time, I think, idly.

– Not me.
I've given up time for the moment.
I'll have nothing to do with it.

The tall girl backs the dinghy in
and I step aboard.

I take the oars and pull
against the wind and tide.
In out, in out. Measuring time
the hard way.

My turn to round the first point,
caught again in the old rhythm –
time and headland, time and headland
and a quiet bay at the end of it.

July 1984*

Bright day, dark centre

The dust silvers and a wind from the corner
brings a dream of clarinets
into the thick orchestra. There's a place
sending messages across the river of people;
and the sullen wharves of buildings
begin to smell of bales and distances.

I have a sad place that nobody enters
but a ragged man hooking the air

443]

with skinny fingers. I sit beside him sometimes,
feeling his despair. His loneliness
infects me.

But today's a day of clarinets and silver
under the lucky horseshoe of the sky.
I leave him and go into the whirlpools of light,
through a jazz of gardens and heliograph windows.

– That house is my monkish cell, my fortress.

I put the key in the door and stop,
terrified that the ragged man
is sitting in my chair with his skinny fingers
tangled in his lap.

July 1984

Over and over again

Tomorrow we'll meet again
as for the first time, though we've not crossed
the river that's both cruel and kind –
that Lethe the ancients spoke about.
And of the buried suns one will arrive
and make bright the fields
where Persephone must have passed:
so many the flowers.
We'll not shrink when we skirt
the entrance to the Underworld
nor be blinded by that shell sauntering in
on to the shore of everywhere.

All myths, with the truth of myths.
We'll do it our way –
with a look, with a touch
and with the space between words
where the truths live
that we can find no words for.

July 1984

444]

A man walking through Clachtoll

He carries a scythe, but he's young,
he doesn't notice symbols.

Packs of waves hold the Split Rock at bay.
He pays no need to their growling and slavering.

He's thinking of Mairi at the dance tonight.
She's his Aurora, she's his Merry Dancer.

They'll whirl in and out of six other lives and end
teetotuming alone. By God, they'll *Strip the Willow*.

He turns into the field and sets to work.
He rejects symbols. But he is one all the same.

And the hay falls and the dances end.
And the scythe cuts, no matter who's holding it.

August 1984*

Plea not to be deserted

Have I taken all I can from you,
books of the masters, printed on the yellowing years?
I know you've hung songs on constellations
I can't visit and under my feet
your minerals are glowing that I can't reach,
dig as I might, furiously, in my midnight room.

Sneak cleverly from behind me, from between
my roving glances, as you did when Catullus
came smiling in and Dante, wrapped in a cloak
of light years, scattered so many shadows
with his white lucidities.

I'm a man waiting to be ambushed.
Take time off to notice me, to step
from a doorway and slip into my hand
a tract of timelessness, a never-ending

exclamation, a single word, like the first one,
of continuous creation, of difficult universes.

August 1984

Memory

Over the turbulence of the world
flies the bird that stands for memory.
No bird flies faster than this one,
dearer to me
than the dove was to Noah – though it brings back
sometimes an olive branch, sometimes
a thorny twig without blossoms.

August 1984

On the pier at Kinlochbervie

The stars go out one by one
as though a bluetit the size of the world
were pecking them like peanuts out of the sky's string bag,

A ludicrous image, I know.

Take away the gray light.
I want the bronze shields of summer
or winter's scalding sleet.

My mind is struggling with itself.

That fishing boat is a secret
approaching me. It's a secret
coming out of another one.
I want to know the first one of all.

Everything's in the distance,
as I am. I wish I could flip that distance
like a cigarette into the water.

I want an extreme of nearness.
I want boundaries on my mind.
I want to feel the world like a straitjacket.

September 1984

Country cameo

Talking (like crows) of crows
three old men by a wall
in interesting attitudes.

The minister passes. He greets them.
They greet him
like doves.

When he's gone, they fall into
new interesting attitudes
and talk (like crows) of the minister.

September 1984

Low tide

Under six inches of water
pebbles, each one of them noble
in the heraldic colours of their ancestry.

Time sits weaving
and unweaving an endless tapestry
for a Ulysses who will one day come.

As I will – not this caricature
who wades in six inches of water.
My true self, my aimless wanderer.

I pick up a pebble and watch
its colours fade – and put it back. Full tide
won't dull its invisible shining.

Repulsive death washes into my mind.
It won't dull the invisible shinings there –
dead friends, noble in the last certainty.

September 1984

Daybreak

Count the lights down,
those lustrous, trembling stars.

If there's an hour whose father
was Proteus, this is it.

The night sky is turning into
a space of pearl. In the East

it faintly flushes, where the hidden sun
sends forward its gentle announcement.

And history, that hasn't slept, yawns
in his workshop – he'll make

a million things today
and be surprised by none of them.

There's one already – a milk bottle waiting
for the door of a house to open.

And another – a baby crying
in the first of all its minutes.

September 1984

Likenesses in a morning

Waves slavering along the sides
of Clett, that great rock,
make it the dorsal fin
of a monstrous invisible fish
travelling south
and not moving at all.

The tide's coming in.
It's being met
by welcoming committees
of mussels who greet it
with slow, lopsided smiles.

Behind us, a buzzard
drifts in slow swirls
across the high hillside.
Somebody on the road
stares up at it
through binoculars.
Young Jamie says, *Look*:
There's a man drinking
from two bottles at once!

We watch from the house
that grips the ground like a limpet
in the tide that never ebbs.

October 1984*

Shetland reel

for Aly Bain

The fiddle bow slides and hops and dances
At a speed that should sound hectic but doesn't.
Down-bow becomes three up-bows in places
I would never have thought of, following
The jags and curves of the tune as though it were
Helicoptering at a hundred miles an hour
Along a drystone dyke on a humpy landscape.

The result – a tune: a witty celebration
Of nimbleness and joy, fit to be played
In a tenement room, in a hall, in the lee
Of a Shetland peatstack where the Aurora
Remembers its other name, the Merry Dancers.

November 1984*

Haymaking

What will the corncrake do now?
Where will the bad hen, the black one, lay her eggs?

Through sunny days we scythed
the trembling grass. We turned it.
We heaped it in small hills.

We trundled barrowloads
to the shed and piled it
high to the roof.

Today, we've pressed it down
in a scent of dust and honey
and piled it high to the roof again.

I lean, sweating, on the hay rake
in the hay coloured sun. My neck
is tickly. My eyes itch.

I am full of joy – and I add to it
with a vast, unmelodious sneeze.

December 1984*

Between mountain and sea

Honey and salt – land smell and sea smell,
as in the long ago, as in forever.

The days pick me up and carry me off,
half-child, half-prisoner,

on their journey that I'll share
for a while.

They wound and they bless me
with strange gifts:

the salt of absence,
the honey of memory.

December 1984

450]

Someone's birthday

So many flowers!
Walk through the rooms – everywhere
their still silent explosions.

Who is the one, the Persephone
to whom they have crowded,
denying dark December?

It's not today she'll be snatched off
to the stony Judge in that grim land.
Not yet. Not yet.

When that day comes it'll be a dark December
where songless Orpheus will wander
his mouth choked with shadows.

January 1985*

On a croft by the Kirkaig

The cock, king of the croft, crowed,
tearing a jagged rip in the silence
that even the river washing by
had failed to disturb.

My mind was like the silence:
an equivalence of peace.

But the cock crowed, ushering in
another day at midday.
What day?

And into my mind came the man
with whom, so often, I'd sat by that river,
now in the most rounded silence of all
where no river shuffles by
and no cock will ever crow again.

I'm sad
but not sad only,
for I share his possessions
and therefore himself.

Cherishingly, I count three of them –
the equivalence of peace,
the cock, carved on tiptoe
on the gold coin of himself,
and the river bundling its sweet vocabulary
towards the swarming languages
of the sea.

January 1985

Crofter

Last thing at night
he steps outside to breathe
the smell of winter.

The stars, so shy in summer,
glare down
from a huge emptiness.

In a huge silence he listens
for small sounds. His eyes
are filled with friendliness.

What's history to him?
He's an emblem of it
in its pure state.

And proves it. He goes inside.
The door closes and the light
dies in the window.

January 1985

Two nights

The real night, the one
that keeps coming back on time,
never begins
with a gash of black.

As though, politely,
it makes a noise on the gravel
and coughs and knocks at the door
before coming in.

Not like the other one, that
on the most summer of days
gashes the light and pours through
a black dark with no moon, no stars.

June 1985

Sounds and silences

The gabbling river
talking to itself –
such garrulities.

– Even the quietest of nights
are never silent: hear
their shadows of sounds.

I've thought no silence
could be deeper than the one
in your sleeping self.

But heft that stone. It has
a language beyond our hearing,
a re-forming of crystals.

And you'll wake in the morning
the one I've known
and the new one, the always new one.

July 1985

Small boy

He picked up a pebble
and threw it into the sea.

And another, and another.
He couldn't stop.

He wasn't trying to fill the sea.
He wasn't trying to empty the beach.

He was just throwing away,
nothing else but.

Like a kitten playing
he was practising for the future

when there'll be so many things
he'll want to throw away

if only his fingers will unclench
and let them go.

July 1985

New flood

For five days and nights
the windows have worn veils
of thin water.

We know the river
is making samurai sounds.
It's swollen, it's apoplectic.

But all we can hear
is the rain, sounding
like dwarfs rushing through thickets.

454]

I'd feel like Noah, but for you,
woman of gentleness
stroking the pale dove.

July 1985

A man and his dreams

I only wanted my dreams to stay
in the iron circle
of reason, of possibility.

They kept going off into far places.
They smouldered beyond horizons.

– But tomorrow will come
with hope, its little child.
And I'll walk in my friendly streets
past the small front gardens,
looking at the sooty snowdrops
and the fool's gold
of daffodils.

And the iron circle will tighten
till I'm content
with the smirched snowdrops
and the daffodils that never think
of Wordsworth's wild ones
and dance the best they can.

August 1985

Getting where?

What so pure
as arrivals,
each a promise
of new beginnings?

455]

We step into a place
we've never seen
or a place
where once we suffered.

And silly hope greets us, She says
What a beautiful Spring day
and smiles charmingly
among the falling leaves.

August 1985

Crew

Three men are pulling
at the starboard oar,
the man I am and was
and the man I'll be.

The boat sails
to a blind horizon.
Who's pulling on the portside oar
that keeps our course straight?

Pull as we may
we're kept from turning
to port or starboard by that
invisible oarsman.

August 1985

Foreboding in Eden

Is it my fault, delicate Eve,
that I'm a man called
Adam?

I'm in life and in love.
The painless wound in my side
has healed.

And I've finished naming the animals,
all but one.

But something's wrong. The night
groans and whirls
in the first storm of all.

Tomorrow will come. Wounded,
it'll thrash in the air.

– Till a silence falls and in it
we'll meet the maker of storms,
the maker of stillness.

August 1985

Buzzard circling

The landscape wheels round
its centre – the buzzard that sees
a hill slide sideways,
a field spin round.

The buzzard wheels
round another, invisible centre,
the black hole that waits
for buzzard and hill –

that will suck in
all circumferences
to the place that was
before chaos was created.

September 1985

Heavenly party

He watches the goddesses dancing
so gracefully and the gods
so elegantly – even, he thinks bitterly,
that lame-footed fellow over there.

He can't be bothered.
He's past it.

And he thinks of the good old days.
Turn into a swan? –
no bother.
A shower of gold? –
all in the night's work.

I'm infected
with humanity, he thinks,
knocking over his nectar.

Ganymede! he bellows.
The same again! A large one!

Poor Zeus.

It's always, always
the same again
in boring Olympus.

September 1985

A happiness

Each second is birds singing in every tree.
Not real birds. Not real trees.

And my room is mornings stretching on forever.
Not real mornings nor that real forever.

A plough went into the ground. Corn rose from it.
I saw that plough. I saw that corn.

They were real. But for this fragile moment
the plough turns over the soil into the future

where the corn sways
that was cut down long ago.

September 1985

Apparition

Before me, the solid cone
of Ben Stack
looks in all directions at once
without needing to turn.

I climb and climb and climb,
disliked by a peregrine,
no friend to a lizard,
shunned by a hind
with two followers.

At the cairn I turn round and scan
the jumbled wilderness
of mountains and bogs and lochs,
South, East, North and then – West
– the sea

where a myth in full rig,
a great sailing ship, escaped
from the biggest bottle in the world,
glides grandly through the rustling water.

September 1985

Thinking of contradictions

Take away the contradictions
and what's left? Heaven.

Only the gods
could settle as happy natives
in that place of no contradictions,
that place of certainty, the place of peace.

And who'd want to be there anyway,
unable to enjoy the darling gifts
of rage, jealousy, cruelty, lust
and that power, the truly godlike one,
of destroying our own creations?

October 1985

In a snug room

He sips from his glass, thinking complacently
of the events of the day:
a flattering reference to him in the morning papers,
lunch with his cronies, a profitable deal
signed on the dotted line, a donation sent
to his favourite charity.

And he smiles,
thinking of the taxi coming
with his true love in it.

Everything's fine.

And Nemesis slips two bullets
into her gun
in case she misses with the first one.

December 1985

February – not everywhere

Such days, when trees run downwind,
their arms stretched before them.

Such days, when the sun's in a drawer
and the drawer locked.

When the meadow is dead, is a carpet,
thin and shabby, with no pattern

and at bus stops people retract into collars
their faces like fists.

– And when, in a firelit room, mother looks
at her four seasons, at her little boy,

in the centre of everything, with still pools
of shadows and a fire throwing flowers.

January 1986

460]

Other self, same self

Such warmth in my mind
where you talk and laugh
and drink drams
and walk amongst mountains

– though I touched your cold brow
on that wintry morning
that went away
and took you with it.

February 1986

Man, rabbit and owl

To see you, little owl,
swallowing that baby rabbit
for two minutes of violent gulping …

I turn away,
I who have fed
on the bread of peace, tender slices
of happiness, comfits of sweet joy.

I look away into the rabbits' world.
They snuffle the air, rubbing together
the halves of their noses;
they rockinghorse forward
and sit straight up, following their ears.

You pay no heed, little owl,
but gulp down your comfits of pleasure,
your fur-ball of happiness,
your sum of present delights.

Too many lessons from one
non-philosopher to another …

461]

I bless you from my other world
and walk away, whistling,
through a scatter of rabbits
bobbing their white scuts
into their dens of peace.

September 1986

On Lachie's croft

On Lachie's croft the cock stands
under the wheelbarrow. What's wrong? – He's bedraggled.
Where are his military elegance,
his gauleiter manners, his insufferable conceit?
I'll call him rooster, it seems more fitting.

I, too, feel bedraggled and haphazard; something
has filched my compass, I'm breathing black air.
I look at that rooster, I look at me.
His hens scratch the ground, step back
and peer at the scratches. They make
motherly sounds, so cosy, so fireside.

But he opens his gummy eyes, looks at me
and utters, no tortured trumpet call,
but a barren croak.

I breathe black air, I poke at
my rumpled feathers, I can't stand on tiptoe.
How I miss my cosy brown hens.
How I miss their motherly clucking.
I'm master of nothing I survey.

October 1986

End of her illness

The stones click their teeth in the darkness,
the darkness of memory, where a skeleton
burns its phosphorus and jeers
at the rising sun.

And animals stumble there, birds fall
with a cry on to the sour clods,
and even friends shrink to Tom Thumb puppets
jerkily greeting friends, jerkily shaking hands.

But now that memory has been rinsed
and laundered. The sun bleaches on curved bushes
and the whole air is a music I can hardly hear
but hear all the time.

A gentle miracle asked for shelter
and I received her in a house suddenly bright
whose shadows only made the brightness clearer.
What's night and day to me?

The unscalable cliff has vanished
as in a pantomime transformation and I
hold Cinderella by the hand and listen
to our friends applauding out there in the world.

October 1986

Seasonal notes – June

Kamikaze swifts dive-bomb the rooftops
(missing them every time) then soar
screaming and wheeling –
if they towed pencils behind them
they'd draw huge baskets in the sky.

Salmon waver behind boulders
and attack waterfalls
with elegant ferocity.

On mountains stags pose
beside lochs, still expecting
Landseer, then huffily
start grazing
beside a chuckling burn.

In the evening villages
men are sucked into pubs
to talk like ruminants
and drink like stirrup-pumps.

And the corn grows
gluttonously towards fruition,
towards the day when the combine harvester
clanks from a nightmare mind
and lurches into the field.

And all the uprising forces
will dwindle and die down,
leaving it to the sleeping earth
to dream them up again.

October 1986

Old shoes

Don't throw them out, don't put them
in the rubbish bin. They're full
of two things, emptiness and journeys.

They're boat-shaped, but (you say) what water
is left for them to swim on? They're empty –
but what chapters of me are curled up in them?

Autobiographies, all mine
who walk the roadless landscapes
of memory. – But there are memories still to be born

and emptinesses to be suffered.
– Don't take them away. I'm balanced
between two times, between two loves –

times past and the ones I've still to meet
that'll give me emblems like old shoes, boat-shaped,
lifeboat-shaped, full of survivors.

October 1986*

Little girl

She wept in a green corner.
The little girl ran into the garden
and sat shaking and weeping
between two bushes.

Because her mother wouldn't give her
a rabbit in a little hutch
with straw to lie on and a dinner
of lettuce and dandelions.

How could she know she would bear
the death of her mother,
the obscenities of wars,
the last illness, the first death?
– with what courage is
and the loss of innocence
and with no green corner
and few tears left for weeping?

October 1986

Perfect evening, Loch Roe

I pull the boat along gently. In the stern
Donald tucks his long rod under his arm
and lights his pipe.

Behind my right shoulder
the cliff Salpioder holds out
its anvil nose
over the sea.

The distances of other times,
the unmeasurable ones,
have withdrawn into nowhere at all.

– A sudden clamour. Oystercatchers
fly off from a gray rock –
their orange-red beaks; their wingbars flashing white.

465]

The desires of other times too
have disappeared
behind the desires that lay beyond them.

And the dreams of other times
are huddled in their false country,
exiles returned to their homeland.

I feel something like love.
I can spare it, for the source of it all
is waiting, there, in the squat cottage.

November 1986

Wild snowstorm

Men dressed like Laplanders
are digging and digging to free
the trapped dragon of the snowplough.

Are they digging in the inside
of a faulty TV screen? They make no sound
that can be heard.

Toss the snow up. Each shovelful
flocks and flies, scattering
to the next parish or settles

behind a wall, behind a boulder,
behind any steepness …
The dragon clears its throat

and roars and moves,
like a nightmare, forward
into a furious whiteness,

into a raging Christmas
where the angels scream and bellow
over all the Bethlehems in the world.

November 1986

Mountain streamlet

Thin splash of water. There should be
red eyes in it or a shiver
of gold grains.

How tiny its water-nymphs would be.
It couldn't trundle away
even the head of Orpheus.
And Ophelia would step over it
singing her sad songs.

I look for the red eyes –
they're there, pebbles
among the white ones.

And gold grains? They're in my mind,
enriching me.

If only I could wrap up
its little music
and take it with me
to my city room.
I'd listen to it and,
if I were Wordsworth,
I'd write something called
Innocence and Independence.

November 1986

Sleepy time

The lamp hisses: a lullaby hiss.
The fire cradles two little flames.
And the world's one room; time
has escaped from the ticking clock.

Somebody sighs. A hand dangles
from a chair arm;
and a man's head droops.
The night outside creeps into it.

November 1986

April day in November, Edinburgh

The sun punches through the cloud gaps
with strong fists and the wind
buffets the buildings
with boisterous good will.

Bad memories are blown away
over the capering sea. Life
pulls up without straining
the jungle tangle between us
and the future.

Easy to forget
the last leaves thicken the ground
and the last roses are dying
in their sad, cramped hospitals.

For gaiety's funfair whirls
in the gray squares. Energy
sends volts from suburb to suburb.

And April, gay trespasser,
dances the dark streets of November,
Pied Piper leading a procession
of the coloured dreams of summer.

November 1986

Slow evening

Night is long in coming. Its soft feet
pause at the horizon. Stars wait
for the light to go out, to perform
their brilliant rituals on their dark stage.

My mind that was sleepy with waiting
begins to waken, to feel small movements
like the tiny waves fudged in a glass of water
carried by a child.

468]

Light drains away. – But there,
sudden windows appear on dark buildings,
small universes wheeling peacefully
with Saturn and the tilted Plough.

November 1986

Like you, like everyone

Forgive me, unknown creators,
forebears whose blood
flickers and dwindles in me.

Like you, I'm a leaf
that hangs down helpless
on the tree of my people.

And like you I move
in whatever wind blows
from whatever spaces.

Forgive the love I feel in only my way
and the griefs I suffer
in only my way of suffering.

For Time's microbes work ceaselessly,
changing you and me and everything
with no thought of forgivingness.

November 1986

A room and a woman in it

It smells of old age,
of a past long dead.
Nothing has changed for so long.

How imagine that chair
is another place? The table
is rooted in years long past.

And the old woman, lonely and sad,
sits wrapped in a shawl of memories,
waiting for the latch to lift
and the door to open
to let in Time with his tall black hat
and a band of crape round his arm.

November 1986

That journey

To make a mark
from the mountain horizon to the sea:
a straight line.

It goes through lochs and fields
and fistfuls of villages.
It goes in the dark and the light.

In the harbour a boat
sets its white sail.
Its anchor crawls aboard.

Those who are left behind
will look out to sea,
their eyes bright with hope –

not knowing when it returns
they'll see approaching
a black sail on the bright water.

November 1986

Emblems: after her illness

They went away, the sad times.
It wasn't I who turned them out of doors,
but another.

The swifts have returned. They've dropped
their burden of long journeys. With what joy
they scream over the rooftops.

Pour the coffee. Sit by the fire
that says *home*. Tomorrow we'll welcome
all the tomorrows there are to be.

Do you hear the swifts? They tie together
the bright light. They nest
in secret places.

December 1986

Still is the night

I'm sleepless. I lie trying to hear
the house breathing, wondering
why the curtain trembles, wondering
what cracked a knuckle outside the door.

Still is the night? Not ever. Its creatures
scuttle and pounce and die.
A tree whispers to the window
and footsteps go by; there's a man on them.

Impossible to think of canoes paddling
on tropical lagoons or caravans
winding over mountain passes.
The night is nearness, it presses down on me.

A godlike car passes in a golden shower:
it throws a handful in through the window.
– Too much is going on. I think uneasily
of a hand twitching the bedclothes.

December 1986

Chauvinist

In all the space of space
I have a little plot of ground
with part of an ocean in it
and many mountains.

471]

It's there I meet my friends
and multitudes of strangers.
Even my forebears dreamily visit me
and dreamily speak to me.

Of the rest of space
I can say nothing
nor of the rest of time, the future
that dies the moment it happens.

The little plot – do I belong to it
or it to me? No matter.
We share each other as I walk
amongst its flags and tombstones.

January 1987

Divider

Greek Atlas is all of us.
He feels the earth
being pushed into him
by the heavenly sky.

But stubbornly
he keeps them apart.
He stands, his own limbo,
always stubborn, always complaining.

March 1987

Curlew

Yesterday, I saw a cousin of yours,
a whimbrel,
that, when close to, looks like yourself
seen at a distance.

But who could mistake its tittery call
for yours, brown bird, as you fly

trailing bubbles of music
over the squelchy hillside?

Music as desolate, as beautiful
as your loved places.
mountainy marshes and glistening mud-flats
by the stealthy sea.

March 1987

Wester Ross, West Sutherland

The mountains swirl water
from their high lochs. It comes down
in fraying threads.

A country of old wars, of clan battles
led by men we call heroes.
The mountains will see them no more.
Yet people remain whose courage is
to live in this hard landscape –
and refuse to leave it.

The sources they came from
have not dried up.

Such few people. Such thin threads
still spilling down
from the high lochs that never dry.

June 1987*

Deception

Dunlins and sanderlings
are dancing with a whole ocean as their partners.
Farther out, guillemots and razorbills,

stumped on rocky shelves,
make an antique shop of the gray cliff.
And four cows shamble across the sand.

473]

Peace has assembled from every direction.
Does the air move? The wavelets
keep saying *hush hush* …

I stare out over the ocean,
trying not to think of the mottled cod
swallowing, swallowing.

Trying not to think
of the bones that lie
under the two hundred feet thick
coverlet of water.

And gentle peace
that should be smiling
grieves over the water,
it trembles, it winces in the broad blaze
of the jovial sun.

July 1987*

Miracles? – no

With no faith in miracles
worked forwards or backwards,
trees grow, buildings decay
and I do both.

The money that used to shower down
from the air still does. I count
my lovely moneybags in the cellar
I call memory.

In the house flowers hold
their colours out, so bright
they seem lit up
from the inside.

And the chairs – each one
is a patriot that needs

no monument. Their arms enclose
dreams of satisfaction.

And the bored miracles emigrate
to seek work elsewhere. What can they do
against the usual, that needs
no witchdoctor, no pale Saviour?

And every thing stays quiet,
sure of itself, asking for nothing –
each one a mushroom
growing in its separate forest.

July 1987*

Fore and aft

Between them we sail
towards the blessed islands
where all voices are sweet
and no door is shut.

Between bow and stern
we enter shop after shop,
we write letters, we sleep:
we love this one and hate that one.

And crystals are always forming
and dead flowers are the mothers
of plenty. There are storms in the hold
and warm beds of love.

That furrow astern
is emigrations and departures.
Its millions of bubbles
die on the broad sea.

And ahead, the blessed islands
are a mirage over it.

We forge on towards them.
They keep their holy distance.

August 1987*

Two sides of a bright day

The Outer Isles are close,
drawn in
by the clear air and the light,
those powerful mesmerisers.

Every leaf asserts itself.
The mountains reveal chimneys and screes
stone by stone.

Yet such clarity makes me think, too,
of the friends
who have gone down among the shades.

I can't get close to them
though their nearness to me
never gets less.

How they would have loved to see
the Hebrides anchored off shore
and those white butterflies
winking and blinking
among the gorse bushes.

September 1987

Poems for her

Take from me these toys I've made
with shells from the depth of the sea.

Aphrodite was born there
from the sea that washed the shores
that Homer dreamt about.

My little baubles would never grace
the neck, the arms of Aphrodite.
Nor will they yours.

But maybe you'll think
of the calm depths
from which I wrested them.

Maybe you'll recognise truths
I could never speak
and look at me
with new knowledge: with a little wonder?

September 1987*

Crystal of women

The room is a crystal of memories.
It glitters, it changes, it makes colours
that don't belong here.

This is no place for sad Iseult –
a boat heads for this shore, its sail
flickers white over the munching water.

This is no place for Persephone
though she's here in this small place.
One king, one courtier would make it royal.

Beatrice sighs, thinking of her empty hours,
thinking of the young man who so stared at her
by the bridge over the Arno.

And Deirdre of the sorrows sits in a corner
singing of her beloved Glendaruadh,
singing of her lover in Ireland.

September 1987*

The many gifts

The gifts keep arriving.

They don't need three Wise Men,
they don't need Bethlehems.

They come from the lips of people
and the touch that lifts
the black burden from bowed shoulders.

Even in the sad lands of gaols and torture
the people sing. They dance
in the middle of desolation.

Hands must close on the strange gifts,
even those that bring tears
to eyes that have been longing to weep.

They wash ashore
from the sea that seems empty.
They emerge from the inner and the outer darkness.

October 1987

Poor world

The round world
carries us through nights and days,
a loving nurse who makes
terrible mistakes. We're volcanoed,
tornadoed, earthquaked.

Ashamed, she brings us bouquets of flowers
and hedgerows of birdsong
and Turner's sunsets.

Poor nurse, she knows no better.
Even if she could sit, rocking her pram,
in the park of space
and chat with other nurses,
what would she gossip about?

– the tantrums of her nurselings
and the loneliness of being a nurse
whose only child, her darling Moon,
is thousands of miles away.

October 1987

Uprising

Quiet among the undergrowth,
like conspirators in a smoky room,
little shoots are assembling.

Some are called snowdrop,
some crocus. Soon they'll be joined
by daffodil.
All different. But
when the vote is taken
all are unanimous.

Winter must be
eliminated!
A call to action.

Small terrorists
with bell-bombs and canisters
of sweet odours.

November 1987*

Her name as everything

The sea lies smooth as a bedspread
and no-one sleeping under it.
On a corner of it
I write your name.

The loudest thing is the gorsebush,
firing its little popgun, scattering seeds.
I arrange their tiny sounds
and hear your name in its music.

479]

The only moving thing is the buzzard.
Its wheelings and driftings
write your name elegantly
on the blank air.

Nothing is not bright, even the roots
of wild iris in the ditch.
They are the brightness of your name
in the darkness that surrounds them.

August 1988*

One day as any day

Let's go back to a day,
any day, much like this one
though different.

It lay all alone
but not lonely,
oiling itself and sunbathing.

It dozed,
it slept,
it dreamed.

And an old fellow called History
shambled up and spoke to it.
It yawned and turned over.

And a little boy called the Future
tripped over its legs and fell on the sand.
Go away, little boy, it mumbled. *Go away.*

But when the sun went down
it woke and shivered and thought
Time to go home.

November 1988

Sargasso Sea

Tangled in weeds.
Far from home.
On an ocean
I've nothing to do with.

How I envy the elvers
who leave their Sargasso and drift
across the Atlantic.

So many will find
the river I know best.
How eagerly they swim
against its rushing torrent

that brings them news
from high places
I once visited
long ago.

                                        November 1988*

Workaholic

He's been bustling
in the dark wood of Time
splitting minutes
as kindling for a bonfire.

– But look at him now,
standing dead still
in the wood
like a grandfather clock.

Something inside him
is chiming the hours.
Terrified, he courts them,
waiting for 11 … 12.

481]

Waiting for the bonfire
that'll burn Time away.
Already he has the taste
of ashes in his mouth.

December 1988*

Reading *The Iliad*

Back from that place
where wine-dark seas still wash at my door,
I watch Troy burning in the darkness.
Its flames flare on the empty wooden horse.

Journey of 3,000 years,
how little time it takes ... Edinburgh, secreted
in my bones, are you outside my window?

It grieves me to see
those topless towers topless at last.
It wounds me to see noble Hector
bumping along behind the chariot of Achilles.

Gray Edinburgh, take me back to you
even though here, too, the stupid gods
are quarrelling – they've learned no subtlety
from wily Odysseus.

And yet, and yet. – Warriors,
keep your swords sharp for the war
that has been won and lost
and still goes on in the green field of my mind.

December 1988

Hope

If only I could say
a new thing, a thing
I've never said before.

482]

Something small as a spoon
or big as a landscape:
as new as a baby.

Hope appears before me, flourishing
as a rosebush.
I pick one of its flowers.

And I look for what resembles
that spoon, that landscape,
that baby.

Nothing there. But the air
smells like a wild rose.
How pleasant its scent.

December 1988*

Maps

Planning a journey
is always a bit frightening –
all those contour lines on the hills:
that blue wriggle meaning a stream:
a small dot that turns out to be a city.

If only one could swallow the map –
including the creatures that aren't in it
and the absence of tomorrow
and the presence of rain showers –
and all the time sit,
a geographer of distinction,
in one's usual chair
lighting another cigarette
and planning such meals,
such expeditions.

December 1988*

483]

Thinker

Thoughts only deceive me.
Some prattle like childish water,
some are balanced and beautiful
as the curled horns on a ram,
some are beggars, they stand against a wall
with a tin cup in their hands
and most are vagabonds disappearing
into the back lanes of the city.

I breed them,
but they have no respect for me.
They leave home as soon as they can walk.

How I wish they would all come home.
How hard I would struggle to hear
what they would talk about
in the next room, always in the next room.

December 1988*

Memory, mother of the Muses

Sometimes my head is full of gloom
because the Muse of poetry won't smile to me
and the world gets dark without words.

But her mother still talks to me
of landscapes and music and friends –
over and over she says joy, she says happiness.

Memory, persuade your daughter to do
what she was born for and the visiting gloom
will go off in a flurry of verses, of whatever worth.

January 1989*

In an Edinburgh pub

An old fellow, hunched over a half pint
I hope he's remembering.
I hope he's not thinking.

Which comes first?

Memory, as always,
Lazarus of the past –

who comes sad or joyful,
but always carrying with him
a whiff of grave clothes.

January 1989

Duncan, bedridden

Big man, what storms you have suffered.
Blind and crippled, you lie there
cut off from all your life has been.

Old man, you who don't know
the meaning of self-pity,
the sea still rages against
your broken body. But your spirit,
that stormy petrel,
dances trippingly along
on the waves that tower over it.

January 1989

London to Edinburgh

I'm waiting for the moment
when the train crosses the Border
and home creeps closer
at seventy miles an hour.

I dismiss the last four days
and their friendly strangers
into the past
that grows bigger every minute.

The train sounds urgent as I am,
it says home and home and home.
I light a cigarette
and sit smiling in the corner.

Scotland, I rush towards you
into my future that,
every minute,
grows smaller and smaller.

January 1989

Depths and heights

What raised these yards of earth
In crocus groups, in shy snowdrops?

Life demonstrates itself in rustling bushes.
In them are nests with coloured promises in them.

But life lies also underground.
We carry it in our own darkness.

How lucky we are when it thrusts up
A snowdrop or one sky-searching tree.

January 1989*

High mountain loch

The cold loch water talks to me
in one of the ways I talk to myself
of chilly depths in high summer
and patience, patience, patience.

History lies in ruins
on the brackeny slopes,

beautiful and dead –
and how are we to escape?

The loch says *No way forward, no way back.*
And tosses a trout into the air.
I make it an argument and a comfort.
I huddle it to myself.

February 1989*

Words, words – and time

In a darkness or a brightness
everyone keeps on speaking.
They gabble and bluster
in the mumbojumbo of days.

At the pier seagulls perch
on boats, on bollards,
gabbling and blustering. They don't know
what more than one day is.

But one after another
the days trundle down the alleys
knocking down the ninepins that at once
spring to attention.

And the voices of everyone
creep everywhere, a fog
of words. Can you see
the lighthouse flashing?

February 1989*

The red and the black

We sat up late, talking –
thinking of the screams of the tortured
and the last silence of starving children,
seeing the faces of bigots and murderers.

Then sleep.

And there was the morning, smiling
in the dance of everything. The collared doves
guzzled the rowan berries and the sea
washed in, so gently, so tenderly.
Our neighbours greeted us
with humour and friendliness.

World, why do you do this to us,
giving us poison with one hand
and the bread of life with the other?

And reason sits helpless at his desk
adding accounts that never balance,
finding no excuse for anything.

February 1989

The Loch of the Peevish Creek

A name like that – how can I not
write about you?

I fished you only once
in your handsome surroundings
and learned why you have that name,
for all I caught were half a dozen trout
and small ones at that.

And how often, in my metaphorical mood,
have I cast flies in other places,
say, over the metaphorical waters of poetry,
knowing the lordly trout that are in them
and catching fingerling after fingerling.

But just because sometimes they relent
and send me stumbling home
with a broad tail

sticking out of my fishing bag
I come back again and again
to their peevish waters, wondering –
my fishing bag, this time, will it be light or heavy?

February 1989*

Nowheres

– Like a fairytale …
Let's take a pile of straw
and turn it into gold.

Much better than a ballad
let's not throw a baby
from a burning castle.

The moonface that hangs
in its nowhere lightens the way
to heaven or hell, two other nowheres.

Let's do a Rapunzel
gazing down from her tower
for any climbing lover.

No. Let's drop all the nowheres
into the water that runs
under the Brig o' Dread.

February 1989

Enemy of time

To stay in a minute
while the horde of seconds gallop by
on their tiny hooves is a way
of trying to forget the night
or the day
when the jaw drops and the eyes
stare into nowhere.

489]

The stupid things we do.
A hand closes on another hand
and a voice says *Forever*
and another voice says *Yes, yes, forever.*

The cruel things we do.

And the clans and tribes of lies
dance in their feathers,
they shout and stamp their feet
to the beating of drums
as they did in the primeval dawn,
as they will in the primeval future.

February 1989*

Spring morning

This girlish morning
comes straight out of old stories
where girls wore sprig muslin
and spent their entire time
being happy.

Even foul streets in the city
comb their hair, walk briskly
and clumsily try smiling,
their forgotten art.

Wherever you look –
in car parks,
by the sludgy canal –
she plays with the light,
sprinkling it in glitters.

And such transformations.
– See, there she is,
perched in a laburnum tree
like a budgie,

490]

where she sings sweet sounds
and, full of vanity,
kisses herself in a mirror.

February 1989*

Idling at sea

I let the boat drift and look around
at the mountains I know best
with their beautiful Gaelic names.

As though I'm sitting on a tiny private star
drifting at a thousand miles a minute
through an uncountable galaxy.

As though a thought revealed
a thousand thoughts that I can observe
but never inhabit.

As though our homely earth
whispers to me *Cousin*. As though
happiness can shelter even in a drifting boat.

February 1989*

Against wind and tide

I pulled with all my strength
at the oars till, exhausted, I couldn't draw ahead
of that boulder on the shore.

"Change places", I said to Big John,
who took the oars,
smoking his pipe and chatting,
and the boat slid forward
past boulder after boulder.

Years later, I think –
Hard labour this

against the forces that oppose me.
Pull as I may I can't pass
that boulder on the shore.
What shame if I start
drifting backwards
with no strength left
and no one to help me.
Then I'll know something
I don't want to know.

March 1989*

Edinburgh stroll

I leave the Tollcross traffic and walk by the Meadows
between two rows of trees, all looking
as grave as Elders of the Kirk – but
wait till the wind blows.

Dogs are hunting for smells. A few men
are practising approach shots
on the dwarfish golf course. Some children
are incomprehensibly playing.

And between two heaps of jackets
a boy scores a goal –
the best one ever,

Past the Infirmary I go back to the traffic,
cross it, and there's Sandy Bell's Bar.

Tollcross to Sandy Bell's Bar –
a short walk with a long conclusion.

March 1989*

Highland ceilidh

In the evening the talking was hushed
while Ishbel sang without trembling
a sad sad song of exile

from the island where she was born.
The anguish and the beauty of the song
were one. How can that be?

Then more talk, more laughter,
more singing in that room
full of "the marriage of true minds".

But what I remember, so long after,
are the two other marriages –
of the anguish and the beauty,
of the singer and the song.

March 1989*

At the foot of Cul Mor

A mountain half a mile away,
and a stonechat twenty yards.
Boulders and deergrass. And a loch
juggling with the weightless sunshine.
I stand among them. They let me
– except the stonechat. He doesn't want me here.
That's his only idea.
The other things have none. And no more have I.
Yet I'm translating
their language which has no dictionary
into feelings that have no words.
I bless them in my pagan way.
They pay no heed, in theirs.
But, without knowing it, they bless me too,
even the stonechat
with his bravado, with his spiky insults
and his dancing flight from boulder to boulder.

March 1989*

Two men at once

In the Culag Bar a fiddler is playing
fast-rippling tunes with easy dexterity.

How do I know? I'm in Edinburgh

On the pier, sun-scorched tourists
hang their bellies over improbable shorts.

How do I know? I'm in Edinburgh.

In the Veyatie burn a man
hooks a trout. It starts rampaging.

And I'm in Edinburgh.

Or so I say. How easy to be
two men at once.

One smiling and drinking coffee
in Leamington Terrace, Edinburgh.

The other cutting the pack of memories
and turning up ace after ace after ace.

April 1989

Dipper

No webbed feet,
but a water bird for all that.

And a gentlemanly one –
he walks on the bottom
of his helter-skelter stream
wearing a white shirt front
and a brown cummerbund.

He hates dry land.
Flying up a twisty stream
he follows the twists
all the way.

When he perches on a stone
it's a wet one.
He stands there, bobbing and bobbing
as though the water's applauding him.

He likes his nest
to be behind a rippling tapestry –
a tapestry? Well,
a waterfall.

Naturally.

May 1989

Kites

They float in the air
like yachts and half balloons
and children's nightmares
– and long-tailed, long-winged insects
more beautiful than the ones
that crawl on the earth.

I watch them gliding and diving
and hovering steady as a nail in a board.
I admire them all. But in the end
I search in the grass for an earwig,
under a log for a woodlouse
or, in a corner, for a spider.

Earth, don't desert me.
Though I walk on you,
separate one,
I belong to you
like an earwig, a woodlouse,
a spider.

August 1989*

Country lover

Back from walking among mountains
where he was alone but not lonely,
he sits by the fire
feeling like three men round a table, all of them drinking and talking.

Each counters a memory
with another one, he tries to listen
to them all.

– Three histories of a day
land in a muddle on the table,
and no waiter in the world
to wipe them away.

Alone but not lonely
he smiles at the fire, in a room
filled with mountains and lochs
and flowery boglands.

September 1989*

Gaps in time

They might have been on Saturn,
those who lived in the spaces of history
I know nothing about.
Could I visit them
I wouldn't expect much –
a floury housewife comes to the door
smelling of bread;
that six feet of suspicion
is a policeman; in learned buildings
learned men foretell the future;
somewhere an army is marching
towards another army;
somewhere children toss up pebbles
and try to catch them on the backs of their hands.

And some fool stares towards the past
and wonders what was going on then
that made today what it is,
what it sorrowfully is.

September 1989*

Sunset at Clashnessie

Two long thin clouds
are cutting the sun in slices.
It's helpless. It's dying in hospital.
And there are no stars yet
to bring it a bunch of constellations
and a coloured box of planets.

Yesterday seems far away.
We've crossed another border
into today, whose language
we're just beginning to learn.

The two clouds thicken
and I stare at the sun
crumbling away
into the darkness that'll finish it off.

How few of today's words
we'll remember tomorrow
when the Lazarus sun
steps out into the glory he died in.

October 1989

Nausicaa

Where is he now, the man
who came from the sea
out of the slippery fingers of Poseidon?

A noble man with not a rag to his back
and a sea-salt beard and a voice to please
even the image of a god.

And the stories! – that sounded so true
he charmed even my father,
even my loving mother.

Even me. And now I hear only
the truths of scholars
that seem false.

Come, girls – the laundry! But
I'll stare out to sea
wondering where he is now.

And I'll pray to Poseidon
to give him a happy landfall.
And I'll never see him again.

October 1989

Impasse

Everything's different now from what
everything was. Good.

But I like it too when I look
at a thing I've known for years,
like a landscape, and you, and think
they're just the same,
they haven't changed a bit.

I know that's nonsense.
Do you hear my voice faltering?
Do you see the moistness in my eyes?

Time loves one child – difference,
and kills another – sameness,
and torments us all
who love both.

November 1989*

Myself after her death

1

I'm exiled from what used to be
my country. It welcomed me
with gifts of peace and of storms,
with heights of mountains
and altitudes of joy.

Not now.
No, says the wall, and I turn back.
No, says the mountain
and I sit sad in the valley
listening to the river that says
Trespasser, trespasser, trespasser.

I stubbornly say, All the same
it's still beautiful.
And I know that's true
but I know also
why it fails to recognise me.

Myself after her death

2

That boulder beside Loch na Barrack,
stuck all over with tiny pebbles,
its costume jewellery
– that's what I'm like.

I have a hardness in me too
of a human kind and –
look close and you'll see
the costume jewellery I've stolen
from the past,
more precious to me
than opals and diamonds
and emeralds.

Myself after her death

3

When she was alive
I had no need for hope,
When she was dying
hope never visited us.

In this cold city snow is falling.
But life works underground and over it
at the endless toil of creation.
Little comfort for me.

But I have blessings; I count them.
They have the names of people.
There are others. But above all
they have the names of people.

They will die, as she did.
They will die, as I will.
And I look at the face of death
and say, I hate you, to destroy such wonders.

December 1990*

Five minutes at the window

A boy, in loops and straights, skateboards
down the street. In number 20
a tree with lights for flowers
says it's Christmas.

The pear tree across the road shivers
in a maidenly breeze. I know
Blackford Pond will be
a candelabra of light.

A seagull tries over and over again
to pick up something on the road.

Oh, the motorcars.
And a white cat sits halfway up a tree.
Why?

Trivia. What are trivia?
They've blown away my black mood.
I smile at the glass of freesias on the table.
My shelves of books say nothing
but I know what they mean.
I'm back in the world again
and am happy in spite of
its disasters, its horrors, its griefs.

January 1991*

Things behind each other

In between the notes of the music
porpoises curve up and over
in the sea I keep thinking of.

That long, savage phrase –
dragonflies by the Fiag burn
are snapping up horseflies.

Pianissimo it goes
and so many daybreaks
quietly spread out from horizons.

Now the slow movement –
sad as the men walking from Kirkaig
to the graveyard at Lochinver.
And the finale – a burst of joy.
And I settle down with the world,
counting nothing, being one of the total.

January 1991*

A sort of thanks

My memory's getting slipshod
Yet it still suddenly reveals
the mile long bank of primroses
by Loch Sal, last spring. Or it produces
from nowhere the acrobatic pair of ravens
I saw near Drumbeg so many years ago.

Like a lost ship that reaches
harbour in a fog
memory unloads cargoes from
hundreds of ports –
bales of words, hundreds of people,
a treasure chest of music – lamps
better than Aladdin's.

Memory, I've not destroyed you yet
and never will –
for whoever heard of a bird
wrecking its own nest?
Whoever heard of a bird
plucking out its own flight
feathers?

February 1991*

A difference (1991)

Times were when, not thinking of
what to do,
I did it.
It was as easy and helpless
as walking into the future.

Migrant birds arrived
on the cliffs of Handa. I didn't think
of where they came from
and where they would go to.

Now I'm troubled by wantings to know
for, having spent most of my years,
that precious wealth, so few coins
are left
they hardly jingle when I count them.

Sad to be a miser limping into the future,
consoled only by thinking
today was the future once – and
look at it
giving me so many gifts
I envy myself.

February 1991*

Contemporaries

It's pleasant to be a contemporary.
– It's the importance of people.

What courage they have
to build a Cathedral in a mess of slums,
to compose even one small tune
like a bird in a thorn bush,
even to say Hello to their neighbour,
and all within a few feet from a grave.

A huge world in space
explodes:– What's that compared
with the first word spoken by a baby,
or the last word spoken by anybody?

March 1991*

In the croft house called The Glen

Where now are the gloomy thoughts? ...

Outside the new lambs
are nuzzling their mothers
and a freezing wind is saying

Stay indoors.
I will. And peace, that old
fashioned thing,
settles herself on the sofa
and looks at me with forgotten eyes.

I love her gray hairs
and her hands clasped in her lap
as though holding a precious thing –
and talking with a quiet voice
that drowns the noisy world
with its gloomy thoughts
and hectoring demands.

It's night now.
I've no fear of going to sleep
I've no fear of waking in the morning.
For peace will say, Today
is like yesterday
and I'll be here for the long
length of it.

                              April 1991*

Languages

A dragonfly speaks to me
in its own language
whose verbs and nouns
are shimmers of four wings
and dazzles of blue.

The little stream it flies beside
talks in lyrics made
of the curves and curlicues of water.

Even the grasses,
those imperturbable philosophers,
explain in solemn paragraphs
how to change

from one green to another.

And my language? – Sounds in the air
and scribbles on paper:
on a bad day each makes
a coffin with nothing in it
and on a good day
a brassbound strongbox of treasures.

April 1991*

Image of a man

Into a tiny bay at Loch Roe, a tall yacht
groped, and anchored.
So many years ago. Why do I remember it?
Is it because of the tinyness of the bay?
Is it because of the size of the yacht
and its sails fumbling down and furled?
Or is it because it was like a man I knew
who lived in the tiny village nearby?
A man splendid as that yacht, with a crew
of thoughts that were sad and merry
until the strange sails that carried him
fumbled down and were furled for the last time.

May 1991*

Assynt and Edinburgh

From the corner of Scotland I know so well
I see Edinburgh sprawling like seven cats
on its seven hills beside the Firth of Forth.

And when I'm in Edinburgh I walk
amongst the mountains and lochs of that corner
that looks across the Minch to the Hebrides.

Two places I belong to as though I was born
in both of them.

They make every day a birthday,
giving me gifts wrapped in the ribbons of memory.
I store them away, greedy as a miser.

September 1991*

Different musics

Extraordinary what's contained
in a bird song, say a skylark's.
It's as though it's a synopsis
of a Beethoven sonata
or a century of folk songs.

Hegel, Kant, Schopenhauer –
I tell you my favourite philosopher
is a blackbird perched on a chimney pot
and explaining to the morning
the meanings of a morning
so simply, so lucidly
and sadly, so untranslatably.

And all the coarse human does
is claim that the yellowhammer
says over and over
A little bit of bread and no cheese
and that a cuckoo
only keeps shouting its own name over a green valley.

September 1991*

By the Three Lochans

I sit, trying to look like a heather bush –
hoping to see
a mewing buzzard or a vole or a dragonfly.
How quickly the days slide away
into where they came from.

It's hard to change anything.

506]

I look into my hand to see
if there's an idea there
giving birth to a strenuous baby.
Only a life-line that's not long enough.

An obstinate old rowan tree
stands on a tiny island.
So many storms, yet there it is
with only a few berries, each determined
to be the last one to drop into the water.

And the light floods down
revealing mountains and flowers
and so many shadows. If only
a merlin would hurtle past, that atom
of speed, that molecule of life.

January 1992*

Processes

The river slides by, looking harmless.
Ask the rock, that gets smaller and smaller
from its stroking.

Birch trees swarm up the opposite bank
in groups that die, so slowly,
from the centre outwards.
The stalker's path up there
is being taken back into the hill.
Quagmires have swallowed what were stones.

These three things are happening to me also.
Yet I happily observe them from the peace
they bring to me, even in their dying.

I'm a crofter in the landscape of time
repairing a tumbling wall
with each dead stone balanced on another.

January 1992*

Deceptions?

To hear a dripping water tap in a house
That has no tap in it, in the dead of night.
To hear footsteps come naturally to the door
And stop there forever. In bed in an empty room
To hear a voice on the pillow say *Hello*.

A wheatstalk dances lasciviously in the fire.
My hand drags its plough across this white field.
My head from a sort of radiance watches a chair
Continually completing its meaning. A picture
Tries to plunge from its nail to the centre of the earth.

Immense tides wash through everything. My knuckles
Are tiny whirlpools in it. I stream sideways.
The room's roots are straining. Sounds of the fire
Unmuffle themselves from black coal, are a theatre.
My foot rocks because my heart says so.

How could things stop? And three plump cheers for distance ...
To shake a hand and be left with it. To see
Sight cramming itself into an eye and wheat
A harrow of fire: and all a correspondence
Shielding the truth and giving birth to it.

Date not known

Small journey

Dragon and damsel fly
Glint above water coloured like them and make
Space into time, by passing. Small waterquake

Rocks the clenched lily and
A trout sinks through ovules of green stain –
One fly won't stand on its six stilts again

On the glassy waterskin.
And Quinag, that hill, that huddle of anvils, puffs
Two ravens from its blue ... A small wave cuffs

My eye with a bang of light
Bounced from the sun. And I am here, inside
My fist of shape – but also wandering wide

Into the being of air or in
The self of feather lisping through it – not
Cramped in the lair of thought and thought and thought.

Date not known

Visiting hour

The hospital smell
combs my nostrils
as they go bobbing along
green and yellow corridors.

What seems a corpse
is trundled into a lift and vanishes
heavenward.

I will not feel, I will not
feel, until
I have to.

Nurses walk lightly, swiftly,
here and up and down and there,
their slender waists miraculously
carrying their burden
of so much pain, so
many deaths, their eyes
still clear after
so many farewells.

Ward 7. She lies
in a white cave of forgetfulness.
A withered hand
trembles on its stalk. Eyes move
behind eyelids too heavy
to raise. Into an arm wasted

of colour a glass fang is fixed,
not guzzling but giving.
And between her and me
distance shrinks till there is none left
but the distance of pain that neither she nor I
can cross.

She smiles a little at this
black figure in her white cave
who clumsily rises
in the round swimming waves of a bell
and dizzily goes off, growing fainter,
not smaller, leaving behind only
books that will not be read
and fruitless fruits.

Date not known

Patriot

My only country
is six feet high
and whether I love it or not
I'll die
for its independence.

Date not known

Old Sarah

What could she live on when her husband died?
He had spent most of his last summers
lying on his elbow on a green knowe, looking
for the black-sailed ship to come into the bay.
But death put no words in his mouth – he spoke only
kindnesses and small jokes. They squeezed past
the permanent pipe in his mouth.

So what could she live on when her world dwindled to
a leaking cottage with five hens
to cluck by the rickety door? She drew

her black memories around her,
her life savings. And fed the hens.
And smoothed the blankets
in the huge dark space of the box bed.

Date not known

It's come to this

For this once I manage, I force myself
to write down the word *light*.
So many times in the last cloudy years
I've tried to and my pen
spelt it *dark*.

Date not known

The tribes of men

They think they walk in their country.
They walk to it.

Ignorant of the earthquake already
swelling its muscles under their feet
or the spark that will bring down a whole forest.

They read the stars overhead
like patterns of stories. All childish tales.
Let them read the darkness between them.

Their country is the one they're walking to,
the one that's the darkness
where they'll hear not even the grass overhead.

They give birth and they murder. They make
music of tears and instruments.
Hate, love and boredom are their companions.

Let them relish them all. Let them be:
those exiled translators of reality
whom the grass neither forgets nor remembers.

Date not known

Gale at Stoer Point

The wind roars through the hot sunlight.
Great waves tower up and smash their foreheads
On the sandstone cliff, savagely exhilarated
As though they thought that this time, at last,
They'd bring down the lighthouse to be chewed at leisure.

They don't think, of course. They're pushed by the wind
And hauled by the moon … Just like me, I thought,
Smashing my forehead against other cliffs.
Forget that. Let me savour the satiny brows
Punched into brain froth by the stolid sandstone.

And the fulmars, feather boats with tubes for nostrils,
Glide and soar on the windy turbulence
With such careless skill I feel like a moorhen,
That red-faced skulker by tame ponds … Have I, too,
Longtoed green legs with neat red garters?

Date not known

Spinning minnow

God in a green legend, I lean over the pool
In a testament of leaves. I dangle my twinkling mood
Before me in a cool cave roofed with branches
And floored with a skin of water. With a delicate hand
I cast it, lose it in a bull's eye ripple,
Let it sink and sidle down the water's shadows.

O moment's darling, I tremble, my hand shakes, twirling
The silvery slip through pale glooms of water.
What savage beauty may rush from its hidden holt,
Swallow you in fire and drench the air with a bitter
Battering of drops, of fire, of its own self curling,
A silver demon, a dancing and dying thought.

Date not known*

It sometimes happens

Change can change everything
except itself.
The one true immortal ….

She woke and the morning was
a net with nothing in it
but herself.

The room, the sunlight,
the doves on the window sill
were nothing at all.

The telephone rang. He spoke.

And the net changed into something
as full of freedom,
as full of wonder

as a room
and sunlight
and two doves on a window sill.

Of the million disguises
change put on that morning
she was the prettiest.

Date not known*

After four sterile months

How I got lost is nothing to do
with broken bridges or lying strangers
or forged signposts.

I was among upside-down hills
and left-handed circles. I could see
only behind me.

I thought, bitterly, if there were
someone to pray to, I'd be
more lost than ever.

Then I met my friend
whom I call *But* …
or *All-the-same* …

And slowly I remembered
my language. Old maps
re-assembled in my head.

From it I chose one city,
one room, one chair.
I sit in it.
I sit in it, smiling and obstinate.
I look in front of me and there's the road
going to its invisible end.

Date not known*

Our neighbour's cat

Night is in the garden.
In both the black cat
is a small black sculpture
in the long grass.

I watch for ten minutes.
She never moves.

A plane flies high
over the city. She looks up.
Her eyes steal the moon.

I'm tired. I go to bed
and stretch out in it.

Sculpturesque, I think,
as my eyes
steal the darkness.

Date not known*

Circles of dreams

In a circle
of what we call dreams
I look trustfully
at my hundreds of companions –
Ahab, pursuing his pursuer,
Madame Bovary, sulky Achilles,
Adam crunching an apple,
Mr Pickwick, round as his own spectacles,
Procrustes, that logical man –
so many, so many, so many.
I'm their homeland, their atlas,
they're whorled on my fingertips.

Or I look out
into the circle of reality
where dreams of so many shapes,
so many passions, whirl
in that dance of life and death.

I see myself there
sitting in a corner, drooping wallflower,
or leaping and skirling
like Burns's Cutty Sark
in the haunted Kirk of Alloway.

Date not known*

A small corner with a space in it

Into the Heather Pool
the river tumbles
over boulders:
a row of white fists.

They open out
into one flat palm
That splays into fingers of water
pointing towards the sea.

515]

A trio of sounds!
angry roar,
gentle plainsong,
childish chattering.

And no summer or winter,
just weather,
quick-change artist
that never leaves the stage.

Date not known*

On Handa

The cliffs are so high I look down
on the backs of seabirds
perched on the narrowest of ledges
or wheeling and diving or
scuttering on the surface,
and all as different as the tribes
of men
from comical puffins
to rapscallion skuas
bullying the gulls to drop
the fish they've just caught.

Date not known*

Married couple

She looks at a tree: it grows inside her.
He looks at a tree and climbs it, fells it,
robs it of its fruit.

If an ugly man passes, she looks
hurriedly away; he stares at him
as if at a chess problem.

She eats daintily, not convinced
she needs to; he passes over the table
like the Angel of Death.

She never knows where the money
comes from; he never knows
where it goes.

They treat life like a spider:
she's little Miss Muffet
he's Bruce in his cave.

Do they know each other? – It says something
of how much there is to know
since they're perefectly happy.
Only this proves he's not
a seal in love with a wren or
an orange on an apple tree.

Date not known

Stifling day

Heat slumps down on the limp grasses
and floats lethargically out over the sea.

Something purplish swells in the place
where memory used to be.
The hand on my knee is a crayfish.
I don't belong to it.

A boat wavers across the bay,
its sight muffled as its sound is.

A new world would have to begin
if a dog barked, a glass shattered
or a thieving breeze came slipping round corners,
lifting the heat to peer under it.

We're insects
in a heavy flower; we lie still
in its choking pollen.

Date not known*

517]

Potter's field

The strangers I have buried there.
I bundled them away because I didn't understand
the language they spoke to me.
All I could give these willing wanderers
was this sad hospitality.

There's no absolution. For the field is mine
and it horrifies me
to think of the pieces of silver
I bought it with.

Date not known*

Discolourations

They move me, the colours
whose birthright has failed them,
starvelings in the haughty economy
of red, blue, yellow and their purebred children.
They are a history of defeat, like the faces
of old people (where we see suffering – but call it
character). They lie in the rain
seeping in ravelled newspapers. They blotch
the stale ceilings of cheap rooms
with bestiaries and maps and feverish roses.
They are the long raincoats of men drinking
in doorways, on benches in public gardens.
They gather in tenement stairs – you never see them
in uniforms marching without bodies to pompous music.
There's more truth in a fisherman's jersey
than in the works of Hegel, more sacrifice
in the washerwoman's shawl
than in a world of vocabularies.

Glossy apple, bulged with red being,
kingfisher, metallic on your dipping twig,
and your shell cousin, mussel, blue beam in lustrous water

– flaring dandelion, voracious lady orchid
– all the loud or delicate statements of colour
vulgarly hoarded in rainbows –
you are of the marvels, you are of the miracles.
The sun in his armour wounds me
with felicities. But he wounds me, too, when withered
to a faded chrysanthemun
that scarcely stains
the brown fog that fades it.

Date not known*

Decaying birch wood

The birch trees by the river
are getting old, are old.
They're no longer like girls swaying
in a dance whose music sounds
only in our dream of them.

They're witches now, a sad coven.
Their branches are talons.
A foul fungus splays from their sides.
Some rot on the ground
snatched from their dance
by a devil with whom
they made no covenant.

On the edge of the wood
young ones are growing.
They sway in their dreamless world.
And the devil waits on the hill
as he waits in a stone, in a mind,
in the seven rings of Saturn.

Date not known*

August 1922

The boy in Scalpay
whirled his sling in circles
behind him –
Celtic David.

That month is a crystal
in the sediment of
a million occurrences.
Its facets glitter.
I stare into it from the future
and see the future
emerging from it and me becoming
what I am now.

Goliath wore feathers
and walked on a stone wall.

The circle of this year.
the smaller one of last year.
the smaller one of the year before last –
they narrow down to a point
and balance on that crystal.
I see in it with
exact clarity
endless things
and endless meanings of things –
boats and peatbanks, the continuous
brooding of the sea, the hard rituals
of labour for men, labour for women –
and Celtic David gazing aghast
at a headless Goliath
walking in his death for four steps
on a drystone wall.

                                        Date not known*

Nighthawk

It's not the strain of living
that makes me haggard: it's the strain
of continually being born. I think,
as I hatch out every morning
covered with a deplorable slime,
weak, bald, toothless
and childishly chirping –
That red cock in the sky
has a lot to answer for.

I grow decently throughout the day.
By midnight I'm my own age.
No wonder I'm an insomniac –
what ghastly reversals happen in sleep
to unfledge me, to face me again with
growing sixty-five years in one day?

Friends, ring my bell at two in the morning.
Keep me from growing young, so that
when dawn breaks I can look the sun in the eye,
man to man,
free, middle-aged and independent.

Date not known*

Index of titles